The Spanish avant-garde

The Spanish avant-garde

edited by DEREK HARRIS

MANCHESTER UNIVERSITY PRESS

Manchester and New York

distributed exclusively in the USA and Canada

by St. Martin's Press

Published by Manchester University Press
Oxford Road, Manchester M13 9NR, UK
and Room 400, 175 Fifth Avenue,
New York, NY 10010, USA

Distributed exclusively in the USA and Canada
by St. Martin's Press, Inc.,
175 Fifth Avenue, New York, NY 10010, USA

British Library Cataloguing-in-Publication Data
A catalogue record for this book is
available from the British Library

Library of Congress Cataloging-in-Publication Data
The Spanish avant-garde/edited by Derek Harris.
    p. cm.
   ISBN 0–7190–4341–7.—ISBN 0–7190–4342–5 (pbk.)
   1. Experimental literature—Spain—History and criticism.
 2. Spanish literature—20th century—History and criticism.
 3. Avant-garde (Aesthetics) 4. Arts, Modern—20th century—Spain.
 5. Arts, Spanish. I. Harris, Derek.
 PQ6073.E94S67 1994
 700'.946—dc20   94–5409
                                           CIP

ISBN 0 7190 4341 7 *hardback*
ISBN 0 7190 4342 5 *paperback*

Typeset by Best-set Typesetter Ltd., Hong Kong
Printed in Great Britain
by Biddles Limited, Guildford and King's Lynn

Contents

Contents

Illustrations

Illustrations

Contributors

WILLARD BOHN is Professor of Foreign Languages at Illinois State University. His publications include *The Aesthetics of Visual Poetry (1914–1928)* (1993) and *The Dada Market* (1993).

JAIME BRIHUEGA is Professor of the History of Art at the Universidad Complutense, Madrid. His books include *Las vanguardias artísticas en España (1909–1936)* (1981). He recently directed the retrospective exhibition of Rafael Barradas, Saragossa–Madrid–Barcelona, 1992–93.

EUGENIO CARMONA is Professor of the History of Art at the University of Malaga. He produced the introductory study to the catalogue of the exhibition *Picasso, Miró, Dalí y los orígenes del arte contemporáneo en España 1900–1936*, Madrid, 1991–92.

NIGEL DENNIS is Professor of Spanish at the University of Ottawa. His latest book is an edition of Ernesto Giménez Caballero, *Visitas literarias de España, 1925–1928* (1995).

GERMÁN GULLÓN is Professor of Spanish at the University of Amsterdam. His books include *La novela moderna en España (1885–1902): los albores de la modernidad* (1992).

DEREK HARRIS is Professor of Spanish and Director of the Centre for the Study of the Hispanic Avant–garde at the University of Aberdeen. He has recently edited Lorca's *Romancero gitano* (1991) and the *Obra Completa* of Luis Cernuda (three volumes, 1993 and 1994).

PATRICIA McDERMOTT is Senior Fellow in Spanish at the University of Leeds. She has recently published a study and edition of Ramón Sender's *Réquiem por un campesino español* (1991).

JOSÉ B. MONLEÓN is Associate Professor of Spanish at the University of California Los Angeles, and author of *A Spectator is Haunting Europe. A Sociohistorical Approach to the Fantastic* (1990).

GABRIELE MORELLI is Professor of Spanish Literature at the University of Bergamo. He has recently edited two collections of essays on the avant-garde: *Treinta años de vanguardia española* (1991) and *Ludus, gioco, sport, cinema nell'avanguardia spagnola* (1994).

C. BRIAN MORRIS is Professor of Spanish at the University of California, Los Angeles. His books include *Surrealism and Spain 1920–1936* (1972). He has edited *The Surrealist Adventure in Spain* (1991).

EDGAR O'HARA is Assistant Professor of Romance Languages at the University of Washington, Seattle. He has recently published

Contributors

From the Mills of Juan Ruiz (1993) and *Cedazo tan chícharo* (1993).

AGUSTÍN SÁNCHEZ VIDAL is Professor of Film at the University of Saragossa. His recent publications include *Buñuel, Lorca, Dalí: el enigma sin fin* (1988) and *El mundo de Luis Buñuel* (1993).

JOSÉ ENRIQUE SERRANO is Associate Professor of Spanish Literature at the University of Saragossa. His publications include *Estrategias vanguardistas (para un estudio de la literatura nueva en Aragón, 1925–1945)* (1990) and *Ramón y el arte de matar: (El crimen an las novelas de Gómez de la Serna)* (1992).

ALISON SINCLAIR is University Lecturer in Spanish, University of Cambridge. She has recently published *The Deceived Husband: A Kleinian Approach to the Literature of Infidelity* (1993).

ANDRÉS SORIA OLMEDO is Professor of Spanish literature at the University of Granada. His books include *Vanguardismo y crítica literaria en España* (1988) and he is the editor of Pedro Salinas–Jorge Guillén *Correspondencia 1923–1951* (1992).

HOWARD T. YOUNG is Professor of Romance Languages at Pomona College, California. He recently coedited *T.S. Eliot and Hispanic Modernity* (1994).

Acknowledgements

The contributions by Andrés Soria Olmedo, José Serrano, Eugenio Carmona, Jaime Brihuega, Gabriele Morelli, Germán Gullón, Agustín Sánchez Vidal, and Edgar O'Hara, have all been translated from Spanish originals. These translations were initially carried out by Gabriel Pérez-Barreiro with the help of a grant from the Research Committee of the University of Aberdeen. They were subsequently reworked by the editor as part of the editing process and any deficiencies they may contain are therefore due entirely to him. The translations of quotations from poems and literary texts, unless otherwise stated, are the work of the editor. Foreign language titles referred to in the text have been translated as a matter of course, unless they are sufficiently well-known or obvious in the original. Where appropriate, however, titles in the footnotes are given in the original languages to facilitate reference.

1. Angeles Santos: *Tertulia*, 1929. Oil on canvas

1 / Squared horizons: the hybridisation of the avant-garde in Spain   DEREK HARRIS

When the Chilean poet Vicente Huidobro gave the title *Squared Horizon* to a book of poems written in French and published in Paris the year before he made an influential visit to Madrid in 1918, he unknowingly indicated one of the essential characteristics of the Spanish avant-garde. Much of the activity of the avant-garde in Spain was an occupation conducted in clothes borrowed from abroad. Just as the Chilean poet wrote in French and sought to integrate himself into the cubist-orientated group of writers in the French capital, so Spanish avantgardists took off the peg the literary and artistic isms fashioned for the most part beside the Seine. But in Spain writers and artists also frequently felt the need to assert an individual identity apart from the dominating pressures from Paris. They were functioning within borrowed

1

horizons and seeking to adapt them to an indigenous circumstance, squaring not a circle but the horizons borrowed, and so the
Chilean Huidobro's image has itself been borrowed to act as title
for the introduction to this collection of essays on the Spanish
avant-garde. It is, moreover, an image of the Spanish avant-garde
which these essays wish to present, rather than a history. No
pretence to be inclusive is intended. The essays deal with precise,
detailed moments in the progress of the avant-garde in the first
third of this century with the aim of providing a sense of the
vitality of the contribution that Spain made, within its geographical boundaries, to the avant-garde activity, even hyperactivity, that
enlivened the European scene of the period.

The military metaphor of the avant-garde that refers, in a
European context, to the radical experimentation and innovation
throughout the arts in the early decades of this century, is not one
widely used in an English-speaking context. The English term
modernism carries some of the connotations of the European
avant-garde, but not all, for the English-speaking world was on
the periphery of such activity, more so, in fact, than Spain, where
the term *vanguardismo* was coined to translate the French original. Spain had made major contributions to the development of
the European avant-garde, in the persons of Spaniards who had
settled themselves in the centre of this activity in Paris. Pablo
Picasso, alone, is sufficient to give Spain a place of honour in the
Europe of the avant-garde. His near contemporary Juan Gris was
prevented from making a greater impact by an untimely death.
The came Joan Miró and Salvador Dalí to occupy prominent
positions in the Parisian context at the centre of such activity. Luis
Buñuel also moved out of the confines of Spain to take a major
place in the cinematic wing of the avant-garde following the first
showing of *Un Chien andalou* in Paris in 1929. Writers, however,
were bound by the limitations of their native tongue, unless they
chose to abandon it in favour of French, and no one who did so,
made much impact on the chauvinist world beyond the Pyrenees.
The activity and achievements of the Spanish literary avant-garde
were therefore muted in the European context, but the deaf ears
outside Spain often were denied access to a considerable concen-
tration of activity and to work which ranks as some of the fore-
most achievements of the avant-garde.

Hybridisation of the Spanish avant-garde

An all-embracing definition of the avant-garde might run to several volumes but some examples can indicate a few broad, widely-recognised features. The cubist painting of Picasso or Braque, the twelve tone music of Schoenberg and his school, the punctuationless poems of futurism and the graphic arrangements of words in Apollinaire's calligrammes have one essential thing in common: they deliberately rupture centuries of hallowed conventions so basic that most people had ceased to be aware of them as conventions. Cubism destroys the convention of perspective that had dominated Western European art since the Renaissance; Schoenberg rips apart the key system of post-medieval European music; the futurist setting free of words from the 'tyranny of punctuation' overturns the controlling linear sequential progression of the poem. Agression and destructiveness justify the military metaphor of the avant-garde. But the attack is more fundamental than an assault on technical organising conventions like prosody, it is a revolution in the relationship of art to the physical world and to human experience. All artistic endeavour since the Renaissance had been based on the Aristotelian concept of art as the imitation of nature and the neo-Platonic concept of art and beauty as the reflection of a divine ideal. The avant-garde rejects these fundamental bases, art and literature are set free from the requirement to copy and reflect something outside itself. Art becomes autonomous, sufficient unto itself and essentially meaningless because it is no longer required to make a commentary on the world or on human behaviour. An avant-garde painting, piece of music or poem simply is; you do not ask what it means. Vicente Huidobro declared as part of his poetics: 'make a poem like nature makes a tree'. You do not ask what a tree means so you do not ask what a poem means. This is the major revolution of the avant-garde, the overthrow of all that artistic endeavour had intended previously, and, most particularly, the overturning of the essential tenets of romanticism which had promoted the neo-Platonic concept of the ideal realm inadequately reflected in the mundane world. The avant-garde rejects transcendence and replaces serious, moral intent with play. Art becomes a game.

The history of the impact of the European avant-garde in Spain has the same characteristics as the entire intellectual history of Spain in the last two hundred years: delayed responses to the latest

3

movements from abroad and a resulting coexistence of different, even contradictory attitudes. The result is a confusion, rather than a fusion, of the different elements, a hybrid creation, a squared circle. The root cause for this is perhaps the late arrival in Spain of romanticism which did not set foot in the Iberian peninsula until 1834, its appearance having been delayed until then by the Napoleonic invasion and subsequent reestablishment after Napoleon's defeat of an absolute monarchy hostile to romantic liberalism. The romantic movement in Spain was short, quickly overlaid by the introduction of realism in the middle of the nineteenth century. Yet the arrival of realism did not dim entirely the presence of romanticism and new waves of romantic influence continued to enter Spanish cultural life, regaining dominance by the end of the nineteenth century in the form of the peculiarly Hispanic movement called inappropriately *modernismo*. This movement has nothing to do with modernism in the English sense of the word. It is the response of the American and European Spanish worlds to the influence, initially, of French Parnassian poetry and, later, French symbolism. All references to this movement will therefore maintain the Spanish form *modernismo*, and the term *modernistas* for the writers associated with it. Along with the sad princesses and Versaillesque gardens of aestheticism, *modernismo* carried a particularly heavy impedimenta of romantic angst, which was responsible for a dual direction in its development, towards the avant-garde and away from it. The continuing dominance of French influence brought a number of writers to the later stages of symbolism where words themselves had come to take increasing importance, acquiring something of the autonomy that the avant-garde would finally liberate. This increasing freedom and arbitrariness of language would also help to prepare the climate for avant-garde experiment. The other direction was more powerful at first, leading writers to take up positions around the romantic heart of symbolism and produce variations on Verlainian 'landscapes of the soul', where evocation of mood and experience were more important than linguistic experiment.

These developments took place in a complex intellectual climate, further confused by Spain's political history. In 1898, under a transparent pretext, the United States of America declared

4

war on Spain, and promptly proceeded to annihilate almost the entire Spanish navy. The humiliating defeat was the death blow of Empire; and Spain's last colonies, Cuba and the Philippines, became Uncle Sam's colonies. The effect on Spain was similar, in British terms, to the loss of India and the Suez adventure combined. The writers and intellectuals of this time are often referred to as the 'Generation of 1898'; Spanish literary and artistic history has a predilection for the long-outmoded generational models of Germanic origin. The central figure of this generation is undoubtedly Miguel de Unamuno who agonised as much about the soul of Spain as he did about his own unbelieving soul. His personal metaphysical anguish reveals the continuing presence, even in such an intellectual giant, of the old shibboleths of romanticism. At the level of national anguish, Unamuno also showed an essentially retrogressive attitude hostile to the modernisation and Europeanisation of Spain. Like almost all the Generation of 1898 he had anti-modern prejudices which, in political terms, created an impossible dream of Spain that nurtured inaction and evasion. Yet while turning his back on Europe as a political model, Unamuno's creative writing showed a marked tendency towards experimentation, especially in his novels where he abandoned the realist model to create a narrative so different that he gave it a new name, the *nivola*. The most striking thing about the *nivola*, in the avant-garde context, is the function of the writer as demiurge, creating characters rather than copying them, and the ability of these characters to acquire autonomy and challenge their creator, as the protagonist of Unamuno's *Fog* does to him in a Pirandellian confrontation of character and author. But Unamuno's interest in this was more philosophical than aesthetic. For him the novel was an existentialist laboratory not an avant-garde playground. However, Unamuno did break the traditional mould of the narrative, as did in other ways his contemporary Pío Baroja, and so introduced some of the principles of modernism, in the English sense, into Spain. The Generation of '98 used to be viewed as in opposition to *modernismo*, a view prompted by chauvinist Spanish critics, but all Spanish writers of the early years of this century share a common intellectual background and romantic inheritance. The principle developments out of *modernista* poetry, for example, represented by Antonio Machado and Juan Ramón Jiménez, re-

5

main fixed in symbolist poetics with a fierce opposition on the part of both writers towards even the slightest manifestation of the avant-garde. An exception is the novelist and playwright, Ramón del Valle-Inclán, who began as a typical turn-of-the-century decadent *modernista*, to later undergo a conversion around 1920 to his own personal version of the expressionist grotesque, which he baptised with the name *esperpento*.

While writers like Unamuno, Baroja, Machado and Jiménez held sway the first clear proclamation of the avant-garde in Spain was made with the publication in 1909 of a Spanish translation of Marinetti's *Futurist Manifesto*, first published that same year in French in Paris. Its translator, Ramón Gómez de la Serna, followed this in 1910 with his own 'Futurist proclamation to the people of Spain' that made a violent appeal for, among other things, 'Rebellion!', 'Antiuniversitarianism!', 'Sidereal violence!', 'Iconoclasm!' and the 'Secularisation of cemeteries!'. For the next ten years he became almost single-handedly the standard bearer of the avant-garde in Spain. In a Madrid café, the Café de Pombo, Ramón, as he simply came to be called, set up what was effectively a centre of avant-garde activity in, paradoxically, the most traditional Spanish medium of the *tertulia*, the regular meetings in a café of a group of friends, acquaintances and visitors to discuss literary, artistic, and intellectual matters. He also invented his own private genre of fragments, the *greguería*, a comic metaphor that rearranged the world into new and unexpected relationships: 'Laboratory guinea pigs say to themselves: I bet they would not do that to polar bears'. 'Dante used to go to the barbers every Saturday to get his laurel crown trimmed'. 'Dogs show us their tongues as if they thought we were doctors'. 'Sculpture museums are places where parents hear their children say surprising things: Daddy, my fig leaf hasn't grown yet!'. 'Nostalgia is neuralgia of the memory'.

Meanwhile, to demonstrate the overlaying of successive and simultaneous elements in the artistic climate, another generation, the Generation of 1914, had arisen to challenge the old guard of 1898. These writers and intellectuals centred around the figure of the philosopher José Ortega y Gasset and the magazine he founded, the *Revista de Occidente*, using the model of the Parisian *Mercure de France* to create a journal that brought to Spain the very latest intellectual, scientific and literary developments of Europe. Ortega rejected the anti-Europeanism of Unamuno and lowered the barrier of the Pyrenees to publish in translation most of the great names of the European intelligentsia. Part of this focus on a broader world included a curiousity towards the avant-garde and a willingness to try to understand it. The Europeanising intellectual attitudes exemplified by Ortega were reflected in the foundation in Madrid of the Residencia de Estudiantes, deliberately modelled on the colleges of Oxford University to provide accommodation and a meeting place for the flower of the country's intelligentsia. This student residence, undoubtedly the most influential location in Spain for the dissemination of new ideas, would later be home for many of the young avantgardists, including, Dalí, Lorca and Buñuel.

All the while the first native avant-garde movement was erupting in Spain, baptising itself ultraism to demonstrate that it had moved beyond the hitherto known into entirely uncharted territory for creation, although it was essentially futurism with a dash of dada. Poems about machines in an outrageous neologistic vocabulary self-consciously flouted convention with the elimination of punctuation and the calligrammatic disposition of the words on the page. The upsurge of activity in the literary avant-garde was matched by the first attempts to introduce the new visual language of avant-garde art. Painting in Spain had previously slumbered in variations on nineteenth-century genre painting or provincial adaptations of impressionism. The establishment of ultraism coincided with the appearance of another avant-garde ism, creationism. A number of young writers, most noticeably Gerardo Diego, had come into contact with Vicente Huidobro during his visit to Madrid in 1918 and had been drawn into the movement of creationism he claimed to have invented, despite accusations that it was just a version of Pierre Reverdy's literary cubism. A bitter rivalry quickly arose between *creacionistas* and *ultraístas*, although the two movements were in many respects almost indistinguishable. The cause of the trouble was a mixture of chauvinism and the characteristic avant-garde problem of leadership and primacy. Guillermo de Torre, the ultraist leader, saw creationism as a foreign implant, this in flagrant defiance of the cosmopolitanism of the avant-garde and of ultraism's own foreign

7

debts to such as Marinetti. He also saw Huidobro as a threat to his position as leader of the avant-garde in Spain. From the violent polemic that ensued came in part Guillermo de Torre's book, *European Avant-garde Literatures*, which, in its first edition of 1925, is to a large extent an attack on Huidobro, although it also served to present the ideas of the avant-garde as a whole to the Spanish public.

At exactly the same time Ortega produced *The Dehumanisation of Art*. Ortega's prestige brought the questions raised by the avant-garde into sharp focus at the centre of intellectual debate in Spain. The proselytising, self-aggrandisement of Guillermo de Torre is replaced in Ortega by an attempt to explain objectively the basic principles of cubism, most particularly the nonmimetic, autonomous aspects of the cubist aesthetic. *The Dehumanisation of Art* is an attempt to bring the avant-garde under intellectual control and this is indeed what occurs in the work of the Generation of 1927,

2. José Moreno Villa: *Travelling stones*, 1930. Oil on canvas

8

the generation of Lorca, who wear the tag of the year that saw the celebration of the tercentenary of the death of the poet Luis de Góngora. Góngora had been a polemical figure when writing in the seventeenth century, a poet of high baroque ornamentation and hyperbolic metaphorical ingenuity. Subsequently, his extraordinarily complex poems had been virtually neglected by the Spanish literary establishment for three centuries. The Spanish Academy had declined to mark the occasion of his tercentenary and so the young writers of the 1920s organised their own celebrations. Some of these events were conventional enough, like poetry readings. Others had a distinct air of avant-garde provocation, like a public burning of books by critics and opponents of Góngora across the centuries, or the communal act of urinating against the wall of the building housing the Spanish Academy, as a gesture of the young writers' contempt for the establishment.

The raising up of a poet of the highest baroque as a symbol and model of what was coming to be called now the 'new literature' is a clear indication of the syncretic character of innovative literature in Spain and it is not as arbitrary as it might seem. The baroque conceit, of which Góngora was a supreme master, has a lot in common with the imagery of the cubist avant-garde. The bringing together in the analogous processes of the conceit of elements that would not normally be seen as comparable, coincides exactly with the definition of the cubist image given by Pierre Reverdy as the conjunction of two normally very distant realities. Neo-gongoresque imagery proliferated in the 1920s: radiators became nightingales because they made singing noises in the night; electric light became a princess imprisoned in the crystal castle of the light bulb. Images such as these use elements of the modern world that might have been celebrated by the futurists for their modernity and machine dynamism, but here the twentieth century is filtered through a traditional literary device that removes the strident clamour of futurist mechanics while at the same time producing imagery that has precisely the playful lack of transcendence identified by Ortega in *The Dehumanisation of Art*.

The Generation of 1927 absorbed the frenetics of the avant-garde into their continuation of symbolism based on the idea of pure poetry borrowed from Paul Valéry; poetry that eschewed any emotional, ideological, moral aims. Thus they maintained the

9

elitism of the avant-garde while abandoning the agitprop attitudes that sought to change the world. The images of the radiator as nightingale and electric light as princess come from the two most bourgeois members of the Generation of 1927, Jorge Guillén and Pedro Salinas. Despite their defiance of proprieties in the celebrations for Góngora all of the rather cosy group associated with the 'new literature' were at that time well on the way to becoming the new establishment, and a number of them did in fact reach this safe haven. But the unity of the Generation of 1927 was about to split with the younger members setting off to sail some very stormy waters.

Violent defiance and provocation of convention re-emerge with the appearance of surrealism in the last years of the 1920s and all the old impurities of ideological, moral, emotional reference flood back on to the artistic scene. New magazines spring up, dedicated specifically to the avant-garde, like *La Gaceta Literaria*, edited by Ernesto Giménez Caballero, himself the author of a provocative novel entitled *I, the Sewer Inspector*. New manifestos attack the old order once again, like the *Catalan Antiartistic Manifesto* of 1928, produced by Salvador Dalí in collaboration with two Catalan literary critics, where futurist exultation of machines and sport is combined with denunciations of the vapid world of bourgeois culture in an attempt to identify with the Parisian avant-garde.

Poetry and painting are invaded by the wounded and wounding images of the surreal. Dalí, after the *Antiartistic Manifesto* does establish himself in Paris, while the young poets of the Generation of 1927 produce some of the most intense, lacerated, rehumanised poetry of their time, like Rafael Alberti's *Concerning the Angels* and Lorca's *Poet in New York*. The younger poets also distance themselves from the cosy and comfortable world of pure poetry by an increasingly active involvement in revolutionary politics, working for the social and educational policies of the Republican government set up in 1931 or writing in some cases, like Alberti, directly in support of Communist revolution. The year 1936 brought death to some and exile to almost all of those who survived. The commencement of the blood-letting in the European cockpit brings a violent end to the Spanish avant-garde, overtaken by the grim realities of the world it had tried to change.

Hybridisation of the Spanish avant-garde

Something of the trajectory of the avant-garde in Spain, and its hybridisation of elements new and old, can be presented most economically in a few examples of poetry. The strident futurist proclamation of the machine's triumph as an aesthetic object is well-represented by the ultraist Guillermo de Torre, who, in 1919 addressed an 'Airmail madrigal'[1] to an automated object of his affections, who wears a wreath of propellors and whose arms unravel on her cubic breasts like a sinusoidal cable. The orgasm which concludes the poem is clearly prompted by the mechanical rather than the human aspects of the lady, but her status as an erotic archetype consecrated by centuries of European art is re-phrased rather than reformed by the transference into technology. The antique model is not replaced, merely transposed. Similarly beneath the fervid, quasi-scientific neologism of such poems there still lurk the old shadows of sentimentalism; the Verlainian 'land-scape of the soul' has just been replanted for the machine age in Torre's 'Aerogram':

Apterygote buzzing in the isotropic night.
The nocturnal concavity saturnly polarizes the paranoid
  enigma.
Invisible ultratelluric cables tremble in a vocal spasm.[2]

In other cases the romantic substratum is not even disguised by the mishmash of a pseudo-scientific lexicon:

    Mine is the star!   Mine!
      Down
          the
              golden
                   stairs
                       pink
                           feet
                              leave
                                 footprints
                                     of
                                        light
From white stars[3]

It is easy to belittle texts such as these, blithely unaware of their self-parody, but from this odd admixture spring the great achievements of the 1920s where superficial lexical experiment is replaced by the condensation of reference associated with neogongorism and where the underlying romantic attitudes are more openly acknowledged in their paradoxical relationship with literary modernity. Rafael Alberti's tryptych of poems, 'Romeo and Juliet', written at the time of the Góngora tercentenary, encapsulates the evolutionary process of the avant-garde in Spain.[4] The initial poem is a gongoresque celebration of Juliet espied through a keyhole while in her bath. The second poem brings her into the twentieth-century world of telegrams and cinemas, bobs her hair in the fashion of the 1920s, and sets her driving at speed in a car down a city street. The last poem destroys both the traditional and modern dream with an image of Juliet as a dehumanised machine, a mechanical rose with a wooden body, nickel skeleton and gramophones in place of lungs. Despite a final throwaway line, 'Wind up the sun, its filament has burnt out', that seeks to reassert the spirit of play, the confrontation of values in these three poems brings together the romantic basis and the attempt at avant-garde restatement into a symbiotic relationship that will lead on into surrealism. The simplistic attempt to reject the old and embrace the new promoted by ultraism has become a problematic involvement in both sets of values.

There is no better example of this problematic quality than the poetry of Vicente Aleixandre in the 1920s who takes the conventional tropes of his romantic inheritance and rewrites them, not with the merely lexical speculation of the early avant-garde that rarely moved beyond neologism, but with the deeper restructuring of relationships that comes from his acquaintance with surrealism.

> Thorn you white hearing
> World world
> Immensity of sky heat remote tempests
> Universe touched with fingertips
> Where an open wound
> Yesterday was bee today rose yesterday inseparableness
> I am you roaming amongst other veils
> Silence or brightness earth or stars
> I am you I myself, I, I am you, I mine,
> Between worlds on the wing beneath cold

12

Hybridisation of the Spanish avant-garde

Shivering in speechless whiteness
Parted from myself like a knife
That parts two roses when it snows

This poem, 'Whiteness' from the collection *Swords like Lips* (1932), quoted here in full,[5] takes many easily recognisable elements of the romantic landscape of erotic angst and then recreates them in a context whose novelty is much more radical than the machine references or scientific neologism of Guillermo de Torre. One is reminded of the landscape in a painting by Yves Tanguy, precise objects in a clearly delineated world, but objects and a world that have never been *seen* like that before. Metaphor has become image, conceit has become icon. The shared world of reader and poet has been transformed, raised to another plane of meaning glimpsed but not comprehended, by either poet or reader. The frantic search for novelty has become creation, the hybridisation of romantic mimesis and avant-garde autonomy is here complete in an integrated new vision. The horizons have been squared not just by lexical or rhetorical sleight of hand but by the production of a literary reality where squared horizons can genuinely exist in their own right.

The essays gathered together in this volume are indications of the process of the arrival, incorporation and development of the avant-garde in Spanish art and letters. The arrival of the avant-garde is represented by two essays on Ramón Gómez de la Serna, without whom the avant-garde might never have established itself in Spain, examining his personal history of the explosion of artistic and literary experiment in Europe, and the originality of his own contribution to the form of the avant-garde novel. Two studies of the way the language of avant-garde painting was brought to Spain and of the relationship between young artists in Spain and the Spanish painters like Picasso and Miró settled in Paris show the complex process of hybridisation resulting from the coexistence in Spain of movements and tendencies that occurred in chronological sequence in Paris. The irreverence and iconoclasm of the avant-garde is portrayed in a study of texts inspired by bidets, baths and lavatories, in calligrammes on sporting themes, and in the playful parodies that celebrate the avant-garde's denial of the seriousness of the romantic tradition against which they

13

were in rebellion. Three essays deal with the image of the urban environment that is the essential *locus* of the avant-garde, examining the idea of modernity in this context and how the social, economic and political world was seen from the avant-garde perspective in Spain. The remaining essays focus on some of the principal figures of the 1920s, Buñuel, Lorca, Alberti and Cernuda, who represent the moment when the avant-garde comes to full fruition as a result of the horizon-squaring synthesis of romantic ethics and revolutionary modes of expression.

Notes

[1] 'Madrigal aéreo' is collected in G. Gullón (ed.), *Poesía de la vanguardia española (Antología)*, Madrid, 1981, pp. 136–7.
[2] G. de Torre, 'Aviograma', in Gullón, *Poesía*, p. 137.
[3] A. del Valle, 'Signo celeste', in Gullón, *Poesía*, p. 143.
[4] 'Romeo y Julieta' is contained in Alberti's collection *Cal y canto* (1926–1927), Madrid, 1981, pp. 37–9.
[5] V. Aleixandre, 'Blancura', *Espadas como labios. La destrucción o el amor*, Madrid, 1972, p. 106.

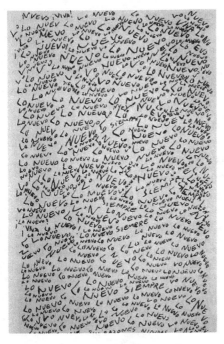

3. Ramón Gómez de la Serna: 'The new always', *Plural* (Madrid), II, February 1925, p. 7

2 / Ramón Gómez de la Serna's oxymoronic historiography of the Spanish avant-garde

ANDRÉS SORIA OLMEDO

Ramón Gómez de la Serna, the founding father of the Spanish avant-garde, produced his own highly personalised account of the European avant-garde under the succint title *Isms*, although many of the 'isms' included are of his own designation, like Archipenkism. As historiography *Isms* is a work as idiosyncratic as its author, a singular work set apart from a context of artistic and literary histories in Spain that was already quite substantial by the time Ramón's book appeared in 1931. The year 1925 had seen the publication of two fundamental critical works, Ortega y

15

The Spanish avant-garde

Gasset's *The Dehumanisation of Art* and *European Avant-garde Literatures* by Guillermo de Torre. Many articles have appeared, especially in Ortega's magazine, the *Revista de Occidente*, from 1923 onwards, as well as several books dealing with the avant-garde in both literature and art. Gabriel García Maroto's *The New Spain 1930* is a curious attempt to develop a utopian 'policy of aesthetic education'. The translation of Franz Roh's *Magic Realism* popularised the ideas of 'New Objectivity', introducing this late version of expressionism into the Spanish avant-garde context where it had been relatively uncommon. Ernesto Giménez Caballero's *Posters* inspired by the practices of futurism, promoted the propagandising power of the advertising poster, while José Díaz Fernández's *The New Romanticism* challenged many of Ortega's ideas from a perspective of left-wing political commitment. In this context *Isms* is a history which is not a history, a case of oxymoronic historiography synthesising a series of paradoxes which shaped the development of the avant-garde in Spain.[1]

Gómez de la Serna had always been both a central and an excentric figure, defining himself in *Isms* with this trenchant statement: 'what I call "Ramŏnism" has always fought against categorisation, and in Spain I always maintained a position as an outsider in my outsider's hovel'.[2] In his reply to the survey of a broad range of writers organised by *La Gaceta Literaria*, the central magazine of the avant-garde, seeking to find an answer to the question 'What is the avant-garde?', he makes a strong defence: 'I will die admiring that word; those who are offended by it will never make me feel ashamed of its meaning. I am sorry that my friends are weakening their resolve; but I remain an enemy of my enemies, I despise them, I spit on them'.[3] With these words Ramón distanced himself from the acceptance of tradition by the 'young literature', while at the some time giving his declaration a defensive ring, like a swan song of avant-garde purity, which sets him apart from any socially committed aesthetic. In 1935 he declared his dissatisfaction with the contemporary situation in no uncertain terms: 'I am about to close Pombo . . . tonight there were too many commies, including some with self-indulgent expressions and a detestable way of sidling up to each other'.[4] This is clearly a symbolic gesture when one realises that the Café de Pombo, from where he had issued in 1915 the 'First Proclamation

16

from Pombo', one of the earliest avant-garde manifestos in Spain, was one of the places where Ramón experimented with the fusion of life and art. It was one of the places which contained his particular conception of avant-garde activity alongside a *fin de siècle* bohemianism and the Hispanic *tertulia*, a place which Ortega described in 1921 as the 'last barricade' of liberalism, beyond which lay the restoration 'of hierarchies, discipline and rules'.[5] Ramón, whose attitudes had come to be concentrated exclusively on artistic revolution, totally ignoring their prehistory which had anarchist and Marxist sympathies,[6] had no wish to see hierarchies restored, although his continuing involvement with the origin of these attitudes in turn-of-the-century vitalism led him to defend in *Isms* the far from liberal surrealism.[7]

These attempts to strike a difficult balance indicate that Gómez de la Serna's situation cannot be successfully explained, as has been the case, by categorising him as a unique, gigantic figure. His 'Ramŏnism' is, in fact, part of an attempt to establish an aesthetic modernism in the difficult, confused context of the early years of this century in Spain. From Hispanic *modernismo* came his scorn for what he termed the gregarious 'Belgian spirit' of the 'littérateurs d'avant-garde', like Baudelaire. Ramón, it must be remembered, had refused to become the leader of ultraism. From *modernismo* too came his adoption of the image of the isolated dandy who defends the Ivory Tower, which in his case was a real tower as well as a symbolic one, where he had accumulated a mythical collection of objects that related him both to the decadent Des Esseintes and to the avantgardist Kurt Schwitters.[8] The avant-garde counterbalance to aestheticism is also found in his adaptation of the futurist concept of the manifesto: he had had installed in the tower in 1930 a microphone so that he could broadcast via the Union Radio company.[9]

Like other authors at the turn of the century he was subjected to the slavery of journalism[10] and like the members of the Generations of 1914 and 1927, he was a traveller. In Paris he took up a position between the Bohemia of the *modernista* Alejandro Sawa, who had once been kissed on the forehead by Victor Hugo and had not washed his face since, and the 'provincial' cosmopolitanism of the two most intellectual members of the Generation of 1927, Jorge Guillén and Pedro Salinas, who both held language assistantships at the Sorbonne.[11] Not since the days of Blasco Ibáñez, the author of *The Four Horsemen of the Apocalypse*, had a Spanish writer enjoyed such fame in Europe. Valéry Larbaud wrote: 'Ramón's window, lit up in the dawn, there in Madrid, shines like a beacon on the prow of the ship of Europe'.[12] His first visit to Paris, in 1910, opened his eyes to avant-garde visual art (in contrast Ortega's favourite painter was the genre painter Zuloaga), and his final visit gave birth to the idea of publishing *Isms*.[13]

A history of the avant-garde, and above all one written by an active participant presents a basic paradox: to what extent is it possible to write a history of the new? Ramón's *Isms*, in fact, centres around the contradiction between history and the avant-garde, as studied by Paul de Man and exemplified in the paradox produced by Baudelaire who, when writing about Constantin Guys, the 'painter of modern life', attributed to him the need to submerge himself in the 'memory of the present'.[14] Ramón sets about this task at the start of the book by praising 'the new', in accord with the path he mapped out around 1909 in his book *My Seven Words*, when he decided that his attitude towards the world should be one of constant vigilance to ensure his ability to 'unmake' all those things which had become petrified. This attitude was further developed through the cultivation of a personal myth of a Robinson Crusoe, like a child alone in a kaleidoscopic world saturated with so many things to see, provoking the excitement of the discovering genius who 'has the ability to reveal the hidden aspects of the visible world'.[15] This revelation is not achieved through the process of analogy the symbolists used, conjuring an essence behind appearances, but rather through the simple establishment of an 'inventory' of reality which itself assumes an 'oneiric' character, as Walter Benjamin noted in his 1927 review of the French translation of Ramón's *The Circus*.[16] Also, the 'new' here relates to a subject with which Ramón was totally in tune, unlike most of his compatriots, and in which he considered himself to be a part rather than an intermediary: 'I lived before the new forms of art and literature were born, and I was in the closest relationship with them afterwards', as he says in the opening sentence of the prologue to *Isms*. This attitude is the result of a personal interpretation that places the text between the projection of the self on to the

18

world and the annulment of self when faced with the spectacle of the world.[17]

From this point of departure the organisation of the book, like many others by Gómez de la Serna, becomes a catalogue or a topography. Borges had noted in 1925:

> Ramón has made an inventory of the world, filling the pages not with exemplary acts of human adventures as is common in poetry, but rather he anxiously describes each of those things which when placed together form the world. Such an abundance is not in harmony nor can it be simplified through synthesis, it is closer to the cosmorama or the atlas than the total vision of life so sought after by theologians and creators of systems.[18]

In the case of *Isms*, the catalogue seeks to establish simultaneous connections between different genres. The essays on individual authors and artists establish an initial connection with biography, so much so that *Isms* becomes the successor to *Effigies* of 1929, which described Ruskin, Baudelaire, Barbey, Villiers and Nerval, that is writers who are precisely the precursors of modernism. There is also an overlap with autobiography and personal testimony: only the portrait of Toulouse-Lautrec is included among those regarded as precursors, because Apollinaire, Picasso, Marinetti, Lipchitz, Lhote, Sonia and Robert Delaunay, Marie Laurencin, Rivera and Cocteau are all considered to be Ramón's acquaintances. Only Archipenko, Léger, Ozenfant and Jeanneret are held to be outside his personal circle.

In addition, the book comprises an inventory of his own personal aesthetic preferences, since its twenty-five 'isms' are framed by the prologue on 'the new', a long theoretical article on 'humourism' towards the centre, in fifteenth place, and by the shorter 'novelism' in penultimate place. At the same time, on the level of rhetorical 'elocutio', the position he adopts is directly connected with the *greguería*, that bond which holds all of Ramón's work together, since 'humour is something that looks to the future, throwing everything into the melting-pot, slightly easing apart the connecting links in the cosmos, softening them through paradox, making them confused, turning them head over heels' (p. 199). This is described as a 'vital function' which reveals the 'family links between all things' (p. 202), and which in Spain 'has the function of making you accept death' (p. 217). The *greguería* is like a compass rose whose tendency to become caricature, as Cansinos-Assens observed in 1918,[19] can lead it into biography. In 1935 Pedro Salinas defined the *greguería* as, 'a sudden brief revelation which by virtue of an unexpected mode of relating ideas or objects, illuminates a new way of seeing things'.[20] This links with the analogic tradition of modern writing, or what César Nicolás describes as the interaction of metonymic metaphors and metaphorical metonyms that can be extended to infinity, and which connects with the irony that is also an ingredient of the modern.[21] Some of the isms dealt with ('Negroism', 'Jazzbandism') either resolve themselves or dissolve themselves into a series of *greguerías*, and this condition of fragmentary writing extends throughout the book, making it into an avant-garde exercise in avant-garde writing, where the idea of organic unity is undermined by the metonymic nature of the *greguería*, which creates a dominance of objects over people and of fragments over the whole that, in Walter Benjamin's view, sets the allegory of the baroque and the avant-garde in opposition to the symbol of romanticism and symbolism.[22]

This attitude also brings the way in which the *greguería* is constructed close to that of the collage, where the objects (or textual fragments) from different sources are held together in their difference so forcing the reader or spectator 'to consider the interplay between preexisting message or material and the new artistic composition that results from the graft'.[23] As a result Ramón's book becomes a double collage: that of the specific objects referred to in the text, and that of the coexistence of the successive 'isms'.

The constellation of the 'isms' Ramón has assembled is not totally arbitrary, the omissions are as important as the inclusions, most especially the omission of expressionism and of the Spanish movements; neither Huidobro, ultraism nor creationism are included. The distinguished linguisticion, Roman Jakobson has linked the predominance of the metonym with cubist representation and cubism occupies the lion's share of this book. Apollinairism (with the fundamental intertextual notion of the antimimetic crusade in *The Cubist Painters*) which exalts the 'simultaneity of the world', Picassoism (two essays published earlier, in 1924 and 1929) which caused, 'the donkey-like certainty of painters who only look and copy and look and copy to be destablilised for ever', and seraphism (about Cocteau), are all concerned with the area of cubism and postcubism. In turn, this is extended, as though in concentric circles, to Africanism, with the view that African sculptures should be the 'backbone of modern art' (p. 127), to Archipenkism and Lipchitzism (about the cubist sculptors), nymphism (about the painter Marie Laurencin), Lhotism (André Lhote provided 'Cubism's bourgeois studio'), tubularism (Fernand Léger), and bottleism (the 'purists' Ozenfant and Jeanneret). Riveraism is about Diego Rivera and cubist 'neoportraitism': 'if there is one thing in us which is allegorical, it is contained in these cubist portraits' (p. 338), and simultaneism, is concerned with the Delaunays, whose art praises industry and the everyday: 'Delaunay's influence is already in the street, but no longer abandoned as a thing ignored by most people as it was in those Sundays of another age, but instead it is on fences, in shop windows and on façades, triumphant in the new magazines' (p. 175).

4. Maruja Mallo: *Easter Fair*, c. 1927. Oil on canvas

The Spanish avant-garde

This last 'ism' provides a link between the cubists and postcubist figure painting and another innovative sequence concerning the diffusion of the new aesthetic and the changes in perception it causes. This sequence reveals a sensibility curiously similar to that of Walter Benjamin; Ramón states at the beginning of the book: 'more than moral propaganda, what has influenced life and habits – which most urgently need to be set free – has been advances in fabrics, lighting, furniture, pictures, literary genres' (p. 13). Luminism concerns new lamps and new light: 'new lamps are like a humorous reconstruction of broken lamps, reflecting the architecture of modern streets, evoking the accelerated development of all new things, balconies like illuminated ocean liners, the sense of brave straight lines which do not resolve into decorative symmetries but rather separate out into flights of steps of different sizes which make anyone who climbs them stay alert' (p. 139). Klaxonism is about car-horns, shelfism about new furniture, then there is monstrousism, machinism, jazzbandism and Chaplinism.

The other historical isms are set apart from these sequences. At the head is futurism, although Ramón is careful to distinguish 'the essential Marinetti . . . who began to shout wildly over twenty years ago' (p. 112) from the Marinetti at the time of the First World War who began to 'say conservative things about the stock idea of heroism that is greeted with official blessings' (p. 117). Then came dadaism, considered in a favourable light and ending with an exaltation for 'Tzara alone' (p. 255), followed by the long, admiring essay on superrealism, as surrealism was called then in Spain, which 'gives a shining light that nobody will be able to extinguish' (p. 264). Ramón values the subversive nature of surrealism, although in a very particular manner and in relation to the contemporary situation of Spain: 'the art this movement produces is one that it is hard to smile at. All the atmosphere of student revolt, the suicides and the most reckless acts of today's youth are acts of superrealism. They should be so in all their purity and thus should not let themselves be caught up in the game of political change mounted by a confused bourgeoisie and vulgar radicals' (p. 288). He also values the opening up of the unconscious and the idea of evasive poetry which Lorca at the time had adopted as an aesthetic emblem: 'Breton and his followers seek evasion, a word heavy with longing, which they present to today's youth suffocated by a stupidly bourgeois world. For them, the real meaning of

22

a poem, its greatest triumph, lies in the extent to which it is evasive poetry and in its ability to enable the human soul to experience evasion' (p. 272). He finishes his essay with a 'practical explanation' in which he attacks the 'bourgeois prattle which puts everything in order' (p. 290) and he affirms that 'the only truth worth paying attention to is the latest one' (p. 293). However, he is dealing with an intercalated story, *The Surrealist Son*, that makes the task of narrating the history of avant-garde art, as he says, sufficiently 'undone'. For the reader, after so many paradoxes, this is particularly pertinent to Ramón's way of narrating the great spectacle of artistic innovation in the twentieth century.

This paradoxical history is, at the same time, involved in other paradoxes like the proliferation of essays and interpretations by Spanish writers relating to the avant-garde compared to the seemingly limited production of the native Spanish avant-garde itself. This imbalance of critical and creative activity is a product of the way modernism, in all its different aspects and characteristics, was introduced into Spain, providing an example of Matei Calinescu's view that aesthetic modernism is both an integral part and also an enemy of modernisation.[24] The arrival of modernism in a Spain that was still in many respects premodern, involved a fairly rapid acquisition of all the sometimes confusing elements of modernism while, with some difficulty, synthesising and absorbing modernism's nineteenth-century aesthetic, decadent and symbolist prehistory, together with the philosophical background in positivism, Nietzschean vitalism and religious modernism.

The complex impact of the dialectics of modernism in Spain can be seen in the intellectual confrontation between Ortega and Unamuno in the years leading up to 1909. As a reaction against the 'wildness' of the turn-of-the-century mentality represented by Unamuno, the later generation of Ortega defended the entry into Europe with their faith in reason and technology, and the need to educate a minority of specialists to face the twentieth century in all its complexity.[25] At the same time, through Gómez de la Serna's translation of Marinetti's manifesto in 1909, futurism, and with it the European avant-garde, was brought into Spain. From this moment the history of the reception of the avant-garde follows a rising curve that leads to the establishment of the first native avant-garde movement, ultraism, that flourished briefly between 1918 and 1921. But from 1922 onwards, with the exception of

23

writers associated with the adaptation of literary cubism known as creationism, there is a notable imbalance between the abundance of theoretical information being disseminated and the limited production of avant-garde writing. This is a result of the dominance of the pedagogical, modernising attitudes of Ortega's generation who wanted, in another paradox, to create a 'constructive avant-garde', in which the assimilation of formalist aesthetics, especially cubism, took primacy over militant subversion. These attitudes helped to establish a free, uncommitted dialogue between the 'avant-garde' and the 'young literature' (later known as the Generation of 1927), which came to occupy the centre-stage of the Spanish literary world in the mid-1920s, and saw itself more in the light of Ortega's concept of a minority than as a militant group, although this is how it was seen from 'outside'. The Generation of 1927 also contributed to this paradoxical dialogue their very characteristic and striking willingness to accept almost the whole of the literary tradition of Spain, which they absorbed into their espousal of a purified form of symbolism.

La Gaceta Literaria's survey on the avant-garde reveals that something called the avant-garde was still perceived to be in existence at that time, although as a phenomenon that had completed its life-cycle. Subsequently the avant-garde underwent a new crisis of assimilation into modernism when some members of the literary minorities reacted against the intellectual climate in which they had been raised by turning to irrationality and a resurgence of romantic attitudes arising from surrealism and the left-wing critique of nineteenth-century liberalism. This is the climate of the 1930s in which, to use recent critical terminology, some members of the 'young literature' stopped being 'modernists' to become 'avantgardists' whose militancy was 'directed towards changing the institution of art'.[26] Some striking examples of this can be found in the statements of poetics which the youngest members of the group contributed to Gerardo Diego's *Anthology* (1932), especially the attacks by Luis Cernuda and Vicente Aleixandre on 'pure poetry'.[27]

This is then a very complex context in which diverse strands of 'the new' are expressed in hybridised forms created by the specific circumstances of the way the avant-garde was received in the Iberian Peninsula. This is the source of the originality of Ramón

Gómez de la Serna's volume of essays and of its singular importance within that context from which it came.[28]

Notes

[1] The first edition of *Ismos*, Madrid, 1931, was augmented in subsequent
editions. Page references, bracketed in the text, are to the most recent
edition, Madrid, 1975. The references to other works mentioned in this
paragraph are as follows: J. Ortega y Gasset, *La Deshumanización del Arte*,
Madrid, 1925 (English translation, *The Dehumanisation of Art*, New York,
1972); G. de Torre, *Literaturas europeas de vanguardia*, Madrid, 1925 (2nd
and subsequent editions were much changed, the latest edition is Madrid,
1965); G. García Maroto, *La Nueva España 1930*, Madrid, 1927; F. Roh,
Realismo mágico, Madrid, 1927; E. Giménez Caballero, *Carteles*, Madrid,
1932; J. Díaz Fernández, *El nuevo romanticismo*, Madrid, 1930 (re-edited,
Madrid, 1985).

[2] *Ismos* (1975), p. 8.

[3] In R. Buckley and J. Crispin (eds.), *Los vanguardistas españoles 1925–1935*,
Madrid, 1973, p. 401.

[4] A. Soria Olmedo, *Vanguardismo y crítica literaria en España*, Madrid, 1988,
p. 288.

[5] 'Palabras en Pombo', *Ultra*, XX, 15 December 1921.

[6] I. Soldevila-Durante, 'Para la recuperación de una prehistoria embarazosa.
(Una etapa marxista de Gómez de la Serna)', in N. Dennis, *Studies on
Ramón Gómez de la Serna*, Ottawa, 1988.

[7] J. C. Mainer, 'Prólogo', in E. Serrano Asenjo, *Ramón y el arte de matar. (El
crimen en las novelas de Gómez de la Serna)*, Granada, 1992.

[8] J. Bonet, *Ramón en cuatro entregas*, vol. 1, Madrid, 1980.

[9] G. Gómez de la Serna, *Ramón (vida y obra)*, Madrid, 1963, p. 159.

[10] N. Dennis, *Studies*, p. 18.

[11] *Crónicas literarias*, Barcelona, 1985, p. 238.

[12] R. Gómez de la Serna, *Antología. Cincuenta años de literatura*, Buenos Aires,
1954, p. 27.

[13] N. Dennis, 'Prólogo', in R. Gómez de la Serna, *París*, Valencia, 1986.

[14] P. De Man, *Blindness and Insight. Essays in the Rhetoric of Contemporary
Criticism*, London, 1983.

[15] A. Martínez Collado (ed.), R. Gómez de la Serna, *Una teoría personal del
arte. Antología de textos de estética y teoría del arte*, Madrid, 1988,
p. 15.

[16] *Critiche e recensioni*, Milan, 1979, p. 35. See also R. Rossi, *Breve storia della
letteratura spagnola*, Milan, 1992, p. 162.

[17] I. Zlotescu, 'Introducción', in R. Gómez de la Serna, *El libro mudo. (Secretos)*,
Mexico, 1987.

[18] J. Bonet, *Ramón en cuatro entregas*, vol. 1, p. 77.

[19] *Ibid.*, p. 36.

[20] P. Salinas, 'Escorzo de Ramón', in Bonet, *Ramón en cuatro entregas*, vol. 3, p. 36.

[21] C. Nicolás, *Ramón y la greguería: morfología de un género nuevo*, Madrid, 1988. See also O. Paz, *Children of the Mire*, Cambridge (Mass.), 1974.

[22] W. Benjamin, *Il drama barroco tedesco*, Milan, 1971. P. Bürger, *Theory of the Avant-garde*, Manchester, 1984.

[23] M. Perloff, *The Futurist Moment. Avant-garde, Avant Guerre, and the Language of Rupture*, London, 1986, p. xviii.

[24] M. Calinescu, *Five Faces of Modernity: Modernism, Decadence, Kitsch, Avant-garde, Postmodernism*, Durham (N. Carolina), 1987.

[25] R. Wohl, *The Generation of 1914*, Cambridge (Mass.), 1979.

[26] C. Russell, *Poets, Prophets and Revolutionaries*, Oxford, 1985, p. 15.

[27] G. Diego, *Poesía española contemporánea* (ed.), A. Soria, Madrid, 1991. The most violent statement comes from Cernuda: 'There was no point in my forgetting reality little by little if I were to remember it now and in the presence of such people. I detest reality as I detest everything that belongs to it: my friends, my family, my country. ǀ I know nothing, I want nothing, I hope for nothing. And if I could still hope for something, it would only be to die in a place not yet reached by this grotesque civilisation that bloats humanity with pride.'

[28] A version of this article was given at the *45th Annual Kentucky Foreign Language Conference* at the University of Kentucky, 1992.

5. Pablo Picasso: *Harlequin*, 1917. Oil on canvas

3 / The theory of the novel in Ramón Gómez de la Serna's *The Novelist*

JOSÉ ENRIQUE SERRANO

Ramón Gómez de la Serna's novel, *The Novelist*, published in 1923, largely accords with the ideas put forward in his essay of 1909, 'The idea of a new literature', where he wrote: 'all works must be principally biographical if they are not to become teratologies'.[1] Given that Andrés Castilla, the book's protagonist, is by profession a novelist, in the light of this remark *The Novelist* itself may be considered to be somewhat 'autobiographical'.[2] In F. Gómez Redondo's view, Ramón in this novel was trying to produce 'a textual metaphor that would reflect his whole existence up to that moment',[3] so that the book would, in fact, become a lucid treatise on the art of writing fiction, although it might be said that it was not all that systematic. The reader is faced with a story that deals with a whole theory of fiction, but which does so from within the novel itself, a 'metanovel',[4] in the final analysis, and one that puts its own theory into practice in itself. The purpose of this essay is to establish the basis of Ramón's theory of the genre he so often used, a genre in need of critical rehabilitation, and also to seek to place his ideas in their historical context.[5]

First, it must be said, as the poet Luis Cernuda pointed out talking about his own relationship with poetry, that the novelist becomes a novelist whether he wants to or not; it is a matter of destiny. This is why we read in *The Novelist*: 'Every day the novelist was more convinced of the need to write that novel',[6] and later, 'he wrote each word as though it had been fired from the gun of destiny' (p. 232). The process of inevitability in the writing of the novel becomes incorporated into the flow of the novel itself. This may be a good point to recall Ford Madox Ford's words: 'Before everything a story must convey a sense of inevitability: that which happens in it must seem to be the only thing that could have happened'.[7]

The results of this inescapable vocation are threefold. In the first place, the novel must 'entertain', which is far from being a trivial aim, as it is only this which will 'distinguish one man from millions and millions of others' (p. 28) and which will cure the serious illness of 'interminable tedium, greater and more expansive than time itself' (p. 287). Also, the novel has an epistemological function, which in Ramón's case can be extended to literature in general, considering that his knowledge of the world is literary: 'I have faith, he said, that I can still understand everything and this alone is enough, and this is all I need. Only if I have this great serenity will nothing distract me from the contemplation of human passion, and it will be now that I will write my finest novels' (p. 286). What we are faced with here is the aim of uncovering things, which is itself a product of the need to understand, even though what we may discover may not be very attractive. The novel 'has done its duty, it has destroyed as much hypocrisy as possible and has, in its own way, held up a mirror to man's insignificance',[8] while it also challenges time, it 'perpetuates' reality (p. 287), so that 'a short life became long in his novel' (p. 103). So we arrive at the central issue in Gómez de la Serna's theory of the novel, the relationship between reality and fiction, or life and fiction if one prefers, which will become particularly important when dealing with his characters.

In the chapter entitled 'Novelism' included in his book *Isms*, Ramón alludes to the immortality of novels as a genre: 'it is the genre that is produced by living and which lets the reader live, because a reader reads a book several times not to learn anything, but to keep living, to live more'.[9] This is an issue that concerned many writers of the beginning of the century who were interested in fiction. Virginia Woolf, for example, suggested that it was 'the task of the novelist to convey this varying, this unknown and uncircumscribed spirit, whatever aberration of complexity it might display, with as little mixture of the alien and external as possible'.[10] Ortega y Gasset in his *Thoughts on the Novel* observed: 'the essence of the novel – note that I am only referring to modern novels – is not in what happens but rather in what "happening" means, in life itself'.[11] As far as the *The Novelist* is concerned, that extension of life, or, more accurately, that creation of a living structure, occurs because the possibility of 'living', albeit in a special form, is present in the novel: 'that was the first stage of *The Novel of Tree Street*, in which a street was going to live through a particular period, a record for the future, when streets would live very different lives' (p. 38).

Later, there is an insistence on the fruitful contact between both worlds. The term novel, therefore, means something like an 'assurance' of life, and we can ask indirectly for some additional services: 'we have to assume life to be healthy and precipitous if we just observe it. In this ideal situation a complementary breeze arises which fixes this life, which traces its outline even if it adds some element of conflict which makes the task of asserting it rather laborious' (p. 111). The 'breeze' is, of course, a metaphor for the novel. As a result, the boundaries between one and the other become hazy and it is even possible for narratives to achieve some sort of predominance over life, since, in a way, narratives are a substitute for life, or at least a definition of it. Ramón does not idly speak of 'the true meaning of the novel of life' (p. 167), and when he talks later about 'novels of life, and of books' (p. 280), the two elements can be considered to be so close that their separation seems somewhat rhetorical. Although Gómez de la Serna's thoughts on the theory of the novel ultimately do not go much beyond the idea that lies behind these words, the disturbing certainty that all life does is conceal a novel, is enough in itself.

Now we must move on to the essence of the novel itself, and to a further element of its life, its unity. In Chapter Eighteen of *The Novelist*, Gómez de la Serna relates the frustration of Andrés Castilla while writing the novel with the title *Everybody*, whose prologue contains the statement, 'life has a complex, rapid and confused unity which should be played in its own key. / One must try to convey that sense of varied boredom which is life' (p. 117). The attempt fails because it tries to be universal and all-encompassing (p. 124), but maybe it is not totally wrong to consider that *The Novelist* as a whole provides a better solution for this problem than this intercalated story. We are facing a question common to many writers of the 1930s. Baroja said in 1925 that the novel was a genre which 'includes everything . . . absolutely everything'[12] and, in the same year, André Gide declared that 'I should like to put everything into my novel . . . everything I see, everything I know, everything that other people's lives and my own teach me'.[13] However, Gómez de la Serna is more interested here in his particular type of unity, and he uses Castilla to make an attack on what is described as the 'deceitful' novelist: 'all his novels lack the light of a soul which would give them unity, however diverse their subjects' (p. 160). A similar attack is levelled at novelists in general, in what could be a reasoned explanation for this demand for stories that have unity: 'you novelists do not realise that the imagination of the world is a compact whole' (p. 251); in other words, compactness leads to unity or, to use a more suitable term for Ramón, unanimousness: 'everything that happens in the world is unanimous'.[14]

All this finally presents itself in the characters because, essentially, 'life' is too abstract a term and what really concern the writer are particular 'lives'. It is now that his wide-ranging powers are revealed: 'the novelist was at that point where he could control destiny and choose between different characters' (p. 165). The genre becomes a trade in characters, to the point where the protagonist says, when he has introduced the characters of his work *Adobe Village*: 'the novel was resolved. He had already caused the two main characters to hurl themselves at each other' (p. 145). Another compulsive writer and fan of newspaper serials, the novelist Pío Baroja, stated that this was the crux of writing novels: 'for me, in the novel as in literature as a whole, the problem is how to invent; above all how to invent characters who have life'.[15] But unlike Baroja, Gómez de la Serna tries to give an account of the process by which fictional characters materialise.

In fact, even if the 'invention' proposed by Baroja does seem similar to the 'creative' impulse quoted in *The Novelist*, we can see theoretical differences emerge once Ramón explains how Castilla obtains characters for his stories: 'I do not create them . . . I find them and I begin to rely on them as genuine and real people' (p. 87). This confrontation between the narrator who invents and the narrator who finds, despite being a subject much commented on by various contemporary writers,[16] is a problem in fiction writing that can have a variety of solutions. It is an issue which specially interests us here, because behind the defence of the 'searching novelist' undertaken by Gómez de la Serna lies his personal vision of the literary universe, not to mention the fact that he comes to discover, as though that were necessary, the *raison d'être* of a text centred on a literary man, who is obviously the human model closest to Gómez de la Serna himself: 'the characters he presents in his novels are simply the images of those he has seen and taken from real life, including himself as the novelist'.[17]

Chapter Ten of the novel, entitled 'In Search of Characters', reflects somewhat mockingly on these issues. It is worth remembering that a couple of times Castilla is referred to as a 'realist' author (p. 287). Obviously, Ramón did not understand the term in

31

a strictly nineteenth-century sense, but curiously his attitude towards fictional characters could be confused with an odd sort of
documentary, a 'living' documentary inescapably bound up with
the fate of the novel. 'He searched for them while they were very
much alive so that nobody could accuse him of creating rag
dolls. . . . He was perhaps the first novelist who had recourse to
newspaper advertisements'. In other words, if he required, for
example, a self-sacrificing woman for his story, he would meet and
interview as many women of this type as possible. The result is
that 'thanks to this method, he could record live voices telling him
things he could never have imagined alone' (p. 61). The idea
behind such encounters was not so much a distrust of the creative
capacity of the writer, unimaginable in one who could himself
sketch out a whole range of passions in a few lines,[18] but rather it
was the belief mentioned above, that novelistic matter is part of
life itself. Still in the same chapter, Castilla says, 'all of you have
lots and lots of different novels but you do all you can to hide them
and not let them be glimpsed' (p. 62), and later he uses a very
powerful image which fuses all these ideas, 'a novelist is a true
detective' (p. 63).

In respect of what the characters in the novel do, Gómez de la
Serna provides a brief but revealing curriculum linked to the city
of Venice, because Ramón's settings are very nearly as important
as the characters who inhabit them:[19] 'in Venice, one can bring
characters to life, one can take them to the theatre, make them fall
in love, marry and kill them with great ease' (p. 194). In other
words, living means frustrating the enemy, time; going to the
theatre is also loving, as subsequent actions in the novel prove, and
finally, life itself becomes a crime at the hands of the creator, be he
the novelist or the demiurge we find in the works of Unamuno. A
couple of quotations will suffice to illustrate the basic aspects
referred to here. The fact that the novel is inseparable from the
area of sensuality is illustrated in the discussion with the false
'noveller', where Castilla states that he creates that part of life
'much more than a woman does' (p. 160). The connection with
violent death, and it is clear that for Ramón all death is violent, is
made obvious at the end of Castilla's novel *The Siamese Twins*:
'He saw that the doll that was his double was broken and felt more
sorry than when he killed other characters' (p. 235). The novelist

is not only a detective, but also a murderer, although that is another story.

We must return to the method of acquiring fictional characters. We saw how the most direct way was for the writer to approach real people to extract their personal experiences from them. Such an approach colours the relationship between the author and his creations in a particular light. If the fictional character is born of a real one, the opposite process can also take place. For the moment, it is worth observing a situation created by searching for possible fictional characters: 'She was, without doubt the protagonist of a novel dressed up in reality. Andrés spoke with her, but when he said he was a novelist, she burst into tears, pleading with him not to tell her anything and, above all, not to kill her at the end of the novel' (p. 64). It is not so much that a person as real as Castilla can be the basis for a fictional character, but that such a person may consider himself to be a fiction. As a result, some of the author's fears are perfectly justified: 'he had always feared meeting one of his characters' and his alter ego holds a conversation with the protagonist of one of his works, 'whom he could not convince of his own inexistence before the book' (p. 27). Observe how, if we assume Castilla's method for collecting material for writing, we must doubt his statement about the non-existence of his visitor before the novel was written. The latter could in fact be right: 'it is not coincidence, sir, it is a complete case which has reached your ears and which you have in turn spread abroad' (p. 27). Remember that the novelist is also a fable-writer.

In this way, the characters of this work are placed on the same level of reality as their assumed creators, just as in Unamuno's novel *Fog*, although in a less conflictive manner,[20] and they ultimately become like permanent accomplices from the bad times through to the glorious old age of the author (p. 283). Naturally, this continuous moving between the novel and the real world ends up affecting the character of Andrés Castilla himself. Thus, it is fairly understandable that, when Castilla comes face to face with one of his inventions, Dr Witterman, this character should look 'at the novelist as his very dear collaborator' (p. 252). What is more, in Paris the author meets Rémy Valey, the distinguished French writer, and as they speak, he asks himself, 'is he the son of the strange characters in his books or are they his sons?' (p. 183). Here

33

we must note that the first possibility considered is that the created being is superior to the creator. This art of narration leads to Ramón-Castilla being referred to by what is a key word. When he explains the necessity of having different houses to write in, he says: 'thus becoming a different novelist and a different *character* of the art of writing novels' (p. 43, [italics added]).[21]

But not only is the novelist a fictional character, he is also a reader, as his dealings with Valey or the English writer Ardith Colmer demonstrate (p. 171). It is not by accident that the two writers he presents as model novelists should be counted among his favourite authors. We must pause to consider the particular role which Gómez de la Serna attributes to readers of novels because, although he does not provide much information on the subject, they are as involved in the whole process of the novel as its creator or the characters he conjures up. Reading, in fact, becomes an act of vital affirmation which is difficult to ignore, as much for the readers as for the author: 'if readers wanted to discover true life, without doubts, they had to search for his [Castilla's] novels and encourage him to continue them' (pp. 109–10). Even more serious implications can be found in an early concern of Castilla's: 'how could he allow him to appear again in a run of thousands of copies, taking new victims, preparing himself to spark off new passions?' (p. 13). Reading, as we have seen, offers a life of special intensity, encompassing all types of suffering, including love, or, at the very least, entails it risks. Not the least of these risks are the doubts which can affect the reader about his own existence itself after reflecting on the issues raised over the degree of fiction which surround the novelist, in theory the reader's equal. What has been reached here through a process of legitimate deduction becomes, in Unamuno's *Fog*, the *raison d'être* of that *nivola*: '. . . the reader of the *nivola* will doubt, even for a brief moment, his own physical reality and will believe himself to be, like us, no more than a character from a *nivola*'.[22]

Andrés Castilla does not explain in any detail how this vocation to which he refers comes about and we can even detect some contradictions on the rare occasions he mentions this subject. At the fountainhead of writing he places Inspiration, personified as one of the regular visitors, a woman, who seems to parade through a somewhat magical house. She is, naturally, largely concerned with providing characters and is variously called 'hunter of life, man-hunter and woman-hunter' (p. 22). Later Castilla abandons her, if only to prove the importance of her absence. In any case, she is 'his personal broker [. . .] a nosey go-between, always causing trouble and interfering' (p. 64). All this does not prevent the work ending up as one way of reaching fictions, whether or not other writers proceed in this manner: 'but all others create their novels without writing, except for me, who has to kill himself with so much work!' (p. 172).

Nonetheless, Ramón's protagonist recognises that although literature is recognised as a 'higher science' (p. 128), he possesses no particular technique to do his job, other than trying to surprise his readers. This, once more, places us in the realm of life and of the *nivola*: 'what he lacked was technique, although his novels were distinguished by certain repetitions and an arbitrary air which showed them not to belong to any identifiable norm' (p. 109). This arbitrariness reveals one of the essential qualities of 'the novel' (p. 128). Unamuno speaks in similar terms: 'I am going to write a novel, but I will write it like life itself, without knowing what will happen next. I sat down, took some paper and wrote the first thing that came into my head, without knowing what would follow, without any plan'.[23] Finally, attention must be drawn to an aspect hinted at by Gómez de la Serna but which does not receive the arbitrary mode of treatment generally to be found in story books; that is, those 'repetitions' which make his texts seem so familiar, especially repetitions related to objects, because, as he writes in another passage, the use of 'detail' in his novels is a fundamental tool, to create, for example, the truth for which he seeks (p. 145).

In order to try to piece together a conclusion perhaps it is best to follow Castilla through the days when he cannot be a novelist: 'he walked amongst un-novelled people who went through a life that was on the whole clean and un-novelled, sneezing from monotony and mediocrity' (p. 88). Just before that he has said that in order to reach this state, one must see the day with 'clairvoyance'.For an instant, the reader of *The Novelist* thinks that Ramón is almost in a repentant mood (note how a positive element such as 'clean' is put together with the repeated term 'un-novelled'), suggesting that novels can give up their privileged position in his personal universe, but the reasons for his bouts of sneezing are beyond doubt. He insists on what those 'non-novellable' days are like: 'they were, apparently days to see everything on the surface . . . On non-novellable days the world turned into a world in which one only lives and dies, just that, nothing more' (p. 89). In fact, he does not predicate any particular advantages for fictions. His tactic here is to hint at the significance of its absence, and what could have appeared as a scene with subdued lighting, becomes, with a few stylistic changes, the landscape of desolation. The meaning of life without stories becomes simply meaningless, underlining the paltry value in living and dying with 'nothing else' and an emphatic 'just that, nothing more'. The consequences could not be more obvious. The novel no longer presents a problem of varying importance, it has become quite simply essential.

At the end of this necessarily brief examination of a book that encompasses the whole development of Andrés Castilla, and also to a great extent of his alter ego, Ramón Gómez de la Serna, we should perhaps recognise that, ultimately, the writer speaks less about the art of writing than it seems, and more about the art of living. Without doubt, this is at the heart of the 'metanovelistic' considerations, the connection between the novel and the world. A special image can help us complete this approach to 'the novel'. In his book *Contemporary Portraits*, Ramón says of Unamuno: 'Unamuno's life as a novelist is a pure mess, a fertile novelistic mess, because a novel is more of a novel the more of a mess it is'.[24] The novel is complex, labyrinthine (pp. 195, 232), but in this it is merely reflecting life itself: 'to present a novel without the true mess of life seems to me to be a waste of time'.[25] The novel also reflects the world, where man loses himself irretrievably. Ortega defined the novelist as 'the man who, as he writes, is more interested in his own imaginary world than in any other possible world'.[26] This, applied to someone whose biography is his literature, presents us with the surprising possibility that Ramón constantly was more concerned with his fictional fields of activity than with any others. To put this simply, the real world, for Gómez de la Serna, was essentially a painful, but passionate novel.

36

Notes

1 R. Gómez de la Serna, *Una teoría personal del arte. Antología de textos y estética y teoría del arte*, Madrid, 1988, p. 62. See also C. Richmond, 'Introducción', in R. Gómez de la Serna, *El secreto del acueducto*, Madrid, 1986, p. 54.

2 Cf. P. Baroja, 'Prólogo casi doctrinal sobre la novela', in *La nave de los locos* (1925), *Obras Completas*, vol. iv, Madrid, 1973, p. 325.

3 'Ramón: greguería y novela', *Cuadernos para la Investigación de la Literatura Hispánica*, XI, 1989, p. 151.

4 N. M. Valis, '*The Novelist*, por Ramón Gómez de la Serna, o la novela en busca de sí misma', in *Actas del IX Congreso de la Asociación Internacional de Hispanistas*, vol. II, Frankfurt, 1989, p. 420.

5 Cf. A. Gide, *Les Faux-Monnayeurs* (1925), in M. Allott, *Novelists on the novel*, London, 1975, p. 79: 'What I want is to represent reality on the one hand, and on the other that effort to stylise it into art of which I have just been speaking.'

6 R. Gómez de la Serna, *The Novelist*, Madrid, 1973, p. 19. All quotations in this essay are from this edition and bracketed in the text.

7 *Joseph Conrad, A Personal Remembrance* (1924), in Allott, *Novelists*, p. 245.

8 Cf. Ford Madox Ford, 'I have always had the greatest contempt for novels written with a purpose. Fiction should render, not draw morals.' *It was the Nightingale* (1934), in Allott, *Novelists*, p. 103.

9 R. Gómez de la Serna, *Ismos* (1931), Madrid, 1975, p. 351.

10 V. Woolf, 'Modern Fiction' (1919), in Allott, *Novelists*, p. 77.

11 J. Ortega y Gasset, 'Ideas sobre la novela', in *La deshumanización del arte. Ideas sobre la novela*, Madrid, 1925, pp. 126–7. R. C. Spires, *Transparent Simulacra. Spanish Fiction 1902–26*, Columbia (Missouri), 1988, p. 108, considers that *The Novelist* can be read as an immediate precursor to Ortega's theory on the dehumanisation of art.

12 P. Baroja, *Obras Completas*, 1973, p. 313.

13 A. Gide, *Les Faux-Monnayeurs*, in Allott, *Novelists*, p. 79.

14 R. Gómez de la Serna, *El hombre perdido* (1947), Madrid, 1962, p. 211.

15 Baroja, *Obras Completas*, 1973, p. 314.

16 Cf. Gide's attitude in *Journal des Faux Monnayeurs* (1927): 'The poor novelist constructs his characters, he controls them and he makes them speak. The true novelist listens to them and watches them function; he eavesdrops on them even before he knows them' (Allott, *Novelists*, p. 291), with that of Mauriac in *Dieu et mammon* (1929): '... for the real novelist is not an observer, but a creator of fictitious life. It is not his function to observe life but to create it. He brings living people into the world; he does not observe them from some lofty vantage point. He even confuses and, in a way, loses his own personality in the subject of his creation, and his identification with it is pushed so far that he actually becomes his creation' (Allott, *Novelists*, p. 80).

[17] M. González-Gerth, *A Labyrinth of Imagery: Ramón Gómez de la Serna's 'novelas de la nebulosa'*, London, 1986, p. 42.

[18] Cf. C. Nicolás, *Ramón y la greguería. Morfología de un género nuevo*, Madrid, 1988, p. 42.

[19] But the novelistic city is Lisbon 'for those types of exhausted life that live there, these totally isolated old men with moustaches belonging to some extinct species, and old women broken by long life. The best ingredients for a novel', p. 201.

[20] Cf. Gonzalez-Gerth, *A Labyrinth*, p. 39.

[21] See M. D. Rugg, 'The Figure of the Author in Gómez de la Serna's *The Novelist*', *Anales de Literatura Española Contemporánea*, XIV, 1989, pp. 143–59.

[22] M. de Unamuno, *Niebla*, Madrid, 1982, p. 167.

[23] *Ibid.*, p. 119. Cf. Gide, *Les Faux-Monnayeurs*: 'X maintains that a good novelist, before he begins to write his book, ought to know how it is going to finish. As for me, who let mine flow where it will, I consider that life never presents us with anything which may not be looked upon as a fresh starting point, no less than as a termination' (Allott, *Novelists*, p. 251).

[24] *Retratos Contemporáneos* (1941), Madrid, 1989, p. 357.

[25] R. Gómez de la Serna, *El hombre perdido*, p. 8.

[26] *Ideas sobre la novela*, p. 138.

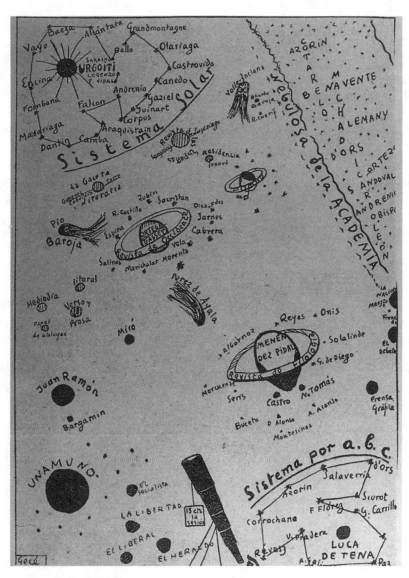

6. Ernesto Giménez Caballero: 'Universe of contemporary Spanish literature', *Carteles*, Madrid, Espasa Calpe, 1927, no. 11

4 / Writers and the bathroom: readings in the Spanish avant-garde   NIGEL DENNIS

The Spanish avant-garde was once described as 'the age of clean-liness' and this description provides a useful starting point for what follows.[1] There is an intriguing emphasis on the principle of hygiene in the definitions of the avant-garde movement in Spain and of the attitudes that fuelled it. In their *Catalan Antiartistic Manifesto* of 1928 Dalí, Montanyà and Gasch referred to the 'hygienic state of mind' prevalent among the young radicals of their generation, and a year later Gerardo Diego praised the 'hygienic, iconoclastic endeavour' of the first wave of subversive literary innovators in Spain.[2] They probably refer back to Marinetti's contention in the Futurist Manifesto of 1909 that war was 'the world's only hygiene',[3] so focusing on some of the guiding principles of the European avant-garde: the hostility towards the aesthetic norms of the past and the belligerent proposition that art and literature should represent only the icons and sensibilities of a stridently new urban, industrial reality.

In the context of the discussion that follows, it is also intriguing to recall a famous definition of Spanish avant-garde writing that circulated in Madrid in the 1920s and was recorded by Max Aub, an alert observer of the literary scene of the time and an active participant in its experiments. Aub recounts how the term 'little literary turd' was coined in order to describe the ideal avant-garde literary text: 'A little literary turd was understood to be a very short work produced with difficulty, exquisite in its choice of adornment, difficult to understand at first sight, a disguise for ingenious, inconsequential ideas and the ultimate goal of the efforts of a young writer'.[4] It is not difficult to discern the truth behind the irony. Even if all parts of the definition cannot be applied to all products of the Spanish avant-garde, they nonetheless signal an ideal literary outlook diagnosed by Ortega in *The Dehumanisation of Art* (1925) and enshrined, on the one hand, in the work of Juan Ramón Jiménez and his constant appeals for conscious, methodical refinement and purification and, on the other, in what Giménez Caballero called the prevailing 'aim of the minority': 'to write little and well'.[5]

Within this framework, it seems somehow inevitable that certain writers of the avant-garde should have occasionally chosen to situate their work in the bathroom, viewing it, apparently, as a kind of *locus amoenus* in which they could painstakingly devise their contributions to the process of literary innovation. At the same time, it seems only appropriate that the production of at least some of these so-called 'little literary turds' should take place within its discrete confines. All the texts reviewed below refer directly to the bathroom, either using it as a setting or dwelling on particular items of its decor. Beyond this convergence at a purely thematic level, the justification for bringing them together here is that they provide points of access to some of the key modalities of avant-garde writing in Spain.

Ramón Gómez de la Serna provides a useful starting point for this discussion since his work, especially in the *greguerías*, directs attention towards reality as a spectacle of objects and appearances with enigmatic properties and incongruent interconnecting relationships. In sifting through those objects and appearances, Gómez de la Serna rejects conventional hierarchies, finding a lyrical dawn sky, for example, as engaging as a prosaic set of false teeth. He once wrote: 'What characterises me is the tenderness I feel in the innermost part of my being towards things . . . A block of wood, a large nail, an ashtray. Things want to tell us something but . . . they are unable to find a single mouth to speak with a single language'.[6] In assuming the responsibility of acting as spokesman for the mutely expressive contents of the world, the writer legitimised any object, no matter how modest. This process of artistic legitimisation rests on the principle of constant interpretation, metamorphosis and embellishment. Seemingly fixed identities are constantly blurred and confused as Ramón tirelessly transforms one thing into another. He attributed this, among other things, to what he called 'the higher understanding of humour' which, he goes on to say, 'accepts that things can exist in a different fashion . . . accepts that in a world of relativities opposites are possible, although reason may find this improbable . . .'[7] His own work can be read at one level as an intense, virtuoso exercise in extreme imaginative transformations, based on the principle that 'today it is necessary to use two images every five seconds of writing so that tomorrow we can use three in the same five seconds'.[8] Many writers of the Spanish avant-garde, even if they lacked Ramón's stamina, seem to have done their best to follow his advice.

Predictably, then, Ramón was the first writer to suggest, albeit implicitly and sporadically, that the bathroom contained as much potential inspiration as any other more conventionally artistic

41

locale. He made use of it, as he did of many other prosaic scenarios, to demonstrate that anonymous, utilitarian objects could be playfully and imaginatively interpreted. As subject matter, for example, the bathroom and its contents surface from time to time in the *greguerías*: 'The wisest invention in the world is the flush mechanism for the toilet whose chain turns us all, when we pull it, into a miraculous Moses .... When you run the water out of the bath it voices its objections .... In bathrooms there is a prison for toothbrushes'.[9] They also occasionally appear in the writer's novelistic prose, enlivening the narrator's descriptions and his characters' observations. In *Cinelandia*, for example, a character named Mary 'claimed that bidets were like fonts of holy water that purified the previous day' while the car in which the stars Max and Elsa cruise around is described in the following terms: 'it was a sort of big, special automobilistic bathroom. When he and she went out in it they looked as though they were having a bath together, all dressed up in an ideal bathtub. Lying back, their heads stuck out of a bath of pure pleasure'.[10]

These are isolated examples, but they point to particular recurring emphases in Ramón's writing and to certain general principles developed by some of the writers under review here. As Luis Cernuda reminds us, Ramón's way of handling metaphor in his *greguerías* and elsewhere had a notable impact on the major poets of the twenties.[11] I would single out as his most fervent and conscientious disciple not a poet but a prose writer, Ernesto Giménez Caballero. Giménez Caballero professed unconditional admiration for Ramón, viewing him as 'the father of all the Spanish *ultras*',[12] and he certainly gives the impression, in his 'Ode to the bidet', for example, of having learned much of his craft while seated at the master's feet. The first part of this text reads as follows:

THE BIDET: NICKEL AND PORCELAIN
The bidet has a guitar's curves.
The bidet has a snake's sinuousness.
The bidet has a woman's thighs.
The bidet has a colt's withers.
The bidet has a bicycle's movement.
The bidet has a black man's hard teeth.

The bidet has a glacier's whiteness.
The bidet has a skate's slipperiness.
The bidet has a rivulet's sound.
The bidet has a lake's way of looking.
The bidet has an infant fountain's basin.
The bidet has a pearl's reflection.
The bidet has unfathomable fauna.
The bidet has stars inside it.
The bidet has a billard ball's shine.
The bidet has an obstetrician's eye.
The bidet has a confessor's mission.
The bidet has the Pope's absolution.
The bidet has everlasting chastity.[13]

This ode can be read as a creative homage to Gómez de la Serna in the way it strings together independent, *greguería*-like interpretative definitions of the bidet, roaming over its parts and dwelling on the full range of its specific attributes (shape, colour, texture, consistency, sound . . .) as well as its abstract associations. The text exhibits that calculated ingenuity and audacity that characterise much of Giménez Caballero's creative writing at the time and recalls how other poets of the decade, Pedro Salinas and Luis Cernuda, for example, riveted their powers of imaginative representation and interpretation on the most unpoetic objects.

However, the adjective 'unpoetic' in this context is notably inapposite since one of the central thrusts of avant-garde thinking was to revise the whole issue of aesthetic status and to propose new standards of beauty. In Spain, as elsewhere, new priorities, new values, new subjects were championed in an attempt to bring art and literature into closer alignment with the realities of a bustling new century. César Arconada, for example, signalled these changing affiliations when, in 1927, he exultantly, if naively, saluted 'the world of our age': 'In opposition to the café, the *tertulia*, politics, the theatre, we proclaim our things: the cinema, action, sport, women with bobbed hair. In opposition to the artist, the politician, the actor, we proclaim the new hero: the footballer, the boxer, the car driver'.[14] It is clearly a question of what Giménez Caballero called 'a new and radical point of view' and involved, among other things, a reconsideration of what constituted the valid subject matter of art and literature.[15]

This point is made even more explicitly in the *Catalan Antiartistic Manifesto*:

> Let us feast our eyes on the marvellous reality we have before us; let us capture the real essence of our time and let us learn to take from it its beauty as did other ages that were true to themselves, so producing their original creations. When people have tried to make art in our day they have turned to the dead, past norms of other times that could be of no use in our hands. The true aesthetic inspiration of our time is, therefore, in the anonymous constructions made with no artistic intention and for utilitarian ends, like the motor car, the aeroplane, the camera, simple mass-produced objects, etc. Their inventors, unsullied by artistic prejudices, have spontaneously caught in their creations the simple beauty of today.[16]

Giménez Caballero's 'Ode to the bidet' is not just a homage to Ramón but also an exaltation precisely of one of those 'anonymous constructions made with no artistic intention'. The writer undoubtedly acknowledged the bidet to be a useful object, but he also considered it worthy of being elevated into the subject matter of the new literature of the twenties, to be handled with the same subtlety, admiration and creative insight that his forebears of the nineteenth century would have reserved, perhaps, for a blood-red rose or the setting sun.

This concept of 'the simple beauty of today' and its implications for the revision of aesthetic norms in the avant-garde can best be appreciated if we turn to what was another probable point of reference Giménez Caballero had in mind when he wrote his ode: Marcel Duchamp's 'ready-made' of 1917 entitled *Fontaine*, his famous urinal turned upside down. Even though a bidet is not a urinal (despite the proverbial confusion of the British abroad), the sense of Duchamp's gesture and the deliberate choice of subject, shed light on Giménez Caballero's text. Duchamp ironically defamiliarises a common object by placing it in a new, incongruous context, thereby endowing it with an artistic meaning and intentionality it would otherwise lack. In an analogous way, Giménez Caballero ironically instates the bidet in an unfamiliar setting (and genre), presenting a new version of what constitutes artistic legitimacy.

It is helpful to remember that Duchamp also devised what he called 'rectified ready-mades', objects or images that are entirely familiar and recognisable in a given context but which have been slightly modified, thereby radically altering their original sense. The most notorious is Leonardo's Mona Lisa with a moustache entitled *L.H.O.O.Q*, a paradigm of 'the struggle against the museum', with its blatant subversion of artistic traditions and conventions. A similar process seems to be at work in texts by Francisco Ayala, 'Susana leaving her bath' (1928), and Gerardo Diego, 'Bathroom' (1932). They too can be read as 'rectified ready-mades': they are firmly anchored in scenes or events that have fixed, pre-established pictorial connotations. Both writers toy subversively with given data, pre-existing artistic realities (to say nothing of pre-existing texts), with the objective of deflating and 'updating' them, bringing them more closely into harmony with 'the world of our age'.

SUSANA LEAVING HER BATH

The two nickel taps – strange birds clinging to the smooth skin of the bath – gazed, pensively, the tub now cold without hot water, on the dramatic angle of her head. Head of red-green seaweed floating away in the porcelain hollow.

The water, neither hot nor cold, sang in her ears, pink and tender shells, a song of mirror-silver. It trembled in the bath to deflect her form; it multiplied each outline in liquid waves, and shut her throat with a green thread: her dead head – her eyes dead in a maritime dream! – on a tray of crystal.

One elastic, imminent minute.

An arm rose, like a signal. Lined with veins and dripping. The five fingers, five roots inserted in the sponge. The hand opened, and the sponge – blond star – sunk into a tepid dawn of flesh and porcelain . . . [17]

Ayala's point of reference or pre-text is the Biblical story of two old men spying lasciviously on the beautiful young married Susanna, while she bathes in what is, naturally enough, an open-air bath. Renaissance painters were drawn to the subject because of its powerful contrasts, pictorial sensuality and moral-didactic

45

potential. Tintoretto painted four versions of the scene, one of which was purchased by Velázquez on behalf of the Spanish crown on one of his trips to Italy and now hangs in the Prado, although Ayala's text seems closer to a version in Vienna.

What Ayala does essentially is to recontextualise the episode: Susanna climbs out of the bath and, as in Tintoretto's painting, looks at herself in the mirror; but in Ayala's version she emerges from a modern bathtub, complete with up-to-date metal fittings, located in a closed and equally modern bathroom. Significantly, Ayala maintains the rich sensuality of Tintoretto's painting by using the most modern of means: the cinematic technique of slow motion. Like a camera lens, the writer's eye lingers over each object, gesture or movement, highlighting and interpreting them as it slowly and self-consciously records the scene. The opening paragraphs, in which the 'nickel and porcelain' of Giménez Caballero's bidet put in an expressive appearance, stand as a fine example of Spanish avant-garde prose. It is interesting to observe how inanimate objects (the taps, the bath, the water . . .) spring to life, becoming alert observers of, or active participants in the scene, while Susanna herself is relegated to the status of mere object, mere spectacle of appearances, dehumanised into pure pre-text for the demonstration of the writer's ingenuity. It is notable too how Ayala strings together the multiple images with absolute discipline and coherence. The reader cannot fail to be struck by the insistent transformations that re-render the identity of each item, embellishing them through metaphor. The outcome is that a basically banal and prosaic scene (a woman getting out of the bath) is changed into something exquisitely artistic while at the same time remaining emphatically non-transcendental. Ayala has deliberately excluded the anecdotal, moral dimension of the scene (gone are the elders and the dramatic juxtaposition of innocence and depravity) and has narrowed the focus to serve his own purely aesthetic ends.

This, then, is a memorable example of neogongorism in prose, but a neogongorism refracted through the sensibility of the avant-garde and informed, above all, by a cinematic mode of perception. In 'Susana leaving her bath', the planes of description accumulate and become superimposed on each other, intensifying the meanings suggested. The slow rhythm of the text recalls an interesting observation on the cinema made by the young Dalí: 'The tree, the street, the game of rugby are disturbingly transubstantiated in the cinema; a sweet but measured dizziness leads us to specific sensual transmutations. The tree, the street, the game of rugby, can be savoured slowly with a straw, like an iced drink...'[18] Ayala's writing is clearly also to be savoured at leisure.

It should be borne in mind that Ayala's text is by no means an aberration of the period. It seems to have inspired other literary versions of this same Biblical scene. In 1929, the writer Agusti Eclasans published in *La Gaceta Literaria* a much longer and more elaborate version under the title 'Susanna in her bath'.[19] It lacks the tautness and discipline of Ayala's text but explores similar motifs and pursues the same stylistic emphases. More importantly, other Spanish avant-garde writers similarly resurrect Biblical characters and re-interpret them in a modern context. One striking example would be the figure of Saul in Benjamín Jarnés's novel *Theory of the Whipping-Top String* (1930). The Biblical Saul's traumatic encounter on the road to Damascus is suitably reorchestrated: he appears as a motorist (perhaps the heroic car driver admired by Arconada?) who has an accident on the highway, the effect of which is to provide him with a direct, mystical vision of God.

Ayala's text draws attention to the way in which the past – artistic tradition, literary convention – is sometimes handled in the avant-garde. The past is clearly present here (in the shape of the Biblical Susanna and of Tintoretto's representation of her), but it is ironically transfigured, disfigured and re-rooted in a modern setting. This curious ambivalence, a simultaneous attachment to the past and a resolve to reconfigure or rectify it, is condensed in one of the statements made in the *Catalan Antiartistic Manifesto*: 'For us Greece continues to exist in the mathematical calculations for an aeroplane engine, in the antiartistic, anonymously manufactured cloth made for golfing clothes, in the striptease of the American music-hall....'[20] The past does tend to figure prominently in avant-garde writing, wearing a disguise that is often as transparent as the moustache of Duchamp's Giaconda.

This ambivalent attitude towards the past is manifest in the early work of Gerardo Diego that swings wildly between the extremes of pure literary tradition and the most daring, ingenious and emphatically modern experimental writing. These conflicting affiliations are brought together somewhat precariously in some of the poems of *True Skylark* (1941), particularly in the sonnet 'Bathroom':

> What brightness of beach at midday,
> What sea shell, what tombs, near and far,
> If, amidst foam, silver and tiles,
> Venus is reborn to mythology.
> Porcelain shell, the bath entrusts
> Her birth to the long love of mirrors,
> Which, dazzled, blinded by reflections,
> Mist with a blush of cold fog.
> Behold, sweet-smelling, the naked goddess.
> Her skin exudes a halo of softness
> That absolves itself and lingers in the air.
> Venus, shyly wrapped in her towel, flees.
> Her soul dissolves in the mirrors,
> Only a tap – oblivion – weeps and weeps.[21]

If, in Ayala's text, a Biblical theme is subjected to a process of 'modernisation', in Diego's sonnet, an episode from classical mythology, the birth of Venus, is resituated and updated. We encounter again a playfully ironic or subversive recontextualisation of given data, also inscribed in a well known painting from the early Renaissance, Botticelli's *Birth of Venus*. The classical myth is delicately respun: Venus is not born in the sea but rather reborn in a bath. She does not emerge from a sea-shell but from a porcelain bath-tub; the foaming waves, plants and flowers of Botticelli's painting are transformed into a backdrop of bathroom tiles; the mist becomes the steam rising from the bath water, clouding up the bathroom mirrors. And the closing reference to the flight of this imaginary, reborn Venus (probably a modern young lady with bobbed hair, of the kind so admired by Arconada) is deftly deflated by the final allusion to the solitary, abandoned, tearful, dripping tap.

In the Spanish avant-garde there are other instances of mythological characters being reborn, albeit in disguise. Hermes is brought back to life in a bizarre way by Antonio de Obregón in his book *Hermes on the Highway* (1934), and the young athletic

Hercules is resurrected by Giménez Caballero in his novel *Hercules Playing Dice* (1928). We might also mention the neurotic central character of Juan José Domenchina's *Nesus's Tunic* (1929).

Miguel Hernández included two poems in his first book, *Moon Expert* (1933), that deserve a place in this discussion because of both their subject matter and the particular emphasis they pursue. These poems are examples of the tortured syntax and allusive complexity of neogongorism, the following translations can only hint at their difficulty:

ABOMINATION

Although bitter and only occasionally,
We shall all have palms in our hands,
Palms, for the eldest ones in the wind
Shall not reach, even by burning, both their elbows.
Then, subsequent sufferings
Will makes us light, free of slime:
The last cheeks, sailing before the wind,
Shall glide briefly over Europa's china.

LAVATORY

That pure moon of the basin
You have only to eclipse completely
Where your existence digs deepest
From the exact cloistered place.
But lower your eyes respectfully
When you find it still and round!
A paired moon, indeed, to urge on serpents,
Perhaps the Virgin has one too.[22]

The fact that the first poem carries a dedication to Giménez Caballero is significant. While it certainly expresses the poet's gratitude for the reception he was given by the editor of *La Gaceta Literaria* in Madrid when he first went there in 1931, it also suggests that the poem was conceived and executed as a complement to the 'Ode to the bidet'.[23] Both poems quoted above have a good deal in common with Giménez Caballero's ode and other texts discussed here as well as with some of the creative drives associated with the Spanish avant-garde: the choice, on the one hand, of prosaic and seemingly poetically unpromising subjects, and, on the other, the artistic transfiguration and elevation of those subjects by means of a dense and highly polished metaphoric interpretation. These poems are prime examples of the hermetic neogongorism of the late twenties, a type of writing that throws out a calculated challenge to the reader, deliberately obscuring its meaning in the expectation that the reader's pleasure will be all the greater when that meaning is finally unveiled.[24] When the poems were first published they carried no titles whatsoever, so reinforcing their secretiveness and celebrating their quasi-unintelligibility. This, in turn, explains how the poetic tradition to which the poems of *Moon Expert* are most closely related is the popular one of the riddle, the text being a set of clues to the identity of the unnamed object.[25]

While valid, these remarks overlook the particular circumstances in which Hernández composed *Moon Expert* and the function that the poems in it ultimately perform. Before his first trip to Madrid in 1931, Hernández lived largely in rural isolation, struggling to combine his poetic vocation, fuelled by his own reading of Spanish poetry, with the modest realities of the world in which he moved. Towards the end of 1932, he wrote to Juan Ramón Jiménez:

> ...For me the song is inevitable. Unlettered, clumsy, I know that my writing poetry profanes divine art... It is not my fault if my soul carries a spark of the fire that burns in yours...
>
> What will you, so refined, so exquisite, think when you see this? Look: I hate the poverty in which I was born, I don't know... I hate it above all because it is the reason for the unlettered condition which does not let me express myself well and clearly, to say the many things I think...[26]

Moon Expert represents an attempt to reconcile poverty and the lowly routine it imposes (milking cows, tending sheep, and, one might add, going to the bathroom, though this particular chore knows no socio-economic boundaries...) with the practice of the sublime art of poetry. Each of the 42 poems in the book is devoted to some item in that rural inventory: a fig, a cockrel, a well, a scarecrow, a cow's udder, an egg, a wooden table . . . All the poems elevate their subject matter artistically, to be sure, but in so doing, they collectively provide the poet with the salvation he seeks, liberation from what he called 'the critical situation of my life made ugly by its foul smell and wretched estate'.[27] Just as in the best of Ramón Gómez de la Serna's writing, reality and the writer become imbued with a sense of redemption.

I would like to close this discussion by returning to Gómez de la Serna and recalling the neurotic, slightly deranged central character in his novel *The Lost Man* who flees from a hostile world and finds his own salvation in the reassuring refuge of the bathroom. There, he gazes lovingly at the pure, silent shapes around him, relishing that same space and those same seductive objects that exerted this curious fascination for some of his comrades-in-arms of the Spanish avant-garde:

I felt my life enclosed like fruit in a tin. I had juice with which to live an entire juice-filled life, but I felt more lost than ever.

Like an aberration in that imprisonment I began to fall in love with the washbasin in the bathroom, its antiseptic porcelain, its shining taps, its appearance of a clean font, with the lunar gleam of porcelain, with the stainless fidelity of the faucets.

If I could say it I would say:

'I have fallen in love with the porcelain thighs of my washbasin, with the tap which responds to the hand that makes it pour water or stop it at will!'

It is the arrangement of the metallic object joined to the watery depths of the earth, a telephone communication with rivers and springs.

Within me I felt a strength coming from the pure and perfect washbasin, with its smooth, delicate curves, with its soapy shoulders.

It was my last hope and salvation: the response of the unpolluted washbasin, graceful in its own right, uncompromising in its solid, compact, shining material.

I have often shut myself in the bathroom just to gaze on its rounded, gymnastic forms and its nickel-plated faucets . . .[28]

The Spanish avant-garde
Notes

[1] Esteban Salazar y Chapela, in his reply to the survey on the avant-garde organized by *La Gaceta Literaria* in 1930; in R. Buckley and J. Crispin, *Los vanguardistas españoles (1925–1935)*, Madrid, 1973, p. 402.

[2] For the manifesto see Buckley and Crispin, *Los vanguardistas*, p. 38. Diego's comment is made in 'La nueva arte poética española', *Síntesis*, XX, 1929, p. 185.

[3] F. T. Marinetti, *Teoria e invenzione futurista*, Milan, 1968, p. 11.

[4] *Discurso de la novela española contemporánea*, Mexico, 1945, p. 95.

[5] 'Los contemporáneos franceses: Proust', *El Sol*, 17 June, 1926.

[6] Quoted by V. García de la Concha, 'La generación unipersonal de Gómez de la Serna', *Cuadernos de Investigación Filológica*, III, 1977, p. 72.

[7] 'Gravedad e importancia del humorismo' (1928), in Buckley and Crispin, *Los vanguardistas*, pp. 269–70.

[8] *Ismos* (1931), Madrid, 1975, pp. 13–14.

[9] Quoted by A. Hoyle, 'El problema de la greguería', *Actas del IX Congreso de la Asociación Internacional de Hispanistas*, Berlin, 1989, II, p. 283. My thanks to the author for bringing this article to my attention and for having given me the benefit, on this and other occasions, of his encyclopaedic knowledge of Gómez de la Serna's work.

[10] *Cinelandia* (1923), Madrid, 1974, pp. 101 and 21.

[11] 'Gómez de la Serna y la generación poética de 1925', in *Estudios sobre poesía española contemporánea*, Madrid, 1957, pp. 165–76.

[12] 'Literatura española, 1918–1930' (1934), in Buckley and Crispin, *Los vanguardistas*, p. 50.

[13] *Julepe de menta* (1929), Madrid, 1981, pp. 64–5.

[14] 'Los futbolistas y la literatura: lo que dice Félix Pérez, del Real Madrid F.C.', *La Gaceta Literaria*, XXIV, 15 December, 1927.

[15] *Julepe de menta*, p. 9.

[16] Buckley and Crispin, *Los vanguardistas*, p. 37.

[17] In *El boxeador y un ángel* (1929), reproduced in *El cazador en el alba y otras imaginaciones*, Barcelona, 1971, pp. 115–16.

[18] 'Film-arte, film-antiartístico' (1927), in Buckely and Crispin, *Los vanguardistas*, p. 225. See also Antonio Espina's comment on 'the infinite slowing down which enables us to analyse slowly the smallest gesture and the most fleeting parts of a movement', in Buckley and Crispin, *ibid.*, p. 214.

[19] *La Gaceta Literaria*, LXXX, 15 November, 1929.

[20] Buckley and Crispin, *Los vanguardistas*, p. 40.

[21] *Angeles de Compostela. Alondra de verdad*, Madrid, 1985, p. 95. This poem, 'Cuarto de baño', dates from 1932.

[22] The original Spanish versions may be found in *Perito en lunas. El rayo que no cesa*, Madrid, 1976, pp. 99 and 123.

[23] A. Sánchez Vidal, *Miguel Hernández, desamordazado y regresado*, Barcelona, 1992, pp. 53–4, convincingly argues that the writer also had in mind an

article by Giménez Caballero of October 1931 entitled 'Nueva moral de lo abominable'.

24 Sánchez Vidal, 'Introducción', *Perito en lunas*, p. 12, quotes the following statement by Hernández on the subject: 'My concept of the poem': 'Poets, keep the secret of the poem: sphynx. Let them learn how to pull it off like peel. Oh orange, such delightful secrets beneath its mundane appearance!'

25 Sánchez Vidal, *Perito en lunas*, pp. 21–8.

26 Quoted by Sánchez Vidal, *ibid.*, p. 10.

27 *Ibid.*, p. 123.

28 *El hombre perdido*, Buenos Aires, 1947, pp. 312–13.

7. Hernando Viñes: Untitled, 1928. Oil on canvas

5 / Visual poetry in Catalonia: Carles Sindreu i Pons　　WILLARD BOHN

Carles Sindreu i Pons was a talented and fairly prolific writer who experimented with a variety of different forms during the early twentieth century.[1] As a member of the flourishing Catalan avantgarde, he contributed to the renewal of poetry in Catalonia alongside such figures as Josep Maria Junoy, Joan Salvat-Papasseit, and J. V. Foix. Sindreu's best known volume is entitled *Irradiations and Poems* (1928), which attracted a certain amount of attention when it appeared and earned him a reputation as an innovative poet. While the majority of the poems are traditional in appearance, the book includes three visual compositions, each of which represents a unique contribution to the genre.[2] Two other visual poems from the mid-1920s that have been rediscovered recently will be examined here.[3] As Michel Foucault observes, visual poetry has a triple role: 'to augment the alphabet, to repeat something without the aid of rhetoric, to trap things in a double cipher ... Pursuing its quarry by two paths, [it] sets the most perfect trap ... as neither discourse alone nor a pure drawing could do'.[5] Sindreu's two poems illustrate the truth of this assertion.

They also reveal that Sindreu was a sports fan who did not hesitate to mix poetic business with pleasure. Whereas only one work in *Irradiations and Poems* is athletically motivated, a poem entitled 'Football', both of the additional texts are devoted to the sporting world, making them almost unique thematically in the visual poetry of any country. Even more unusually the two poems were published not in a literary review but in a publication devoted to sporting events. To appreciate the radical nature of Sindreu's gesture fully, we should ask ourselves how many avant-garde poems have ever been included in *Sports Illustrated*.

The simplest of the two poems appeared in the sporting magazine *L'Esport Català* on 20 April, 1926, with the enigmatic title 'NOBLOM' (Figure 1). The title means nothing to the reader of today, but the average Catalan sports fan in 1926 would have known the name of the then famous athlete. Today's reader of the text soon discovers that Noblom was a talented tennis player. At the visual level the composition adheres to the poster aesthetic. In addition to the prominent title, which advertises the poem's 'product', it includes a visual diagram and two boldface slogans: 'ORGANIZACIÓ' (ORGANIZATION) and 'PERFIL PUNXANT' (SHARP PROFILE). As if to emphasise the resemblance to commercial posters, Sindreu even provides a rectangular frame. While this device can be seen as an effort to ally poetry with painting, its function is not to enhance the text but to delimit it. According to a common convention the viewer reads the rectangle's four sides as the edges of a sheet of paper.

As one soon perceives, the design occupying the lower half of the poem reproduces Noblom's footwork during a typical match. Zigzagging down the page in a series of interlocking curves, it retraces his path as he battles his way to victory. Not only does

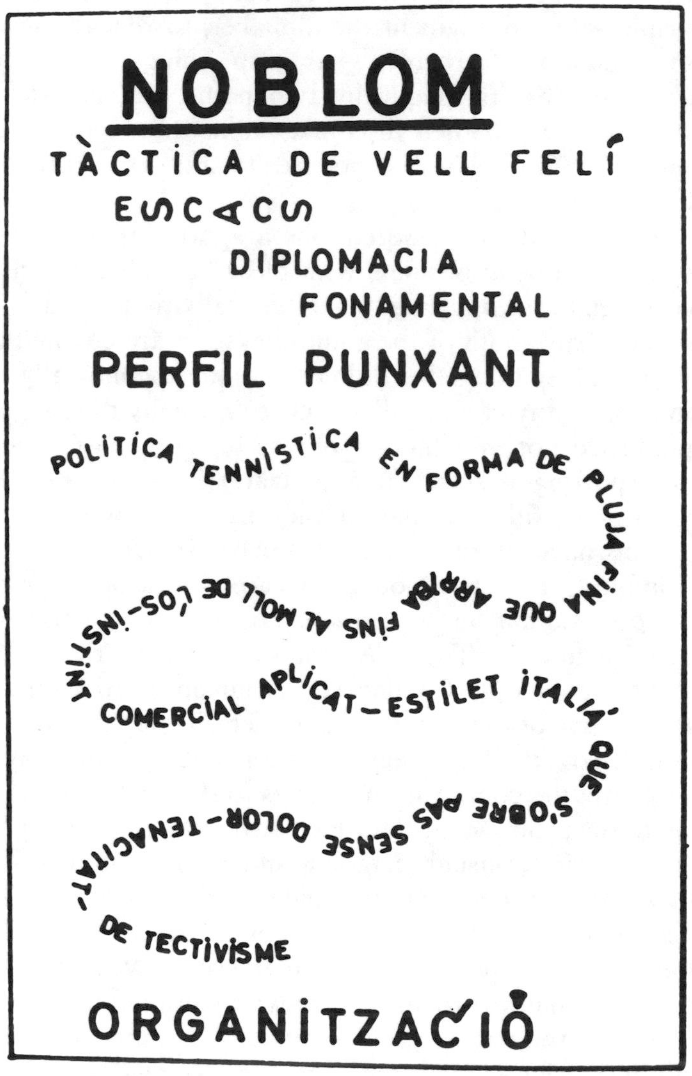

Fig. 1

it reveal that the champion possesses excellent reflexes, it documents the strategy that has made him a winner time after time. Although the text reads from top to bottom, the drawing itself progresses in the opposite direction. Following his initial serve at the bottom of the page, Noblom returns each one of his opponent's volleys while advancing toward the net. Like his opponent, he directs the ball first to one side of the court, then to the other in order to exhaust the other player and keep him off balance. Once he reaches the net, he finishes his adversary off in one of two ways. Either he delivers a powerful smash that is too fast for the other to counter, or he hits the ball behind him where he cannot reach it. In the last analysis, therefore, the rectilinear frame represents the tennis court itself. Like the printed text, the players are enclosed by a visual rectangle whose borders they may not exceed. The play of the text coincides with the text of the play and vice versa.

'NOBLOM' requires a surprising amount of manipulation on the part of the reader. Despite its simple format it needs to be subjected to ten separate operations in order to extract its message. Not only must the composition be rotated constantly from beginning to end, much of it is upside down. One of the areas that demands the most attention is the second line, which consists of a single word: 'ESCACS' (CHESS). For reasons that are not entirely clear every other letter is turned on its side, rendering the term illegible. To spell it out one must rotate the page 90° five separate times in the space of only six letters. The fact that this dislocation is so systematic suggests that the poem may contain a visual analogy after all. Conceivably the alternating pattern could represent a row of black and white squares on a chess-board. Thereafter the need to turn the poem this way and that is dictated by the footprints in the lower half. In order to reconstitute the verbal trace of Noblom's activity the diagram must be rotated 180° four times in succession. Forced to choose between literary and artistic conventions, Sindreu opts for the latter as a means of establishing a continuous flow. Although the reader is inconvenienced to some extent, once he rotates the page he discovers that the formerly upside down lines now read from left to right. Ironically, the divorce between artistic and literary conventions tends to disappear during the act of reading. Unexpectedly, both models

57

play a decisive role in guiding the reader through the verbo-visual labyrinth.

Although the mechanics of reading the poem are complex, the signifying process itself is largely unaffected. Despite the work's visual pyrotechnics its underlying structure is relatively simple, as this 'straightened-out' translation reveals:

NOBLOM

THE TACTICS OF AN OLD FELINE

CHESS

FUNDAMENTAL

DIPLOMACY

A SHARP PROFILE

TENNISTIC POLITICS IN THE FORM OF FINE RAIN THAT SOAKS YOU

TO THE BONE – AN APPLIED COMMERCIAL INSTINCT – AN ITALIAN STILETTO

THAT NEVER OPENS WITHOUT CAUSING PAIN – TENACITY – SLEUTHING

ORGANIZATION

We can now see that the poem is essentially a catalogue. Consisting of a series of unrelated images presented in a telegrammatic style, it portrays the individual whose name appears in the title. Despite the fact that the images normally have nothing in common, they are linked together here by their common subject, Noblom. Although their function is cumulative, they are related to the latter, and often to each other, by relations of equivalence. As a portrait of the tennis player begins to emerge one notes numerous examples of duplication and reinforcement. Qualities that are associated with one image turn up in subsequent images as well. This exercise in redundancy is essential in literary portraiture since it allows the author to achieve a certain basic consistency.[4] It should be noted, however, that not all the images in 'NOBLOM' are equally effective in establishing the subject's character. Some play a major role, some contribute relatively little, and some add nothing at all. On the whole the poem turns out to be fairly heterogeneous. In general one can distinguish three different ways in which the various elements contribute to the final portrait. The elements themselves, both implicitly and explicitly, may be divided into the following categories: descriptive, abstract, and metaphoric.

As one would expect, the singly descriptive term in the text, that he has a sharp profile, is useful in determining Noblom's physical appearance but reveals nothing whatsoever about his character. It is helpful to creating a visual portrait to know he has a sharp profile, but the psychological value is dubious. The history of numismatics proves that both saints and sinners may have prominent silhouettes. In contrast the abstract terms are more informative but lack the solidity that one associates with description. That Noblom is tenacious and well organized, for example, almost goes without saying. Since these qualities describe most successful athletes, they come as no surprise. In other words, the problem with the abstract terms is that they are lacking in specificity. This situation is exacerbated by the fact that they occupy isolated positions in the poem. Without verbs or adjectives to contextualise the concepts they express, their usefulness is limited. The reader thirsts for additional details that will flesh out the portrait. What form does Noblom's tenacity assume during a typical match and how does his organisational ability express itself. How does Noblom compare to other tennis players? What impression does he make on the average spectator?

The answers to these and similar questions are furnished by the metaphoric terms, whose presence is crucial to the poem. Despite the marked scarcity of verbs throughout the work, they comment on Noblom's athletic ability and establish a network of relations between the various parts. In addition, since the essence of metaphor is comparison, they relate Noblom to society at large. Upon reflection many of the terms that appear to be abstract turn out to contain implicit metaphors. With relatively little difficulty, for example, one can perceive the figure of an ambassador concealed in the expression 'DIPLOMACIA FONAMENTAL' (BASIC DIPLOMACY). Similarly the word 'DETECTIVISME' (SLEUTHING) conjures up images of a private eye lurking in the background.

The very first metaphor sets the portrait's tone and introduces at least two dominant themes. By comparing Noblom to an old feline, Sindreu implies that he is crafty, patient, and experienced. In some respects the metaphor anticipates the concepts of tenacity and organisation, discussed previously, which are presented at the end of the poem. Just as tenaciousness requires patience and vice versa, organisational ability presumes a certain amount of experience. Compared to these abstractions, however, the concrete metaphor is much more effective in establishing Noblom's merit as a strategist. The image of a lion or a tiger sneaking up on its prey has undeniable visual appeal. The second, third, and fourth metaphors continue the themes of craftiness and patience, which they illustrate in several different ways. The comparison with a chess-player, for instance, stresses Noblom's ability to develop intricate combinations several moves in advance and to predict his opponent's reactions. Like a devotee of chess, moreover, Sindreu's diplomat and politician are skilled in dealing with various adversaries. On the one hand, the former engages in delicate negotiations that depend on careful planning. On the other, the latter devises one strategy after another in order to ensure the defeat of a particular bill, the adoption of his own legislation, or his eventual re-election.

At this point in the poem the author reverts to a non-human metaphor to introduce another idea entirely. Noblom also resembles a rainstorm, he announces, the kind that drenches unwary pedestrians to the bone. Although this is an unusual image, to say the least, it seems to be intended as a tribute to the champion's ability to overwhelm his opponents. The fact that Sindreu evokes a fine rain rather than a heavy deluge is likewise significant. Instead of storming all over the court in an effort to intimidate the other player, Noblom relies on superior reflexes and technique. Because his style is so highly refined ('FINA') he is able to penetrate his opponent's defence time after time. The following metaphor, which praises his 'INSTINT COMERCIAL' (COMMERCIAL INSTINCT), evokes the image of a successful businessman. Like the previous individuals who figure in the poem, the latter stands for craftiness and patience in the service of a larger plan. Like the diplomat and his associates, the businessman carries out complex negotiations over a period of time that require tenacity as well as organization. Where he differs from his predecessors, at least in the author's view, is in his instinctive feel for what he does. He not only enjoys his business career, but he possesses a natural aptitude for commercial affairs. Whereas the first metaphor stresses the value of experience in playing tennis, the present example stresses the importance of instinct. Not only is Noblom an accomplished veteran, but he is a natural phenomenon like the rain.

The next to last image, which again is non-human, involves neither an animal nor a natural phenomenon but a man-made object. If Noblom resembles the gentle rain in his ability to insinuate himself into his opponent's mind, his resemblance to an Italian stiletto makes him downright murderous. In his hand a tennis racket is not simply overwhelming – it becomes a lethal instrument. That the stiletto comes from Italy, of course, is a sign both of professionalism and of excellent workmanship. Although it appears near the end of the poem, the weapon activates an additional seme retroactively. In retrospect one perceives that the anonymous feline possesses the same killer instinct as the stiletto's owner. Like an experienced criminal or a hungry lion, Noblom zeros in on his adversary and swiftly dispatches him. Sindreu prefers to end on a more positive note, however, and so returns to the paradigm developed at the beginning of the poem. Like the chess-player and his numerous descendants, the figure of the detective personifies the triumph of craftiness and patience. Only by carefully piecing together numerous clues (some of which are misleading) and by interviewing various witnesses (some of whom are lying) does Sherlock Holmes succeed in identifying the guilty party. While Holmes' reputation has increased immeasurably over the years, that of Noblom has been totally eclipsed even in Catalonia. The only trace of his exceptional ability that survives is the present poem, which serves as a final monument.

Published the previous year on 16 June, 1925, the other poem (Figure 2) is considerably more complex than 'NOBLOM' and thus more difficult to interpret. At the visual level the work presents obvious analogies with commercial posters and yet manages to leave the viewer unsatisfied. Try as he may, he succeeds in identifying only one visual form: a stringed instrument juxtaposed with the work 'VIOLONCEL' (CELLO). Like the title, whose meaning is not readily apparent, this word is printed in large boldface capitals but it too provides no immediate access to the text. The same thing is true of the other words that catch the reader's eye, including 'CALLÍGRAMA', 'PERNOD', and 'SON' (SLEEP / DREAM). While the first term describes the genre to which the poem belongs, it tells us nothing about the work itself. The second and third terms are even

FLAQUER. CALLÍGRAMA

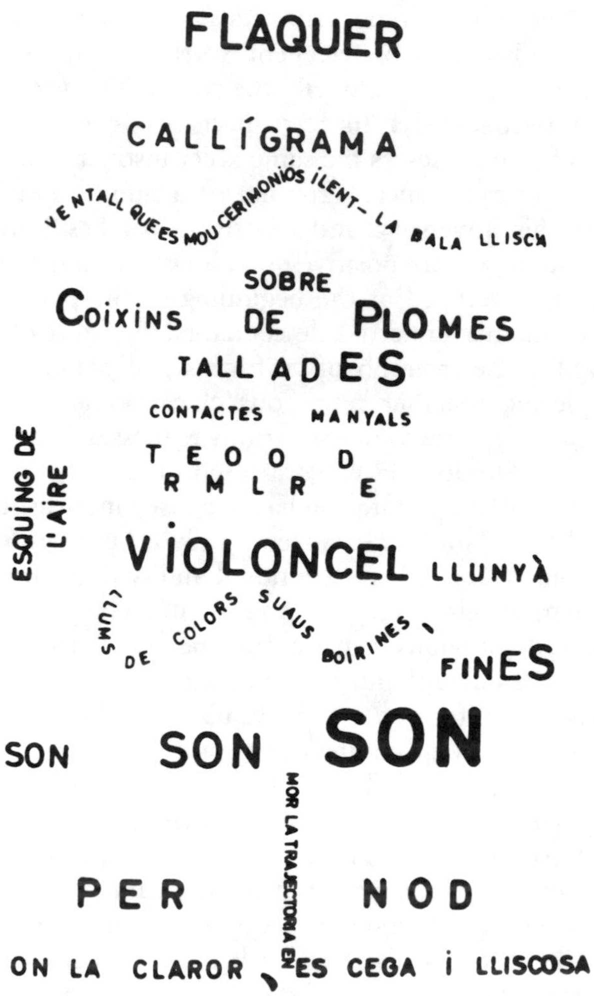
FLAQUER
CALLÍGRAMA
VENTALL QUE ES MOU CERIMONIÓS ILENT- LA BALA LLISCA
SOBRE
COIXINS DE PLOMES
TALLADES
CONTACTES MANYALS
ESQUING DE L'AIRE
T E O O D
R M L R E
VIOLONCEL LLUNYÀ
LLUMS DE COLORS SUAUS BOIRINES
FINES
SON SON SON
MOR LA TRAJECTORIA EN
PER NOD
ON LA CLAROR ES CEGA I LLISCOSA

Fig. 2

8. Nicolás Lekuona: Untitled, 1934. Photocollage

less helpful and have little or nothing to do with the previous words. At most they evoke a popular French drink and seem to introduce the theme of sleep. Ironically, as we will discover, 'SON' reflects the vagaries of Catalan spelling at this date and signifies something other than appears at first sight. Although the poem seems initially to be under the spell of Morpheus, nothing could be further from the truth. Despite its considerable visual appeal, therefore, 'FLAQUER' possesses little visual coherence. In contrast to works whose pictorial elements conform to an overall pattern, the visual details simply accumulate as the poem progresses. Thus the poem disguises itself as a poster but embraces a rival aesthetic. As will become increasingly evident, it consists of a series of visual analogies that are linked together at the verbal level.

Like the rest of Sindreu's visual poetry, 'FLAQUER' facilitates the act of reading by adhering to a series of conventions. Although one must occasionally rotate the page to the left or to the right, in general the text follows the literary model. Where difficulty arises is not in reading the work but in interpreting it. The greatest problem is to determine the relationship between its individual parts, on the one hand, and between the text and the title on the other. The latter task is complicated by the discovery that *flaquer* does not belong to the standard Catalan lexicon. Ironically, the single greatest stumbling block in analysing the poem turns out to be its title. Without some clue as to its subject the reader is reduced to pure speculation. Only after extensive research does one discover that the word is an obscure dialectal form and that it should be translated as 'pond'. Since the title is crucial in interpreting subsequent events in the poem, it is included in the translation given below:

POND: CALLIGRAM

A fan that moves ceremoniousilent – the bullet glides

OVER

FEATHER PILLOWS

Manual contacts

THE AIR TORN ASUNDER

T E O O

R M R F

A DISTANT VIOLONCELLO

Softly coloured lights FINE mists
Sound SOUND SOUND
The trajectory dies in
PERNOD
WHOSE LIGHT IS BLIND AND SLIPPERY

At first glance the poem appears to be hopelessly obscure. Even with the aid of the visual elements and the information provided by the title one can make out very little. Drawing heavily on ellipsis and metaphor, Sindreu challenges the reader not just to understand the text but to duplicate his original thought processes. The function of the printed words is thus analogous to that of a musical score. The poem does not consist of the marks on the page but must be recreated mentally. If this operation describes aesthetic response in general, it is especially true of 'FLAQUER' which makes heavy demands on the reader's imagination. Fortunately two important clues are provided by the double frame enclosing the poem. In the first place, the fact that the text appeared in *L'Esport Català* implies that it involves some sort of sport. In the second place, the title indicates that it is associated with a body of water. These facts suggest that the work is concerned, not with the pond itself but with an activity located in, on, or near the pond. In other words, the title's role is metonymic rather than tautological. Although this reduces the number of possibilities to manageable proportions, it fails to identify the sport in question. The poem's subject could be anything from ice skating to swimming to fishing or boating. Re-reading the text in an attempt to identify the elusive sport, one eventually realises what Sindreu is describing. Concealed behind a camouflaged blind on the edge of the pond, the author and at least one other person are hunting waterfowl.

The visual processes at work in the poem become immediately apparent as the first line resembles a snake writhing across the page. Sindreu is not alluding to a serpent, however, but to another image in the poem. More precisely, the line is motivated by an implicit metaphor concealed in the initial phrase. Its shape is dictated, not by the speeding bullet, which proceeds in a straight line, but by the arrival of a flock of waterfowl who are preparing to land. The analogy itself is generated by the observation that their wings appear to 'fan' the air. What one sees, therefore, is not the birds' flight path but the silhouette of their extended wings, represented here by a single individual. The latter is depicted from the front rather than from the side. True to his futurist model, Sindreu combines two different terms to form a portmanteau word: 'cerimoniósilent'. While the aesthetic value of this combination is minimal, it provides more information about the birds in question. The fact that their flight is silent, for instance, indicates that they have long, powerful wings. Unlike ducks, which must flap their stubby wings rapidly (and hence noisily) to support their weight, the birds move slowly and elegantly as they approach the pond. According to all indications, therefore, the line evokes a flock of geese.

As soon as the geese come within range of the hunters' shotguns, however, they become targets instead of aesthetic objects. Like the avian ceremony, the sentence is disrupted by the sound of gunfire before it can be completed. Switching his attention from the birds to the hunters, Sindreu describes one of the shotgun slugs as it streaks toward its target. The second visual analogy concerns the geese themselves which are compared to a pile of feather pillows. Since the former are soft and plump and the latter are often filled with goose down, the metaphor exploits both shape and substance. Avoiding any hint of figuration, the author evokes one of the links between them visually. Taking the expression 'PLOMES TALLADES' (FEATHER PILLOWS), he decreases the size of successive groups of letters in the first word and increases them in the second to form a crude analogical portrait of two feathers.

The 'contactes manyals' (manual contacts) in the next line are puzzling until one suddenly realises to what they must refer. As before, Sindreu alternates between the geese and the group of hunters. Not only does the phrase parallel the previous reference to hunting syntactically, it is linked to it through the principle of cause and effect. Judging from appearances, at least one of the hunters, perhaps the one who fired the earlier shot, has managed to bag a goose. As is customary, the others crowd around him and offer their congratulations. The latter contact is 'manual' in the etymological sense that their words are accompanied by handshakes.

The vertical notation 'ESQUING DE L'AIRE' (THE AIRE TORN ASUNDER) is considerably more ambiguous but presumably refers to additional shotgun blasts. The force of the blasts is so tremendous, Sindreu implies, that they threaten to rip the atmosphere to shreds. By contrast, the tremulous violoncello in the distance is more difficult to identify. Were the poet writing at an earlier date, it could represent the universal complaint of nature saddened at the sudden violence. However, the hunters are not presented as agents of destruction but simply as ordinary sportsmen. As such, they are not the villains of the poem but exemplify a desirable way of life. Whatever the role of the cello metaphor, it must coincide with this basic scenario. On the one hand, it may record the honking of another flock of geese in the distance. On the other, as Derek Harris has suggested in conversation, it may represent the echoing of the shots, resonating in the still morning air. In this instance, 'TREMOLOR' would serve as another portmanteau word (trèmolo + dolor), evoking the tremolo effect and sorrowful tones so characteristic of cello playing. However one chooses to interpret the image, one thing is certain: the drama is situated at dawn. Wreathed in the first mist rising from the pond, the hunters are bathed in the soft light of early morning.

Although the cello itself is depicted realistically, it is framed by visual analogies on either side. Like the previous examples, these are constructed according to a variety of principles but are based on futurist models. Directly above the instrument, for instance, the word 'TREMOLOR' has been decomposed into its constituent elements. Oscillating between two different lines, it resembles one of the cello's vibrating strings. Whether one conceives of the instrument as 'trembling', 'shivering', 'shuddering', or simply responding to the cellist's touch (all of which are possible), the device serves equally well. Situated below the cello, the next example recalls the analogical plumes in several respects. Among other things the word 'FINES' resembles the first visual analogy ever composed – by Francesco Canguillo in 1914.[6] Like Canguillo, who took the term 'fumare' (to smoke) and made each successive letter larger than the one before it, Sindreu employs a word that appears to be expanding. In both instances the point of this procedure seems to be the same. Just as the smoke expands to fill the second class railway compartment in the earlier Italian poem, here the mist increases in response to the rising sun until it fills much of the landscape. Interestingly, the word that is actually subjected to the analogical process is not the term for mist ('boirines') but its accompanying adjective. Although the verbo-visual relationship is not tautological, the effect is identical.

At first glance the next visual analogy seems to be governed by the same principle. Extending across the page from left to right, the word 'son' (not 'sleep' as it turns out but 'sound') is repeated three times in increasingly larger type. Whereas progressive typographical enlargement was associated previously with physical expansion, at present it has another function altogether. The size of the letters bears no relation to spatial phenomena but corresponds to the rising intensity of the sound. Although the latter is never identified, the context leaves little doubt as to what it must be. While the metaphoric cello is still reverberating in the hunters' ears, another flock of geese flies over the pond. As soon as they come within range the hunters open up with their shotguns again: 'BANG BANG BANG'. Despite the apparent precision of the visual device, the reader is free to imagine two scenarios. On the one hand, the hunters may fire three separate blasts corresponding to each of the words on the page. On the other, they may fire a whole series of blasts that quickly rise in a crescendo of sound.

As before, the visual analogy is tied to a following line by cause and effect. Once again one of the hunters succeeds in downing a goose, which plummets to earth in a straight line. Not only do we see its vertical trajectory, the presence of the verb *morir* (to die) confirms our initial impression. The hunter has been successful. The poem ends with a resounding splash as the goose falls into the water. The pond is so murky, the poet adds, that it resembles a glass of pernod. Sindreu is thinking, not of the liquor itself (which is clear) but of what happens when one adds water to it. Like the pond the cloudy suspension that results is bright, opaque, and slippery.

Visual poetry, Foucault reminds us, 'lodges statements in the space of a shape, and makes the text *say* what the drawing *represents*'.[7] As Sindreu's poems demonstrate, it is capable of a wide variety of aesthetic effects, ranging from simple tautological constructions, which mean exactly what they say, to complex interdisciplinary dialogues. Despite the design's instantaneous impact on the reader's retina, processing the entire poem takes much longer. Indeed, Mary Ann Caws points out that one of the genre's functions is 'to slow down the glance . . . impeding the linear rush from beginning to end, forcing attention to sides and centre'.[8] The effort to relate the visual elements to their verbal counterparts imposes a creative delay on the interpretive process, ultimately allowing the reader to gain greater insight. Since visual poetry is a hybrid genre by definition, the area of its greatest interest is normally where the two domains meet. Whether this phenomenon is envisioned as intersection, overlap, or interference, it is what gives the genre its identify. On the one hand, visual poetry combines two types of sensorial experience, sight and sound, which are viewed as complementary. It 'aspires playfully to efface the oldest oppositions of our alphabetical civilization', Foucault proclaims, 'to show and to name; to shape and to say; to reproduce and to articulate; to imitate and to signify; to look and to read'.[9] On the other hand, visual poetry encourages readers to bridge the gap between these categories themselves by expanding their aesthetic horizons. As much as anything, poems like 'NOBLOM' and 'FLAQUER' seek to inaugurate new cognitive patterns based on new modes of perception. In this way, author and reader collaborate to produce a synthetic vision of the world.

Notes

[1] The first volume of his *Obra poética* was published in Barcelona in 1975. No other volume has appeared to date.
[2] For an analysis of these three works see W. Bohn, *The Aesthetics of Visual Poetry, 1914–1928*, Cambridge, 1986.
[3] J. Molas, *Literatura catalana d'avantguardia*, 1916–1938, Barcelona, 1983, pp. 243–4.
[4] M. Foucault, *This Is Not a Pipe*, Berkeley, 1982, pp. 20–2.
[5] This phenomenon is discussed in Bohn, *Aesthetics*, pp. 92–3.
[6] See Bohn, *Aesthetics*, pp. 16–17.
[7] M. Foucault, *This is Not a Pipe*, p. 21.
[8] M. A. Caws, *The Art of Interference: Stressed Readings in Verbal and Visual Texts*, Princeton, 1989, p. 167.
[9] M. Foucault, *This is Not a Pipe*, p. 21.

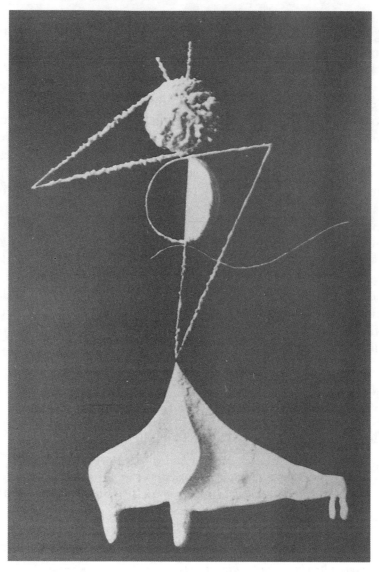

9. Angel Ferrant: *Mountaineering femenimity*, 1935. Wax

6 / The ludic element in the Spanish avant-garde: Gerardo Diego's *jinojepa*

GABRIELE MORELLI

Max Jacob's declaration that art is a form of amusement, is widely echoed throughout the avant-garde. The idea of art as an amusement is clearly present in the word games played in the nonsense poems called *jinojepas* that were produced by Gerardo Diego, one of the central figures of creationism. The attention-grabbing alliteration, the repetition of the letter 'j' in the *jinojepa*, like its Latin American cousin the *jitanjáfora*, declares both its ludic intentions and its esoteric significance: the affirmation of an entirely gratuitous value in the phonetics of language at play.[1] The dominance of phonetics over semantics produces the term's semantic obscurity and the limited relevance of what it might convey. In addition, the difficulty of pronunciation that it presents has the immediate effect of requiring a physical–mental effort on the part of the speaker, a circumstance that is shared with any type of initiation ceremony.

The three fundamental elements that characterise the figure of the *jinojepa*: its phonetic substance, its ludic aspect and its elitist nature, throw into relief by contrast the semantic void in its depths, or what might be better described as the neutral and open area towards which its meaning tends to gravitate, so leaving a space for other elements that are irrational, easily created and designed to provide a shared amusement.

In the literary scene in Spain in the 1920s one of the cultural groups where such burlesque linguistic exercises were produced was to be found in the Madrid Residencia de Estudiantes.[2] In the highly-charged creative atmosphere of this centre for cultural exchange, young writers, artists and intellectuals established a surrealist language *avant la lettre*, continually using neologisms like the term 'vidista' (lifeist), which they opposed, as an existentialist antithesis, to the term 'putrefacto' (putrescent). Dalí claimed to be preparing a collection of drawings to be published in book form under the title *Los putrefactos*, with an introduction by Lorca.[3] There were also other rythmic and rhyming games, like the so-called *anaglifos*[4] that invented a collectively created lexicon constructed on a basis of irrational analogy, producing something that is part *divertissement* and part pure poetic invention. The *anaglifo*, in its basic form, consists of four nouns, the first two being repeated, the third must be 'chicken', the fourth something

71

widely improbable, for example: 'Tea, / Tea, / Chicken, / And Teotocopuli'.

The importance of the game for the militants of the 'isms' is its ability to bring things together in new and surprising associations, a capability that augments the liberating power implicit in the game. This is the freedom of the mind to seek to regain, as André Breton proposed, the true life that is betrayed by the meanings imposed by culture and its false ideologies. The theoreticians of these new ideas put forward the act of play as a form of protection against the process of denaturalisation by society's morality. In addition to its liberating, imaginative values the act of play thus acquired an intrinsic therapeutic value. This is why in the 1920s, the verbal game in a variety of forms (puns, spoonerisms, *cadavres exquis*, anagrams, calligrammes, *anaglifos*, etc.,) became an obligatory exercise for any artist who wished to fight against 'common sense' and seek freedom from its shackles.

The game, envisaged in the context of a wide range of activities and often understood as a cumulative series of repeated elements capable of being taken apart and rearranged, has the ability to conjure up and reveal the unexpected and the fantastic through the process of random variation. André Breton, along with Marcel Duchamp and other pioneers of automatic writing, insisted on the importance of the ludic in this practice, claiming the revenge of pleasure over reality, of nature over culture, as in the work of Lautréamont. Johan Huizinga's *Homo Ludens* of 1938, the theoretical justification for this activity, was a vital, dominant presence in Breton's work right up to his last books, such as *L'un dans l'autre* of 1952, where he insists on the potential for socialisation in such ludic practice, since the game is 'one of the most extraordinary meeting grounds' and is like a 'pooling' of thought.

The *jinojepa* itself, as a manifestation of this ludic spirit of the avant-garde, is particularly associated with Gerardo Diego, who is sometimes considered its inventor. Certainly the use of the *jinojepa* is restricted, by and large, to Diego who frequently published these joke poems in his light-hearted and easy-going magazine *Lola* ('relaxed, determined and Spanish' as it was described), the younger sister of the more serious magazine *Carmen*, (*Lola* is a highly popular-flavoured diminutive of the girl's name, Dolores). However, Mario Hernández, one of the few critics to have made a serious and determined approach to Diego's burlesque work,[5] has connected Diego's practice of the *jinojepa*, which was born out of 'a collaborative effort at regular meetings of a group of friends', to use Diego's own words,[6] with Lorca's well known imitations of various authors (Juan Ramón Jiménez, Antonio Machado, Jorge Guillén, Rafael Alberti, Manuel Altolaguirre, etc.) and his parodic poems written earlier in a collective manner with his circle of friends from Granada, which they attributed to an imaginary poet, Isidoro Capdepón Fernández, described as 'the epitome of all bad rhetoricians'. The link between Diego's burlesque *jinojepa* and Lorca's Capdepón jokes and parodies is confirmed in a letter, dated 12 December 1927, from Diego to Lorca in which, after an opening based on a verse by Lorca, he asks his friend to send some *jinojepa*s for the magazine *Lola*, and announcing in the same letter that he is writing three new comic compositions: 'The real one, the declension of Chabás and the one about *Milord Acrostic and Milady Charade*'.

The declension of Chabás is a schoolboy-like parody of a Latin noun's declension, based on a string of mutations of the name of the poet Juan Chabás for the singular forms, culled from actual printers' errors, and a sequence of arbitrarily chosen Italian words for the plural.

THE DECLENSION OF CHABÁS

SINGULAR	PLURAL
Nom. -Chabás	*Nom.* -Aprile
Gen. -Chalás	*Gen.* -Velaggio
Dat. -Mabús	*Dat.* -Palazzeschi
Acus. -Chavá	*Acus.* -Bontempelli
Voc. -Chaves	*Voc.* -Pensile
Abl. -Chafás	*Abl.* -Don Giovanni

NOTE. The singular is made up of genuine printers' errors. The astonishing irregularity of the plural is being studied by a committee of philologists comprising Messrs Vighi, Vegue, Goldoni, Alberti, Sassone and Pittaluga.

In his prologue to the modern reprint of *Carmen* and *Lola*, as a part of an explanation of how the first *jinojepa* was produced, Diego reveals that it was based on an example of a schoolboy mistake, something that imbues the substance of many *jinojepa*s perhaps because Diego was by profession a school teacher.[7] The unintentionally creative mistake, which we might refer to as the '*qui* pro quo' of the *jinojepa*'s birth, occurred in the course of an oral examination.

A VARIANT OF THE *JINOJEPA*

(Place where the incident occurred: the Jovellanos Secondary School, on 4 June of this year).

The Teacher: Give me the title of a poem by the Marquis of Santillana.

The Examinee: His famous 'Mountain-Girl Songs'.

The Teacher: Can you remember any of them?

The Examinee: I never saw, I never saw a maid so fair . . .

The Teacher: I never saw along the border . . .

The Examinee: Like a cowgirl with phyloxera.

(The pupil was given the grade of excellent and appointed as an honorary contributor to *Lola*).

The prompting of the teacher with successive lines of the poem provokes the pupil's panic stricken memory into a wild grab at a linguistic straw suddenly created with total illogicality by the vagaries of phonetic imaging. 'Finojosa' in the original is replaced by the partial homophone 'filoxera', which at least has the virtue of having rustic connections; the phylloxera plant-louse had destroyed a huge sector of the vineyards of France. But not all the phonetic pressure here comes from the student; the 'Finojosa' of the original is an almost complete homophone of Hinojosa, that is José María Hinojosa, the author of one of the first surrealist books in Spain, *La Flor de California* (1928), a title whose erroneous stress on the last 'i' of California was designed to rhyme with María in the poet's name. Hinojosa, from Málaga and part of the Andalusian section of the Generation of 1927, was rather unpopular with the group in the Residencia de Estudiantes and the poets linked with Madrid, like Diego. Lorca, Dalí and Buñuel were particularly disparaging about him.[8] A further arbitrary phonetic shift, associated with Hinojosa, between 'Europa' and the non-sense phonetic recreation 'Eurepa', is the source from which comes in part the nonsense word *jinojepa* itself.

The game of variants and phonetic substitution played in the oral examination just quoted sees the same materials elaborated further in the 'Mountain song of the jinojepa', one of the most successful and amusing compositions of all of Diego's burlesque production, which appeared in *Lola*, no. 2. The basis of the parody is again the type of folksong favoured by the fifteenth-century Marquis of Santillana, including an imitation of the archaic language, over which is laid the same butt for the joke, José María Hinojosa:

> *Musa tan fachosa*
> *non vi en la Poesía,*
> *como la Hinojosa*
> *de Jose María.*
>
> *Faciendo la vía*
> *desde el surrealismo*
> *a California*
> *– y lo cuenta él mismo –*
> *por tierra fangosa*
> *perdió la sandía*
> *aqueste Hinojosa*
> *de José María.*
> . . . .
> *En la catoblepa*
> *se encontró a Picasso*
> *y díjole: – Paso.*
> *Europa es ya Eurepa.*
> *Y viva la Pepa.*
> *Ya no hay más poesía*
> *que la Jinojepa*
> *de José María.*[9]

Both the signature, the Marquis of Altolaguirre, which refers to the youngest poet of the Generation of 1927, Manuel Altolaguirre, and the note at the end which indicates that the famous bullfighter 'El Tempranillo', referred to at one point in the poem, was also called José María Hinojosa, help to situate this and the other burlesque inventions in a very specific literary scene. On the one hand they allude to members of the poetic pleiad of the Generation of 1927, while on the other hand they are based on existing models of well-known song poems by the Marquis of Santillana, as in this case, or in others by Góngora himself and even by Rafael

The Spanish avant-garde

Alberti, the poet of the Generation of 1927 most closely associated with the non-parodic imitation of this type of song poem, indicating the hybridisation of the avant-garde and poetic tradition.[10] The imitative, parodic intentions are clear, since the authority of the literary source used is revealed at the outset, and it is almost always a famous composition which would have been memorised over a long period of time during Diego's years as a school teacher. This gives the composition of the *jinojepa* something of a mechanical character as well as placing it in the realm of oral production, and so rendering it susceptible to transliterations and continual variation, as new readings reorder the material in accord with its rhyme and rhythm.

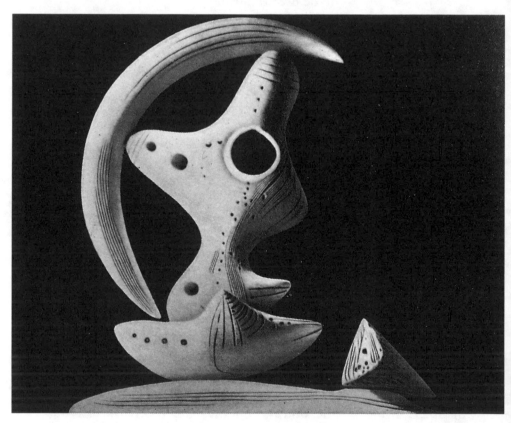

10. Alberto (Alberto Sánchez): *Volume that flies in the silence of the night and which I could never see*, c. 1933

The ludic element: Diego's *jinojepa*

As a further example of the effervescent, carefree attitude which uses satire and provocation as a form of amusement and literary horse-play we have the rewriting of a very well-known poem by Góngora into a burlesque exercise that lists together the group of friends who attended the celebration of the Góngora tercentenary in Seville in 1927. One can almost hear the youthful, collective laughter of the group ringing out behind the lines.

JINOJEPA OF THE ALTOLAGUIRRES
(The strange physical resemblance of the youngest Sevillian poets with little Manuel Altolaguirre inspired the brilliant pleiad, in collaboration with Don Luis de Góngora, to write the following *jinojepa*.)

> Not all the juanramons
> Are those that sing, nor villalons.
> Some are silver altolaguirres,
> Cheekbones, little eyes,
> Some are golden altolaguirres,
> Keen wits, sharp set,
> Who come and go stage rear.
>
> Not all the merry voices
> Are from plumed guillens
> Nor do manuals of spume
> Sing in shaded grove.
> If you hie acernuding
> To their songs at morning . . . [11]

The poets hidden behind the neologisms of noun and verb are very clearly Juan Ramón Jiménez, Fernando Villalón, Manuel Altolaguirre, Jorge Guillén, Luis Cernuda, and Gerardo Diego himself disguised by the reference to *Manual of Spume*, the title of Diego's most well-known *creacionista* book. It is not by chance that Diego wrote, 'The good jinojeper jinojeps himself'.[12]

Gerardo Diego is careful to emphasise the benevolent and self-mocking nature of the humorous comment. In his own words, 'A *jinojepa* is not exactly a satire, it is more of a joke, a good humoured chaffing that holds no spite. If anyone thinks otherwise,

77

let him think on his own condition and purge himself before casting the evil eye on his neighbour'.[13]

However, as the history of literary relations illustrates and as Mario Hernández points out, the creation of a *jinojepa* is not always so innocent and burlesque. At times, in spite of the author's own declarations, his subtle satire is strongly pointed at some distinguished writer. Juan Ramón Jiménez's refusal to be involved in the homage to Góngora provoked a sharp response in the second issue of *Lola*. Ortega y Gasset is the target of the *jinojepa* 'The espectorator and his saliva', which appeared in the first number of *Lola* and which begins with the quotation, taken from, as it indicates, Ortega's work, *The Spectator*: '. . . the poets who salivate their little poems'. Diego refers to this reaction in a letter to Lorca of 28 December 1927.[14] Lorca must have felt a similar annoyance with Diego for the joke played on him by the publication in *La Gaceta Literaria*, XI, 1 June 1927, of the 'Apochryphal Ballad of Don Luis on Horseback', over the signature of Federico García Lorca. Diego described this to Lorca as 'a just punishment for your despicable desertion from the homage to Don Luis'.[15] The ballad is a parody of the Andalusian imagery, sensual metaphors and sometimes arcane allusions found in Lorca's poetry in the mid-1920s.

> Por el real de Andalucía
> marcha D. Luis a caballo.
> Va esparciendo su manteo
> negra fragancia de nardos,
> y luciendo un repertorio
>
> en los pliegues de sus paños
> el viento, escultor de bultos
> y burlador de romanos.[16]

In another letter to Lorca, dated 13 September 1927, Diego defends his burlesque attitude, referring both to his attack on Valle-Inclán in *La Gaceta Literaria*, VII (1927), for his lack of interest in Góngora, and to the joke on his friend, by saying they were, 'isolated cases, not ill-intentioned: miscalculated flowers of youth, in a complacent atmosphere of a rotten academic garden'.[17]

The ludic element: Diego's *jinojepa*

While Diego was keen to emphasise the collective character of the creation of *jinojepa*s, in fact, other than the '*Jinojepa* of the Altolaguirres' and possibly the apocryphal ballad attributed to Lorca, all the compositions are by the same author, sometimes disguised as 'Chiclet', 'The Marquis of Altolaguirre', 'Fray Luis de Pato' and later, 'Jaime de Atarazanas' (Atarazanas was the name of the street where Diego lived at the time in Santander). The matter of the poem's authorship was the subject of these comments by Diego:

> The *jinojepa*s appear in the issues of *Lola* with different signatures and were the work of different authors, occasionally of just one, although most are the result of a collaborative effort by a group of friends working together. We can name Alberti, Lorca, Altolaguirre, Villalón and Pepín Bello amongst those who had a hand in the little creatures. They were produced under the supervision of the person who finally gave himself the name Jaime de Atarazanas, the friend and supplement of Gerardo Diego. Once this name had been fixed on, and with the swiftness he had learned with *Lola*, Jaime de Atarazanas has carried out his perverse *jinojepic* torpedo-attacks right up until the present day.[18]

This emphasis that Diego places on the collective effort of several individuals does not so much undermine the authorship and question the legitimacy of the text's paternity as turn the text inevitably into a spontaneous, ephemeral product, whose collective authorship places the writing process outside any fixed paradigm and opens up for it other possibilities of expressing itself, especially at an oral level. This hint of instability which can be detected in the texture of the burlesque composition, written in an unfinished, fragmented form that is open to modification, is established initially by the strong, insistent use of rhyme and the tone of voice, i.e. interchangeable elements that create a range of possibilities, which, while obeying some general rules, come together in order to strike out in different directions and unexpected variants.

At a time when Ramón Gómez de la Serna's *greguería* was trumpeting its new incisive formula of metaphor plus irony that modified the traditional view of an inert reality, Diego's *jinojepa*, with its vitalist, carefree attitudes offered another important example of comic satire. 'Variations for four hands', the title of the piece which appeared in the fifth issue of *Lola*, eloquently displays the euphoric atmosphere in which a group of friends create and play the games of rhyming parody. The two variations are burlesques of poems by Rafael Alberti that had achieved a certain notoriety. 'That fool Raphael', which is the text and pretext for a satirical burlesque mixing other verses by Alberti with coded references to Juan Ramón Jiménez, based around Alberti's well-known song poem, 'Were Garcilaso to return'. In the original poem Alberti posits the wish to be the squire of the sixteenth-century knight-poet, should he return; in the *jinojepa* this is replaced by a wish to be his butler or his barber. The parody of Alberti is followed by an attack on the then well-known literary figure Ricardo Baeza which uses the simple form of eight-syllable couplets associated with the doggerel verses of popular prints to mock the figure of the literary pedant, an example of the *putrefactos* the young turks of the Generation of 1927 despised so much. Ricardo Baeza was the author of a wide variety of works that displayed his diverse, but essentially superficial erudition. His publications on Dostoyevsky, Casanova and Oscar Wilde are alluded to, along with many others of his endeavours, all subjected to the deflation of their importance by being attached to the most outrageous rhymes in the couplets. Many of these are lost in translation but two that survive the passage between languages accurately give the flavour of the rest: 'Lorca' is rhymed with 'Menorca' and 'Miró' with 'K. O'. The parody comes to a halt with an incomplete couplet, whose first line ends with the word 'miaow!', followed by an invitation to 'the ingenious reader' to add the missing final line and find a rhyme for 'miaow', something that is as difficult to do in Spanish as it is in English while maintaining some modicum of semantic coherence.

The cheerful, bantering attitudes that characterised the social and literary relations of the young writers of the Generation of 1927 eagerly interested in the new ideas of the European avant-garde, provided a welcoming environment for the burlesque practices started by Lorca and his friends and which were carried forward onto the national scene by the success of the *jinojepa* in the 'relaxed, determined and Spanish' *Lola*, from there becoming incorporated into the everyday literary life of the period. As a final example of the generalised use of the *jinojepa* I will quote one directed against Gerardo Diego himself, made the victim of comic satire on the occasion of the publication of his *Anthology* of 1932 which caused a violent and bloody literary controversy.[19] This outrageously rhyming poem, a mock lament for all those poets of the 'old school' who had been excluded from this gathering of the Spanish avant-garde poetic clan, appeared under the acronym E. S. y Ca. (Esteban Salazar y Chapela) in the section entitled 'The torpedo on the track' of the *La Gaceta Literaria*, CXXIII (1932). The editor of the magazine, Ernesto Giménez Caballero, frequently referred to by his initials in Spanish as 'Ge. Ce.', was himself the inventor of an outrageous and exaggerated lexicon, had had a poem dedicated to him by Diego in *Lola*, nos. 3–4, entitled, 'Ode to Ge-ce-be-de-o and Ge-de-te-be-o', which was constructed on the model of two poems by the sixteenth-century poet Fray Luis de Leon: 'A *Santiago*' and '*La profecia del Tajo*'. Salazar y Chapela's 'Ode to the very arbitrary poetic anthology which Gerardo Diego has just published, and we still don't know why', with its language full of childish jargon and with its allusion to the question 'Gerard, why do you rhyme with thistle?, asked by Jorge Guillén in a poem directed to Diego ('thistle' in Spanish is 'cardo'), shows how the satirical–burlesque *jinojepa* was enlivening the lexicon used by the new generation of young Spanish poets, bonded together both by friendship and their espousal of avant-garde exhilaration:

> Oh Gerard, despotic thistle
> Of earth, stone all gloomy,
> Oh to be your friend and bard,
> Oh Gerard, dart hard,
> And be in your anthology!

Notes

[1] Diego himself admits this in the prologue to the facsimile reproductions of the magazines *Carmen* and *Lola*, Madrid, 1977, p. 26. Under the title '*Jinojepas* and parody', he writes: '*jinojepas* are unexplainable. *Jinojepas*, like *jitanjáforas*, say everything with their name'. For the nature and practice of the *jitanjáfora* see A. Reyes, *La experiencia literaria*, Buenos Aires, 1969.

[2] For details of life in the Residencia de Estudiantes see J. Moreno Villa, *Vida en claro. Autobiografía*, Mexico, 1944, p. 117; V. Bodini, *I poeti surrealisti*

81

spagnoli, Turin, 1963, pp. XXXIX–XL; R. Alberti, *La arboleda perdida*, Buenos Aires, 1959, pp. 175–7.

3 Letter from Dalí to Pepín Bello, dated 17 November 1925, in A. Sánchez Vidal, *Buñuel, Lorca, Dalí: El enigma sin fin*, Barcelona, 1988, p. 153.

4 On the use of *anaglifos*, see the anecdotes recorded by J. Moreno Villa, *Vida en claro*, p. 113, and R. Alberti, *La arboleda perdida*, pp. 214–15.

5 G. Diego *et alii*, 'Jinojepas', *Boletín de la Fundación Federico García Lorca*, II, 1987, pp. 51–67.

6 'Prólogo', *Carmen* and *Lola*, p. 26.

7 *Idem.*

8 For details of the derisory attitude some of the generational group had towards Hinojosa see M. Altolaguirre, *El caballo griego*, Madrid, 1986, pp. 54–8. Vicente Aleixandre commented ' . . . we poets of the Generation of 1927 never took him very seriously as a poet' (J. L. Cano, *Los cuadernos de Velintonia*, Barcelona, 1986, p. 250). A. Sánchez Vidal, *Buñuel, Lorca, Dalí*, p. 159, refers to a letter of September 1927 from Buñuel to Pepín Bello which was an 'unmerciful comic attack on José María Hinojosa', and also quotes Altolaguirre's memory of the poet: 'Hinojosa read his disastrous poems very badly, and so at the end of each one he would say "that's all". If he had not said this, he ran the risk of nobody realising the poem had ended'.

9 Editor's note: The following lame English translation inevitably loses almost all the forced rhymes of the original, which produce such nonsense links as 'watermelon' with 'Maria'. 'A muse so striking / Was ne'er seen in Poesie / Like the Hinojosa / Of José María. // On his pilgrim way / From surrealism / To Californía / – As he himself relates – / He lost his watermelon / In muddy ground / Did that Hinojosa / Of José María. // In the catoblepa / He met Picasso / And said to him: I give in. / Europa is now Eurepa. / Long live the fair Pepa. / The only poetry now / Is the *jinojepa* / Of José María'.

10 *Boletín de la Fundación F.G.L.*, p. 51.

11 Diego's Spanish original reads: 'No son todos juanramones / los que cantan, ni villalones. / Sino altolaguirres de plata, / pómulos, ojos menudos, / sino altolaguirres de oro, / afilados, agudos, / que entran, salen por el foro. // No todas las voces ledas / son de guillenes con plumas / ni los manuales de espumas / cantan por las alamedas. / Si acernudado te quedas / a sus tempranas canciones . . . '. It is calked on a very well-known song poem by Góngora: 'No son todos ruiseñores.'.

12 *Carmen* and *Lola*, p. 27.

13 *Ibid.*

14 *Boletín de la Fundación F.G.L.*, II, 1987, pp. 23–4.

15 *Ibid.*

16 Editor's note: The following English translation gives the sense of the original but fails to convey its esoteric allusiveness. 'Along the Andalusian highroad / Don Luis goes on his horse. / His cloak spreads round him / Black fragrance of spikenard / While the wind in the cloth's folds / Displays a sculptor's repertory of forms / That mock Roman statuary'. There are specific echoes of well-known poems by Lorca, including 'Arbolé, arbolé' from his

Canciones and from several of the ballads of the *Romancero gitano*. The parody is so good it might be taken for a genuine Lorca poem.

[17] *Boletín de la Fundación F.G.L.*, II, 1987, p. 22.

[18] *Carmen* and *Lola*, pp. 26–7.

[19] On this subject see G. Morelli, 'Recepción de la *Antología española* de Gerardo Diego en España (y en Italia)', in *Actas del Congreso Internacional Iberoamérica y España en el génesis de la vanguardia hispánica (el modelo vanguardista de Gerardo Diego)*, Cáceres, 1993.

11. Salvador Dalí: *Honey is sweeter than blood*, 1927. Oil on canvas

7 / The Language of Avant-garde Art in Spain: A Collage on the Margin

JAIME BRIHUEGA

In a game which is probably played all over the world, a group of children sit in a circle; one sits in the middle and quickly whispers a sentence to one of those in the circle, who then passes the message on to his neighbour, who does the same, and so on. When the message has gone full circle, the last one to receive it says it out loud. When this is compared to the original version, then disclosed, it is found to have gone through a process of distortion: the order of the words has changed, new ones have been added together with unintelligible new sounds, and parts of the original phrase have disappeared. The outburst of laughter with which the game ends can be understood in terms of the feelings of shared guilt created by the comparison of the two phrases in the full light of the logic of the language shared by all the players.

Let us now play with this example. We can imagine these children, and others, in different parts of the world playing this game using three or four recently acquired foreign languages. Let us also imagine that, paradoxically, the distorted final versions arrived at in each of these circles are similar. Without doubt, we would have contrived a situation that would be so incredible as to be absurd. However, the old anthropological theories of polygenism used such models to explain a certain parallelism discovered within primitive societies. Although polygenism is now out of fashion, and I would not dare to pronounce in public on the value of methodologies which fall outside my own specialist field,[1] I would soon find I had a circle of compliant listeners if, in a light-hearted conversation with a group of modern art historians, I were to point out that when I visit the modern sections of museums as diverse and as isolated as those in Havana, Prague, Lisbon, Copenhagen or Madrid, I discover that local artists have, unknown to each other, painted the same pictures.

Today we all accept the fact that the process of modernism has been ruled by a dialectic between centre and periphery, between creative nuclei and various receptive foci which, across the length and breadth of the Western cultural map, imported the different poetics of the avant-garde and, through a process of emulation and assimilation, re-elaborated them in different ways. This process of incorporating into modernity areas far from the centres of avant-garde activity resulted in much confusion, the juxtaposition of similar, or even contradictory aesthetics, and the hybridisation of elements taken from theories, praxis and languages which, in their original contexts, would sometimes have appeared incompatible. What is surprising is how these peripheries produced works of art which, like the rings of Saturn, are closely related to each other. It would be irresponsible to try to go beyond a mere suggestion of this subject in so few pages,[2] above all after having allowed myself to use as a metaphor the concept of polygenism in anthropology simply as an act of provocation in a context for which it is perhaps entirely unsuitable. What I will try to do is to present some ideas about the character of this process of emulation and hybridisation of aesthetics from diverse primary sources in a peripheral situation exemplified by the artistic avant-garde in Spain.[3]

Picasso, Gris, Miró, Dalí and Julio González were all artists who contributed new directions to the course of modern art, some of which have left a permanent mark. However, they only achieved this once they were working as part of a larger context, which, in these specific cases, was Paris in the early decades of this century, when it was such a productive centre of new visual theories. What will be examined here are not these names, but others, less significant if one attempts to view in global terms the history of contemporary art, but who were none the less key players in the process of artistic modernisation which took place in Spain between 1909 and 1936.[4]

When, in March of 1928, Salvador Dalí, Sebastià Gasch and Lluís Montanyà published their *Catalan Antiartistic Manifesto*,[5] they were launching a frontal attack on the existing hegemony of the Catalan cultural system. Each word was planned as deliberate agit-prop, directly inspired by the provocative methods of the dadaists and the futurists. In fact, the model for this manifesto is the one Apollinaire published in 1913 with the title *Futurist Antitradition*.[6] However, at that time, Dalí had already entered the realm of surrealist poetics, something which is only hinted at in the manifesto where, in the last section, some of the names listed belong to this movement. The rest of the manifesto is a simple attack on local 'backwardness', quoting from a list of various figures and activities considered emblematic of international modernism, or of visible signs of 'mid-cult' such as rugby, jazz, or sports stadia. In other words, it is a display of avant-garde syncretism born from the desire to give their activities an impact of simplicity and directness. These same three figures continued re-elaborating existing textual models in their *Synoptic guide to commercial advertisements and publicity material*, a manifesto calked with elements taken from a text written by Blaise Cendrars in the previous year.[7] The assertive joviality with which both texts deal with the phenomenon of advertising does not accord with the surrealists' solemn and bloody battles against the status quo.

This was not the first time that such a thing had happened in Spanish avant-garde writing. Most of the writing of the ultraists combined within its curious structures elements taken from dada, futurism, expressionism and cubism. Such a complicated mosaic of influences was transformed within the Spanish cultural ecosystem so that it could all be accommodated under the single heading of 'the new'. Any analysis of the arguments or forms of literary criticism, art history, the explanations of educational reformers, or any type of defensive or programmatic writing which was produced by the promoters of the Spanish avant-garde, would continually encounter this amorphous mass of elements of diverse origin, linked into a persuasive discourse which is sometimes innocent, sometimes Machiavellian and sometimes merely opportunistic.

This is similar to what happened in the generative syntax of the Spanish avant-garde's visual language. If we leave to one side the formative periods of Picasso and Miró, or the interlude of planeism which Celso Lagar brought back with him from Paris,[8] the first avant-garde language coined and baptised in Spain was Rafael Barradas's vibrationism.[9] Between 1913 and 1914, the Uruguayan artist had spent several months in the cultural milieux of Paris and Milan where he began to absorb the spirit and forms of the broad range of avant-garde aesthetics he discovered there. After his arrival in Spain, towards the middle of 1914, his style returned to the *fin de siècle* aesthetic ideals which had been the basis of his training in Montevideo. However, after his move to Barcelona at the beginning of 1916 and, above all, after 1917, he started again to develop avant-garde principles through his vibrationism.[10] His work from this period combines clear references to Severini, Marinetti, Carrá, Depero, Magnelli, Gliezes, Picabia, Delaunay, Nevinson, Bomberg, Cursiter, Russell, and MacDonald-Wright, and we could also include Richter, Schad, Janco, Heckel, Schmidt-Rottluff, Cocks, Uitz, Pechstein and Derain, if we take into account his work as engraver for the ultraist magazines.[11] The idea of a collage of poetics is evident from the very origins of the Spanish visual avant-garde.

Clearly, the transmission of visual languages through hybrid forms is something of which historians have always been aware, whether we are dealing with the Renaissance, the Bronze Age, or the rococo. What probably deserves to be examined with special attention is the development of printed visual material from the beginning of the twentieth century which enormously expanded the range of possibilities for knowledge, adding itself to direct experience of the work as the only convincing means of gaining information and increased the possibilities of combining information in a 'visual cocktail'. What also happened was that this extra information acquired the magical persuasion of 'documentary truth' implicit in photographic reproduction. In fact it acquires something of the insolent quality that comes from knowledge in a state of change. On the one hand, while the artistic theory and praxis of modernism achieved equality in their ability to function as poetic expression, information about theory and practice did not always arrive together and at the same time. On the other hand, graphic visualisation in the first third of the twentieth century is done through reproductions in black and white which need to be completed by the imagination, which acts on the basis of an assumed original reality, guided by some strength of conviction. Also, information arrives divorced from its original cultural and chronological context, wrapped up in a vague package where the avant-garde is presented as compact and homogenous, just as those in a peripheral situation will wish, and indeed require it to be.

What is more, this phenomenon of real 'importation', through which the avant-garde is transmitted from creative centres to peripheral contexts, is not always a simple connection (directly or photomechanically relayed). Often, the peripheral avant-garde takes material for its poetic bricolage from another peripheral avant-garde which can, in its turn, have taken it from a third, which could, perhaps, have had the opportunity of direct experience or have the memory of relayed information to which he had privileged access.[12] There are, and it has often been noted, avant-garde expressions which are based on residual and displaced visual stylemes that often do not fit with the other elements which create the language of any particular work. Now we can begin to see the relevance of the image of the circular children's language game.

The Spanish avant-garde offers several instances of this, especially after 1925 and the Exhibition of the Society of Iberian

The avant-garde language of art

Artists, a milestone in collective consciousness which, from that moment, began to consider Spanish artistic culture as having entered the ranks of that 'modernity' which was creating shock-waves internationally. We can take as an example the body of work produced by the avant-garde artists in the Spanish peninsula and compare it with the work of the so-called 'first school of Paris'. There is much that moves from one context to another; stylemes are transmitted and then deposited as visual themes, with that air of authority which comes from being first-hand witnesses to the cultural scene. In this body of works a clearly identifiable series of stylemes and 'iconograms' can be found over and over again. For example, there is a particular way of representing a bowl of fruit which comes straight out of the last cubist works of Picasso, Braque and Gris,[13] and which can be seen in Cossío, Moreno Villa, Palencia, Peinado, de la Serna, Pelegrín, Olivares, Angeles Ortiz, and Caballero, in fact in almost anybody who went in for that type of still life. The non-figurative fill-in in the backgrounds of these and other similar paintings were also taken from a mixture of 'pre-digested' options which had been developed by the three painters of the Paris school or by the plethora of artists who, in Paris and other centres, worked in a similar idiom. In fact, one can come up with some really quite surprisingly exact examples; meshes of parallel vertical, horizontal or oblique lines (Moreno Villa, de la Serna, Cossío); meshes of perpendicular or parallel lines (Moreno Villa, Esteban Vicente, Caballero, Cossío, Rodríguez Luna); areas of fairly regular monochrome dots (Moreno Villa, Peinado, Angeles Ortiz, de la Serna); passages of small circles which contain half-moon shapes of a different colour (F. Domingo, Bonafé, Caballero, Angeles Ortiz, Cossío, Moreno Villa); sinusoidal segments grouped in parallel (Moreno Villa, Cossío, Peinado); the list is not exhausted. These are elements which appear time and again in *Cahiers d'Art* or in *L'art d'Aujourd'hui*. It is also a sign of complicity and emblematic intercommunication, such as we see in certain urban tribes today when they express their particular identity through different styles of graffiti. It is important to note that we can see almost all the stylemes which have been described above in two single works, Picasso's *Mandolin and Guitar* (1924) and Braque's *Still Life (Fruit bowl, pipe and ace of clubs)* (1917). It is also worth recalling Picabia's use of the same stylemes in his 'Bad Paintings' of 1914–

12. Francisco Bores: *Nude in grey*, 1927. Oil on canvas

1927, although he used them for an ironic attack, aware of their emblematic value for much of European painting: a refined tautology as opposed to the elementary tautology of the peripheral artist.

These specific examples are only applicable to the repertoire of Spanish neocubism which was so widespread in the 1920s, but the import and hybridisation of stylemes was a usual mechanism through almost the entire development of the Spanish avant-garde. A clear example is the metaphysical carpenter's square made popular by Giorgio de Chirico which acted as an explicit emblem in Dalí's early surrealism,[14] also in the later surrealism of José Caballero and of other artists who, like Massanet, sought a surrealist connection for their avant-garde work from the early 1930s. The drilled hole of the wooden carpenter's square, used for hanging it on the wall, appears as a sort of visual shorthand in so many works by so many artists that to list them here would be impractical. The exact meaning of each appearance varies within the semantic field opened by De Chirico, but it coexists with totally different aesthetic aims which freely move between the broad boundaries of metaphysical painting, surrealism, neocubism, or simply 'modernity', understood in the broad sense it acquires in a peripheral situation.

The same thing occurs with some of the visual elements of Yves Tanguy's language, such as the horizontal or vertical concentrations of 'worm-like segments' which appear in his compositions from 1925, along with severed hands and fingers, drops of blood, wiry corpuscles like roots and other visual annotations, all within the gravitational floating world of his conception of pictorial space (these elements, in turn, relate to certain graphic characteristics used by Miró c. 1924). These components reappear, in an almost identical manner, in works by Lorca and Dalí from 1927 and continue in Lorca's drawings up to the 1930s.[15] However, in this last case, we must also take into account the fact that this influence from the first orthodox surrealism was also acting to express a web of suggestions born out of a microcosm of extremely complex personal relations between the poet and the painter.[16]

What have been listed so far are a mere genealogy and childish puzzle compared to the problems which are raised by the birth of the 'new wave of realisms' which flourished in Spain between 1925 and 1936. It is necessary to be aware that Spanish surrealism of the 1930s, like the activities of ADLAN (Friends of New Art), the sophistication and specificness of the debates on modernism in the pages of the *Gaceta de Arte* of Tenerife, the poetic ideas of the so-called 'Vallecas School', the literary–visual identities involved with the Generation of 1927, or the intense debates on the political function of art, are only the more visible extremes of the post-1925 Spanish avant-garde when seen from our current historiographical viewpoint. Faced with these manifestations, which were sharply perceived by the small elite at the centre of the cultural debate, the image of modernisation of Spanish art found its clearest expression in the development and multiplication of new forms of realism which developed from the Exhibition of the Society of Iberian Artists in 1925.

The Spanish avant-garde

This flourishing of new realisms was born at the heart of a labyrinth of circumstances and it resulted in a mirage where apparently very diverse aspects of Spanish culture appeared to overlap in the same formal space. The background to all this was again the international scene, where there was a plethora of examples of neoclassicism, revisionism, or new understandings of realism: Picasso, De Chirico, Severini, Derain, new objectivity, magical realism, *valori plastici* and the Italian *novecento*, the general 'return to order' in France, precisionism in the USA, Mexican muralism, and the forced crisis of the Soviet avant-garde in the 1930s. Around 1922, the first avant-garde generations in Spain found themselves at a crossroads which would force them to revise the neophyte fervour that had motivated them until then.[17] The Catalan avant-garde had been losing members since 1918 while the ultraists in Madrid, finding their fireworks had died down, began their own particular return to order, which was something of a paradox if one considers that in Spain they had never achieved much disorder, but understandable in the light of the foreign developments they followed. The transformation of Barradas's language from 1922 or of Dalí's from 1923 to 1926 are clear examples of this situation, as is the fact that Vázquez Díaz was being considered by the younger generation as a beacon of modern visual art.[18] On another front, Catalan *noucentisme*, which had stagnated after its initial flowering in the early 1920s, began to bounce back in new forms, encouraged by foreign developments and fanned by nationalist sentiment which the Primo de Rivera dictatorship was trying unsuccessfully to repress.[19] For a variety of reasons Basque painting, which had been caught in an awkward balance between tradition, avant-garde and a search for identity, now appeared to fit perfectly into this context.[20] In their turn, the artists of the new generation who began to adopt avant-garde attitudes[21] discovered a scenario in which, for the first time, local models matched the information received from abroad.

For this reason, everything was ripe for the Exhibition of the Society of Iberian Artists to raise the flag of integrationist eclecticism which could also establish contact with the public through a wide range of less strident varieties of modernisms.[22] But some other sectors also came to operate under this mirage of 'common ground'. Official academicism in Europe was losing ground on all fronts, under attack from its own obsolescence, its own intellectual, aesthetic and moral degradation. Also, it was under attack from the increasing diffusion of the avant-garde and hounded by its populist and demagogic enemy, Art Deco, a recipe for modernising both the high- and middle-cult.

Although in Spain the process was limited, it is true that Spanish academic painters began to feel the need to offer the public paintings less rooted in the reactionary traditionalism of the figurative painting of the International Exhibitions, the Autumn Salons, and the regional exhibitions devoid of cultural identity which took place in Catalonia and the Basque Country. To take this step of including little hints of modernism in technique and subject matter would be no great effort for a painter fully trained in representational methods. For this reason, the aesthetic panorama of modernising eclecticism represented in the nearly five hundred works shown at the Exhibition of the Society of Iberian Artists was something of a starting point for the development of a regeneration of national consciousness based on toning down the aesthetic differences between the various tendencies. This situation was even more the case during the Second Republic, which was created with the aim of regenerating all areas of culture. What we could start to call '1925 Style' found several advocates in the Republican government[23] and these new realisms began to be a central point of reference for all the artistic languages circulating in the cultural field. If we add to this the general rise of social and political realism from the debate over the political role of art, which was also an issue in Spain in the 1930s, or if we consider the overlap between the new forms of realism and the *trompe l'oeil* techniques used by many of the surrealists, the scene is set for us to understand the potential for the rise of the 'new realisms' of Spanish art between 1925 and 1936.

But this aesthetic common ground, given a sense of unity by the proximity of its linguistic variants, was not in fact anything other than a fiction produced by the alliance between elements, whose origins were geographically, chronologically and ideologically very far apart. The poetic 'collage' had reached its point of maximum complexity, a point which at the same time showed it at its most surreptitious and deceptive. This situation is interesting not only for the origins of the varieties of visual languages now present but also for the complex ecosystem of communication which they inevitably created. The exponents of a pure avant-garde saw in this range of realisms the danger of an irresponsible, opportunistic or simply paralysing regression. The 'experts' carried out a complex decoding of the matrix of different stylistic wavelengths, reaffirming in the process their elitist identity. Those who were socially committed to the process of modernisation of Spanish culture were forced into a Machiavellian double-interpretation, which depended on the character of the audience they were addressing, seeing that for the first time, the public was not openly rejecting 'new art', in spite of what Ortega said.[24] It was certainly not ignored. Now the general public could see in these new realisms the golden bridge that would, symbolically, connect it with the activities of a Europe seen as a more developed universe.

Notes

[1] Nonetheless, even C. Levi-Strauss takes up this question when he writes 'no ethnographer has failed to notice how, across the world, totally different societies conceptualise initiation rites in the same way'. *La pensée sauvage*, Paris, 1962, p. 350.

[2] On this issue, see F. Calvo Serraller's article concerning the similarities between Munch and certain Spanish artists at the turn of the century, 'Edvard Munch y España', in the exhibition catalogue *Edvard Munch*, Madrid, 1984; or the similarities between the work of Zorn and Sorolla which were recently shown in an exhibition at the Sorolla Museum in Madrid (1992); or (to stay on a Nordic theme), the work of the Finnish painter Gallen Kallela and the Basque Anselmo Guinea.

[3] For more details see J. Brihuega, *Las vanguardias artísticas en España. 1909–1936*, Madrid, 1981, pp. 415 *et seq*. and 431 *et seq*.

[4] I have always distinguished between the terms 'avant-garde in Spain' and the broader term 'Spanish avant-garde'. The former assumes the proper delineation of a real cultural context. The latter may create historical confusion, for example, the attempted revisionist view of the first three decades of Spanish art in the exhibition *Le siècle de Picasso*, Paris, 1988. The date of 1909 (the translation of the *Futurist Manifesto* in the magazine *Prometeo*) and 1936 (start of the Spanish Civil War) are chronological limits which nobody seems to challenge.

[5] Also known as the *Yellow Manifesto*, it was handed out to the public in the streets of Barcelona and mailed to various supporters and opponents of the avant-garde. The most recent photographic reproduction can be seen in the catalogue of the exhibition, *Las vanguardias en Cataluña, 1909–1936*,

Barcelona, 1992.

6 The similarities between these two manifestos are analysed in J. Brihuega, *La vanguardia artística española a través de la crítica (1912–1936)*, Madrid, 1982, pp. 699–715.

7 S. Dalí, S. Gasch, L. Montanyà, 'Guia sinóptica: L'Anunci comercial, publicitat, propaganda', *L'Amic de les arts*, March 1928. B. Cendrars, *Aujourd'hui*, Paris, 1927.

8 Celso Lagar, born in Salamanca, returned from Paris in 1914. From early 1915 until 1919, the year he returned to Paris, he exhibited in Barcelona, Gerona, Madrid and Bilbao. He named his aesthetics planeism, mixing elements of cubism, fauvism, futurism, primitivism and the richness of Cézanne. This was how he saw what he was doing, and how it was understood by his contemporaries. Cf. J. Minguet and J. Vidal, 'Las vanguardias en Cataluña. Cronología crítica', in the catalogue of the exhibition, *Las vanguardias en Cataluña. 1906–1936*. Barcelona, 1992, p. 479.

9 For a recent detailed general overview of Rafael Barradas, see the catalogue, *Barradas. Exposición Antológica. 1890–1929*, Saragossa, 1992, with texts by A. Kalenberg, C. Lomba, R. Santos Torroella, F. Miralles, E. Carmona, A. Peláez, and one by myself ('Saturno en el Sifón. Barradas y la vanguardia española'), in which I specifically deal with the issue of Barradas's merging of languages.

10 Although never developed as a coherent philosophy, vibrationism informs most of Barradas's work between 1917 and 1919, developing continuously from dynamic cubism, to be replaced by a peculiar expressionist fauvism which he himself called 'clownism'.

11 The visual arts of ultraism have been systematically examined in E. Carmona's unpublished doctoral thesis, *El movimiento renovador de las artes plásticas en España. Del 'momento vanguardista' al retorno al orden. 1917–1925*, Malaga, 1988/89. What has been said about the convergence of elements in Barradas's ultraist work also applies to the other artists who produced engravings for the movement: Norah Borges, Bores, Santa Cruz, Jahl.

12 A good example is the manifesto entitled 'Presentació' which opens the first issue of the avant-garde review *Art* (Lérida, 1933/34). The number of coincidences with the *Antiartistic Manifesto* of 1928 is very revealing.

13 Fundamentally in the still lifes produced by these artists from 1917.

14 It appears in his first important surrealist compositions, such as *Honey is Sweeter than Blood* (1927), *Apparatus and Hand* (1927) or *Little Cinders* (1928), but it had already been present in many works from 1924.

15 From Lorca, it will pass to other artists, for example, José Caballero, the José Viola of the 30s, and many others. This is a good example of the delayed circulation of information to which I have referred.

16 Cf. R. Santos Torroella, *La miel es más dulce que la sangre*, Barcelona, 1984.

17 Cf. E. Carmona, *El movimiento renovador*.

18 Cf. J. Moreno Villa, *Vida en claro*, Mexico, 1976, p. 169.

19 Cf. F. Miralles, *L'época de les avantguardes, 1917–1970*, Barcelona, 1983, pp. 21 *et seq.*

95

[20] Cf. P. Mur, *La Asociación de Artistas Vascos*, Bilbao, 1985. In this book many of the clichés through which the development of Basque painting in the first thirty years of the twentieth century were examined are revised.

[21] It so happens that, because of age or means of entry into the avant-garde, most of the artists who form the modernist movements 'in' Spain appear in the public arena at this time. Until 1925, the number was very small and was concentrated intermittently between Madrid and Barcelona.

[22] Some names which I have chosen intentionally from diverse groups illustrate the mirage of the 'common ground', these are: Ponce de León, Rosario Velasco, Servando de Pilar, Luis Muntané, Togores, F. Elíes, F. Domingo, Angeles Santos, Ucelai, Cabanas Eurasquin, Landeta, Maruja Mallo, García Maroto, Genaro Lahuerta, Quintanilla, Fernández Balbuena, Martín Durban, Suárez Peregrín, Pelegrín . . . and this is without mentioning more well-known names, Arteta, Vazquez Díaz, Dalí, Barradas, or the reappraisal of Solanas which took place from this period.

[23] The naming of Juan de la Encina as Director of the Museum of Modern Art and the participation of Manuel Abril in various official operations (both were related in some way with Exhibition of the Society of Iberian Artists), were factors that greatly promoted change in spite of the antagonistic inertia the dead weight of academicism.

[24] Remember that all the arguments which Ortega proposed (*La deshumanización del arte*, Madrid, 1925) as representative of the entire contemporary art scene were written precisely after the event of the Exhibition of the Society of Iberian Artists.

13. Josep de Tagores: *Nudes on the beach*, 1922. Oil on canvas

8 / From Picasso to Dalí: 'Arte Nuevo' and the Spanish masters of European avant-garde painting

EUGENIO CARMONA

On 27 October 1928, at a function in Granada organised by the avant-garde magazine *gallo*, which he helped to edit, Federico García Lorca gave a talk called 'Sketch of the New Painting', a brief survey of the development of the European avant-garde. Lorca's opinions derived from his own recent experience of drawing and were strongly influenced by the ideas of his Catalan friends, Salvador Dalí and the critic Sebastià Gasch. Lorca's text is still rich in implications today, but it might seem surprising that, in concluding, he confidently states:

> We Spaniards have been graced with the three great revolutionaries of contemporary painting. The father of all painters, the Andalusian Pablo Picasso; from Madrid Juan Gris, the creator of the Theology and the Academy of Cubism; and Catalonia's son, Joan Miró [. . .] there can be no doubt that Spain continues generously to bestow her genius. Her genius of eternal life which inspires, and will continue to inspire all activity with her own very peculiar and unexpected light.[1]

Were this statement not signed by García Lorca, we would probably consider it to be repulsive, negative or unacceptably chauvinistic, but the emphatic and 'nationalist' tone the poet uses must be understood in the context of very specific circumstances.

During the first four decades of this century, Spanish art was divided between those who worked 'outside' and those who remained 'inside' Spain itself. Although both worlds were connected by a common aesthetic endeavours, they were also very distant. On the 'outside', in Paris, there were many Spanish artists, but it was above all Picasso, Gris, Miró, González and Dalí who changed the course of modern art with their work. On the 'inside', those artists who wished to link their activities with those of the avant-garde or the modern movement in general gave the name 'Arte Nuevo' (New Art) to their efforts.[2] The delayed arrival in Spain of Arte Nuevo sometimes makes it hard to analyse systematically the attempt to emulate the general European experience that characterises it.

This peripheral character of Arte Nuevo made it quite unlike any similar artistic experience. Among those involved with Arte Nuevo there were many who justified their activities by stating that the incorporation of the forms of the European avant-garde into Spanish painting made a contribution to the modernisation of the country by increasing its connections with Europe. This is the idea which is present either implicitly or explicitly in many manifestos, declarations, magazine editorials, and critical texts, as well as in the works of the artists themselves. The aim was one of social regeneration, linked to a certain 'nationalistic' sentiment, and this is what we can see in Lorca's text. Although it may seem paradoxical, the desire on the part of Arte Nuevo to communicate with Europe coloured this 'nationalism' with the internationalist aspirations that were an integral aim of modernism itself.

As a result, the existence of Spanish artists playing a central role in the European avant-garde was of vital importance to the artists developing 'inside' Spain. The Spanish masters of the European avant-garde were not merely models to copy but, more importantly, they acted as confirmation that the ideals of Arte Nuevo, which were so difficult to develop within Spain, had a historically important *raison d'être* in contemporary circumstances. Arte Nuevo imported en masse the formulae of European art, but there can be no doubt that those 'inside' wanted most particularly to assimilate and to make their own the experience of the Spanish masters of the European avant-garde.

However, the attitudes from 'inside' towards Picasso, Miró and Dalí were different to those toward Julio González or, in particular, Juan Gris. Picasso, Miró and Dalí all went through a 'Spanish period' before their absorption into the European scene. This was not the case with Juan Gris and Julio González who began to produce their 'significant' work after moving to Paris. The Spanish period of Picasso predates the very foundation of the avant-garde, while Miró and Dalí's work in Spain coincided with two crucial periods in the internal development of Arte Nuevo. This fact may have conditioned the relationship between Arte Nuevo and the Spanish masters of the European avant-garde. This relationship was different in each case and so to explain it, it is necessary to place it within each of the periods or 'moments' which marked out the history of Arte Nuevo.

The first attempts to emulate the European avant-garde 'inside' Spain occurred around 1917 in Barcelona and around 1918 in Madrid. Before 1917, Spanish art followed a fluctuating rhythm of development through the 'prehistory' of Arte Nuevo. Since the turn of the century, the precociousness of the young Picasso had caused him to experiment with every possible variation of Catalan and Spanish modernism in the intellectual climate created by the Generation of 1898. All of this was dressed up with a watered-down, but still active, affinity with libertarian ideals. Until 1905 he was continually moving between Catalonia and Paris, not forgetting his brief stay in Madrid in 1901. Picasso at the turn of the century quickly and deftly passed through post-impressionism, his particular brand of 'pre-fauvism', the pink and blue extension of symbolism, and the purified Parisian classicism of 1905, pushed to the extreme in the ochre Gosol landscapes of the summer of 1906. However, after 1907 and *Les demoiselles d'Avignon*, the start of the cubist adventure, any art that did not respond to the rupture implied by this painting ran the risk of rapidly becoming out of date and redundant. The appearance of the first wave of the avant-garde in cubism meant that European art could not avoid being transformed. Art 'inside' Spain, though, was isolated from this experience and its evolution would remain out of step with the latest developments for more than a decade.

What is more, Picasso's new art could not be seen in Spain at the time. The only people who could see it as it was being created were those Spaniards in Paris who frequented the Bateau-lavoir, and the small number of Catalan artists who lived with Picasso in the Summer of 1911 in Ceret, in French Catalonia. In contrast, Juan Gris's cubism could be seen in Barcelona in 1912, thanks to the *Exhibition of Cubist Art* organised by the gallery owner, Josep Dalmau. However, Gris's work did not provoke much comment. None the less, cubism was related to Catalan culture in a curious manner. Eugenio D'Ors and Josep Junoy, the theoreticians of *noucentisme*, a movement of new Catalan Mediterranean classicism born around 1911, identified both cubism and *noucentisme* as having the same normative aesthetic aims, in contrast to *fin de siècle* aesthetics.[3] D'Ors even included Picasso's pre-cubist works in the 1911 *Almanach dels noucentistes*, one of the fundamental texts of the movement. Junoy made clear references to the painter in his book *Arte & Artistas* of 1912. Picasso, whether seen or not, and understood in a particular manner, was reincorporated into the new Catalan culture. Juan Gris remained apart.

From 1917 to approximately 1919, Celso Lagar, Joaquín Torres-García, Rafael Barradas and the young Miró developed the possibilities of avant-garde painting in Barcelona. From 1918 until about 1922, the visual artists involved in ultraism did the same in Madrid. The directions these artists followed took used elements from the first avant-garde movements, although in Catalonia echoes of futurism came to dominate to a certain degree.

However, in 1917, at the same time as this avant-garde sparkle was beginning to show itself, Picasso was back in Spain with Diaghilev's *Ballets Russes*. This was no longer the same Picasso. Some *noucentista* reviews were ready to announce that Picasso had readopted the language of classicism. *Noucentisme*, as a classicist movement, was very interested in this about-turn by Picasso. In Madrid in 1918, Guillermo de Torre reproduced and commented on both cubist and classicist works by Picasso in the magazine *Reflector*, without being able to explain very well the reasons behind this duality. In ultraist circles in Madrid, the 'return to order' also arrived late. When it reached the capital, around 1922, Picasso's classicism was presented as an example of the end of the avant-garde and of a purified or renewed reconciliation with visual tradition. Spanish art was badly affected by the delayed adoption 'inside' Spain of the attempts to emulate the avant-garde, which meant that the avant-garde and neo-classicism arrived at the same time, and that as a result of this the effects of the 'return to order' would be dominant in Arte Nuevo until 1925. All of this occurred with Picasso as the guiding star.

Someone who was not convinced by the ideals of neo-classicism was the young Joan Miró,[4] and this despite the fact that many critics have wanted to see in his very detailed 'realism' between 1919 and 1922 a trace of this 'return to order'.[5] Perhaps this trace does exist, but Miró was more interested in the avant-garde and was fascinated by Apollinaire's calligrammes. In fact, although his early work is referred to as 'fauvist', it is a reworking of ideas from the first 'isms', using very personal themes which appear time and again. This attitude set the young painter apart from the dominant influence of *noucentisme* and from the confusion created in his contemporaries by the 'return to order'. It is true that with this attitude, Miró could only develop his work after about 1920, when he moved to Paris. But it is also true that it was precisely thanks to this attitude that he was able to enter the most radical groups of the European avant-garde, without the stigma of being 'peripheral', then to return years later to Arte Nuevo as a model to be copied.

The Spanish avant-garde

The development of the Picasso myth took on the form of dogma. Joan Miró's star was in the ascendant. Where then was Juan Gris? In 1920, Guillermo de Torre wrote to the painter requesting a theoretical article for the ultraist magazines. Gris turned down the invitation, writing in his reply: 'anyway, you are the first writer in Spain to acknowledge my existence'.[6] At that time, there was no particular reason why Juan Gris's work should have been rejected by the innovators 'inside' Spain, but it was. For Gris it was the start of his 'course of neglect in the land of cubism'.[7] He would have to wait until 1923 for the critic Manuel Abril to write favourably about him[8] and for the magazine *Alfar* to publish a lecture he had given at the Sorbonne called 'The possibilities of painting', illustrated with reproductions of his recent work.[9] 'Inside' Spain in the early 1920s, Gris's influence is perhaps only traceable in that part of Barradas's work which 'returns to order', or in some drawings by Daniel Vázquez Díaz, but this is a minor element in both painters' work compared to the global and formative influence of Picasso.

In 1925, still influenced by the 'return to order', a great deal of art from 'inside' Spain was presented in Madrid in an exhibition organised by the recently established Society of Iberian Artists. This exhibition in a way opens and closes chapters in the history of Arte Nuevo. The chapter which is now opened is undoubtedly influenced by the increasingly important Generation of 1927. The aesthetic coherence of this generation is debatable, but it was in their magazines that Arte Nuevo, always lacking a means of reaching the public, found one of the best platforms from which to promote its own survival and self-discovery. This was largely thanks to the deliberate decision of the editors not to draw up geographical frontiers where Spanish art was concerned.[10]

Even more important was the fact that Giménez Caballero, Lorca, Sebastià Gasch and Lluís Montanyà were capable of offering 'a' revision of the Modern Movement, which suggested the pictorial aesthetic to be followed, as well as 'a' rehabilitation of the Spanish masters of the European avant-garde. This phenomenon appeared in the pages of *La Gaceta Literaria* and *L'Amic de les Arts*, one of the most important Catalan avant-garde magazines, fostered by Gasch's abilities as a theorist, and aided by Dalí, Lorca and other critics of the time.[11]

14. Julio González: *Woman combing her hair*, c. 1936 or 1937. Steel

103

The Spanish avant-garde

Put simply, Gasch and his circle held the view that painting in the European avant-garde in 1926 had arrived at a genuine impasse. Neither the 'cold' and 'rationalist' tradition of cubism, nor neo-classicism, nor New Objectivity were acceptable alternatives. For them, the way out was to take the concept of 'pure painting' from cubism, but filter it through the exaltation of 'instinct', 'spontaneity' and 'poetry' which surrealism embodied. This was the solution proposed in the recent works of Picasso and Miró and it was adopted, under their influence, by many Spanish painters on either side of the Pyrenees. The 'truth' of this proposition does not matter. The fact is that it was transformed into a formula, which is applicable to or which explains the work of many members of Arte Nuevo during this period. Above all, it re-established Picasso and Miró as models, although their works could hardly be seen in Spain.[12]

In all of Gasch's writings, Dalí is presented as one of the principle exponents of this new 'redeeming' tendency, and some of Dalí's writings before 1929 endorse and comment on this new tendency.[13] However, his own painting shows little trace of this solution, unlike Francisco Bores, Pancho Cossío, Hernando Viñes, Benjamín Palencia, and so many others. In fact, Dalí's painting between 1923 and 1928 is a working through of all the possibilities of Arte Nuevo. This working through was, however, challenging and critical. Dalí reworks, in his own way, some of Barradas's concepts: *noucentisme*, neo-classicism, new objectivity and metaphysical painting. In 1926, he also quoted in his own paintings, *pro domo sua*, Picasso's late cubism, and in 1927, Miró's painting with signs. Both these painters were already immersed in surrealism, as was Dalí to be himself in his 'antiartistic' manifesto of 1928. Dalí's initial suspicion of surrealism was merely a result of his narcissism. The quotation in his own paintings of Picasso and Miró was an attempt to be at their level. By playing a game of love – hate with surrealism, he wanted to bring it under his control. He achieved both things. Before leaving for Paris, Dalí was already the most respected young painter in the Arte Nuevo circle. For his personal development, Dalí had to break his links, both real and theoretical, with Gasch and Lorca. But his inclusion into the Parisian group of surrealists was seen by most as a glorious triumph.

104

From Picasso to Dali: 'Arte Nuevo' in Europe

Picasso, Miró, and now Dalí have been considered. Only Juan Gris and Julio González are left. González began his 'significant' work as a sculptor in the second half of the 1920s. From 1928 to 1931 he worked with Picasso, in an association which was important for both artists. González's early reliefs in cut metal and his later 'drawings in space' were to some extent related to the artistic option described by Gasch, and also to the more recent production of Picasso and Miró. However, in the second half of the 1920s, González was still totally unknown in Spain, and, indeed, his work was hardly commented on by French critics until 1930.

As for Gris, his was not a case of being an unknown figure like González. Throughout these years, the 'black legend' of Gris's relationship with Arte Nuevo became more entrenched, and was maintained even at the time of his death in 1927. His obituaries reiterated the idea of his separation from Spain. Although Gris had a few defenders,[14] his work was often overlooked or was the subject of negative criticism. For example, in the circle of Lorca, Dalí and Gasch, Gris was criticised for practising that 'cold' and 'cerebral' style which had led cubism and avant-garde painting to the extreme from which it had now been rescued by Picasso and Miró. Lorca's opinions on Gris in his 'Sketch of the New Painting' are filled with these clichés. However, the fortunes of Gris and González were to change in the last chapter of the transformation of Spanish painting during the first half of the 1930s.

Arte Nuevo reached maturity after the proclamation of the Second Republic in 1931, when there was a desire for 'internationalisation' which brought with it the definitive 'rehabilitation' of the Spanish masters of the European avant-garde. The new mood had been anticipated in 1929 with the *Exhibition of paintings and sculptures by Spaniards resident in Paris* in the Botanical Gardens in Madrid. For the first time in Spain, Picasso, Gris, Miró and Dalí were exhibited, along with some of the more important defenders of Arte Nuevo. In the following year, the *Exhibition of Contemporary Art and Architecture* in San Sebastian repeated the formula, adding new architecture and showing works by Picasso, Gris and Miró.

As a consequence of the increasing desire for internationalisation the Society of Iberian Artists re-emerged in 1931 and, in this new phase, managed to organise exhibitions of new Spanish art in

105

San Sebastian and Madrid, and also in Copenhagen, Berlin and Paris. Equally important for the resurgence of the 'Iberians' was the foundation of ADLAN (Amics de L'Art Nou – Friends of New Art) in Barcelona in 1932, which then spread to Madrid and other centres with the same initials in Castilian (Amigos de las Artes Nuevas). The programme of exhibitions by ADLAN became very intensive, with an emphasis on the avant-garde which was by then so necessary for the transformation of painting 'inside' Spain. Also in 1932, in Santa Cruz de Tenerife, the magazine *Gaceta de Arte* was founded, which was something quite unlike its predecessors because of its clear support, without any of the peripheral impedimenta, for the main movements in European art in the early 1930s. Its principal achievement in Spain was to be the first to organise an avant-garde event of the calibre of the Second International Surrealist Exhibition.[15]

The aim of removing frontiers from the experience of Spanish art began to bear fruit. Miró and Dalí continued to be key points of reference for Arte Nuevo, despite the fact that neither had a one-man exhibition in Spain in this period. Juan Gris's 'destiny' remained unchanged,[16] although the *Gaceta de Arte* did try to reappraise his memory.[17] Thanks to an article by Luis Fernández published in the magazine *AC* in 1931, González was seen in Spain for the first time. The following year one of his sculptures was shown at an exhibition of the Constructive Art Group which had been 'invented' by Joaquín Torres-García for the Madrid Autumn Salon. In 1934, Ricardo Pérez-Alfonseca's book, *Julio González, escultor en hierro y espacios forjados*, appeared in Madrid and revealed the importance of the sculptor to his Spanish contemporaries.

Undoubtedly, the attempt to 'normalise' the relations between new Spanish artists 'inside' and 'outside' Spain was centred on the 're-establishment' of Picasso and his work.[18] In January 1936, ADLAN in Barcelona managed to exhibit 25 works by Picasso in the Sala Esteve. These works, according to the organisers, showed Picasso as a 'poet' and a 'revolutionary',[19] in a clear attempt to correct the first perception of him in Spain, which mistakenly saw in his works the possibilities of a 'return to order'.[20] As part of the activity surrounding the exhibition, texts by Picasso himself,

Luis Fernández, Julio González and Dalí were broadcast. At the opening, the speakers included Miró and Jaime Sabartés; Paul Eluard gave a lecture. It was the first event 'inside' Spain which brought together the names of Picasso, González, Miró and Dalí. Once again, Gris was absent; he had died nine years before.[21] The exhibition then travelled to Madrid and Bilbao and, in the same year, monographs were written on him by Guillermo de Torre[22] and Sabartés,[23] while the *Gaceta de Arte* (XXXVII) dedicated a whole issue to Picasso who, a few months later, was named director of the Prado Museum.

The rehabilitation of Picasso in 1936 was an initial, but crucial gesture in the attempt to cure the schism which had split modern Spanish art. The works of art themselves were not isolated from this phenomenon. During the first half of the 1930s, most Spanish painting and sculpture which displayed elements of surrealism did so under the influence or support of Picasso, Miró and Dalí. We can even trace certain affinities between some works of Julio González and those of Spanish surrealists influenced by Picasso or Miró. In that same year of 1936, the Spanish masters of the international avant-garde and the artists 'inside' Spain showed their work together in the *Exhibition of Contemporary Spanish Art* at the Jeu de Paume in Paris. It was the first time that the Spanish government had supported a project of this type. Spanish art was presented in Europe as a single experience. The next time this would happen was in very different circumstances. It was in the Pavilion of the Spanish Republic in the Paris International Exhibition of 1937. The aim of the Spanish presentation here was a call for solidarity with the cause of democracy and the Spanish people, and a clear rejection of war. This was because in the same nineteen thirty-six of the homage to Picasso, the year the ground was prepared for the rehabilitation of the Spanish masters of the European avant-garde, the army had risen in Africa, sparking off the Spanish Civil War. The winners were never sympathetic to the effort for transformation which had always so clearly inspired Arte Nuevo. After the war, a new frontier had been erected. The complex history of relations between Spanish art on the 'inside' and the 'outside' of Spain had to start all over again.

107

Notes

[1] Reproduced in Francisco García Lorca, *Federico y su mundo*, Madrid, 1981, p. 464.

[2] I prefer the term 'Arte Nuevo' to 'avant-garde' because, of all the alternatives proposed, it was the one most popular with artists on the 'inside' to describe their activities. Also, the concept of avant-garde requires a more rigorous examination than is usually allowed by historians.

[3] See E. Carmona, *Picasso, Miró, Dalí, y los orígenes del arte contemporáneo en España. 1900–1936*, Madrid, 1991, pp. 17 *et seq.*

[4] See G. Raillard, *Conversaciones con Miró*, Barcelona, 1978, p. 235.

[5] Cf. R. S. Lubar, 'Miró before "The Farm". A Cultural Perspective', in *Joan Miró. A Retrospective*, New York, 1987; with V. Combalia, *El descubrimiento de Miró. Miró y sus críticos, 1918–1929*, Barcelona, 1990.

[6] D. Cooper, *Letters of Juan Gris: 1913–1927*, London, 1967, letter LXXXIX.

[7] For Miró's relationship with Spanish art see: F. Calvo Seraller, 'Proyección de Juan Gris en la vanguardia española: el rastro del olvido en el "país cubista"' in *Juan Gris (1887–1927)*, Madrid, 1985, pp. 389–409.

[8] 'El pintor Juan Gris', *Alfar*, xxxiv, 1923, pp. 3–7.

[9] *Alfar*, XLIII, 1924, pp. 24–30.

[10] From 1925 onwards several young Spanish painters (Bores, Cossío, Viñes, etc.) moved to Paris. None the less, their works were always part of the history of Arte Nuevo and they contributed to it through contemporary magazines.

[11] See, Carmona, *Picasso, Miró*, pp. 54–66.

[12] Picasso had a substantial presence in *La Gaceta Literaria* through the texts of Gasch, D'Ors and other critics. Simultaneously, two important artists 'inside' Spain, Palencia and Alberto, chose to make Picasso a key point of reference in the foundation of the so-called 'School of Vallecas'. In *L'Amic de les Arts*, there was a veritable 'Miró promotion' through the texts of Gasch, Foix and Dalí. The magazine reproduced many contemporary works by Miró.

[13] See, for example, 'Nous limits de la pintura', *L'Amic des Arts*, xxii and xxiv, 1928, pp. 167–9 and 185–6.

[14] The only supporters he seemed to have 'inside' Spain were the critic Manuel Abril and the painter and poet José Moreno Villa. Gerardo Diego and Juan Larrea dedicated poems to Gris, on the occasion of his death, in the magazine *Carmen*, I, 1927. In the issue dedicated to Góngora of the magazine *Litoral*, v–vii, 1927, there is a colour print by Gris on the cover with the inscription, 'A Don Luis, Juan Gris, 1926'.

[15] For more information on what happened after 1929, see J. Brihuega, *Las vanguardias artísticas en España. 1909–1936*, Madrid, 1981, pp. 301 *et seq.*

[16] Gómez de la Serna in *Ismos*, Madrid, 1931, heaps praise on Picasso in a long chapter while he hardly mentions Gris.

[17] Manuel Abril, *De la naturaleza al espíritu. Ensayo crítico de la pintura contemporánea de Sorolla a Picasso*, Madrid, 1934, remains faithful to the

eulogistic memory of Gris.

[18] Gómez de la Serna had already noted this in 1929 with his 'Completa y verídica historia de Picasso y el cubismo', *Revista de Occidente*, xxv, 1929. A. Bonet gives a rich summary of the relationship between 'Picasso and Spain' in *Picasso 1881–1891*, Madrid, 1981, pp. 137–53.

[19] Text from the issue of *Cuadernos de Arquitectura*, LXXIX, 1970, p. 19, dedicated to ADLAN.

[20] Even between 1925 and 1936 Eugenio D'Ors continued to insist on the primacy of a 'classical' Picasso. On the other hand D'Ors did dedicate some space to Gris in his writings, but he was never especially favourable.

[21] Encouraged by ADLAN, the general interest magazine *D'ací i d'allà* dedicated an issue to avant-garde art in the Winter of 1934. This is really the only time that works, albeit in reproduction, by Picasso, Gris, Miró, González and Dalí were presented together in an initiative arising from 'inside' Spain.

[22] *Picasso. Noticias sobre su vida y arte*, Madrid, 1936.

[23] *Picasso en su obra*, Madrid, 1936.

15. Alfonso Ponce de León: *Accident*, c. 1936. Oil on canvas

9 / Góngora, Buñuel, the Spanish Avant-garde and the Centenary of Goya's Death AGUSTÍN SÁNCHEZ VIDAL

Not all the members of the Spanish avant-garde made the seventeenth-century poet, Luis de Góngora, into one of their heroes, thereby prompting for themselves the label 'Generation of 1927' the year of the tercentenary of his death. Some thought that, if they were looking for precedents, the centenary of Goya's death falling in 1928 offered a more attractive and relevant one, because he was

110

less sterile and aestheticist. This was the posture adopted by Valle-Inclán and Ramón Gómez de la Serna, among older writers of the avant-garde. While from the younger generation, it was Luis Buñuel, who planned two filmscripts about his compatriot from Aragon; one in 1926 for the Centenary Committee of Saragossa, and another written in English, *The Duchess of Alba and Goya,*which he submitted to Paramount in 1937. The aim of this essayis to trace some of the tendencies behind the competition between Góngora and Goya as illustrated in the context of Buñuel's frustrated project.[1]

The reappraisal of Góngora in 1927 was far from being monolithic. He was clearly susceptible to many different re-readings. But one of the central elements of the interest in this adopted precursor was the hangover left by the first wave of the avant-garde. This had resulted in a return to the use of regular verse forms in Cocteau's 'return to order', in the purism of Ozenfant and Le Corbusier or Giorgio de Chirico and Alberto Savinio in magazines like *L'Esprit Nouveau* and *Valori Plastici*, in the strict sextets of Valéry's 'Marine Cemetery' (translated by the 'purest' of the Spanish poets, Jorge Guillén), and in the debate on 'pure poetry' itself started in Paris by the Abbé Brémond in 1926. All these were symptoms of a common aesthetic climate which Jean Cassou called 'new intellectual classicism' in an article of July 1926 in the *Mercure de France* about the influence of Picasso's neoclassicism on Salvador Dalí and on Lorca's 'Ode' to Dalí published in the April number of the *Revista de Occidente*, that same year.

The surrealist film-maker Jacques Brunius, one of the first to welcome the audacity of *Un Chien andalou*, went even further in his book, *En Marge du cinéma français* when he used the expression 'photographic gongorism' to attack the stylistic affectations of some avant-garde films. In *How a Novel is Made*, Unamuno denounced the link between this neoclassicism and the then dictatorship of General Primo de Rivera. For Unamuno, the commemoration of Góngora was a tacit support for the 'dirty old camel', as he called the General. For this reason, after attacking the article the avant-garde novelist Benjamín Jarnés wrote in the issue of *La Gaceta Literaria* dedicated to Góngora declaring: 'all this homage to Góngora, due to the circumstances in which it has

111

occurred, the current state of my poor country, appears to me to be a homage of submission to tyranny, a servile act, and in some people – obviously not all! – an act of begging. And all this poetry they are commemorating is nothing but a lie'.[2]

By distancing themselves from such 'modern lyrical tendencies represented by groups from the east coast and Andalusia', some people started to introduce a geocultural element, like the novelist Ramón Sender who opposed this jendency with an Aragonese tradition, recommending to the Saragossan group of the magazine *Noreste* (*North-East*) that they should adopt the heritage of Goya and the seventeenth-century writer Gracián: 'two men who are far removed from current lyrical tendencies'. From such a position, we can infer that those who chose Goya, preferring him to Góngora, did so because of their resistance to 'dehumanisation', which they tried to fight through expressionism, surrealism, neoromanticism or political commitment. This was the case with Valle-Inclán, Ramón Gómez de la Serna and Luis Buñuel and, respectively, their aesthetic positions, biographical comments and film projects.[3]

The split was evident in the most respected organ of the Spanish avant-garde, *La Gaceta Literaria*, which, to be safe, played to both sides of the house. As was to be expected, it dedicated its eleventh issue to Góngora on 1 June 1927 (to coincide with the death of the poet on 23 May 1627). What was less expected was that it almost coincided with an issue dedicated to Goya, number thirteen of 1 July 1927, which had been announced in a footnote on the first page of the Góngora issue.

On that first page of the Góngora homage, the senior members of the 1898 or the 1914 Generations said exactly what they thought of Góngora, or they apologised for not sending anything, pleading lack of knowledge or lack of sympathy. Unamuno wrote: 'I have never felt the need to think with Góngora nor to feel with him'. The novelist Baroja confessed to not reading him often, and showed little intention of changing his habit. Antonio Machado, a fellow poet, found he had no time to read him. Valle-Inclán was more explicit: 'I re-read Góngora a few months ago – last summer – and I felt totally desolate, he was so far from having any literary merit. Unbearable! Incredibly cold, forcibly over-elaborate'. Ortega y Gasset, despite his support for the 'Gongorine' poets from the *Revista de Occidente*, could also hardly hide his doubts, urging the young disciples of Góngora to control their enthusiasm: 'we have to admit Góngora's grace but also his horror. He is wonderful and unbearable, a Titan and also a fairground monster: the giant cyclops Polyphemus and then just someone who is one-eyed'. Juan Ramón Jiménez, a poet who had been a guide for the younger generation of writers, was thoroughly suspicious and even had his doubts about Ortega's role in this matter, believing that the homage to Góngora was a plot by the *Review of Disorient* (as he cuttingly named it) to claim leadership of the new poetry.[4]

Shortly afterwards, Antonio Obregón, himself an avant-garde novelist, dismissed the whole commemoration of Góngora as a mere 'intellectual conspiracy', adding, 'in 1928, let us learn to do without him'. He did this in the issue of *La Gaceta Literaria,* 15 January, at the start of Goya's year. However by then Goya, who was never exactly ignored, had become so talked about that Ramón Gómez de la Serna said ironically, 'the centenary has been anticipated to such a degree that anyone who does not act quickly can be sure that what they do will be lost in the saturation coverage on the day of the actual centenary'.[5]

By dealing with Goya on 1 July 1927, *La Gaceta Literaria* itself was more forthcoming than it had been with Góngora, aware of the contrast it was emphasising by bringing forward an anniversary which, by rights, should have waited a year. Thus, the leading article which dominates the first page says: 'with our ears still ringing with the tercentenary of the death of Góngora, the great Andalusian poet (May 1627), our antenna are picking up the waves from another centenary, outstanding in the annals of Spanish culture, that of the death of Goya, the great painter from Aragon (March 1828). Sometimes, the coincidence of two dates, by the nature of coincidence, produces unexpected, unimagined and basic connections between cultural figures who otherwise, would not have met. Such is the case with Góngora and Goya. Two artists from different centuries, with different professions, opposite aesthetic aims, yet who, caught off guard by the coincidence of consecutive commemorations, force one to consider them both, relate them together and even replace one with the other'.

On the one hand, the author of the article contrasts them: 'all contemporary and past writers on Góngora have wanted to show him as closing the door on an age. A peak of excellence. A splendid conclusion for a period.' Of Goya, the opposite is said: 'an opener of doors. A new dawn. A conquest of totally new horizons in art'. But on the other hand, the author suggests that maybe Góngora was not such a conclusion and Goya was not so free of tradition, and that both were attracted by the popular and even the plebeian. The author then proceeds to run through a whole series of clichés of the painter's romantic legend, '... the libertine genius of Fuendetodos (a town with a Communist name) who seduced its young women, ran his sword through its husbands, mocked its magistrates and transgressed all the solemn values of the nation, setting himself to wait, at critical moments, alongside the knives of *majos*, the bullfighter's cape or the common people's demand for justice'.

This text, although unsigned, betrays the identity of its author: the editor of the magazine, Ernesto Giménez Caballero, and it is next to an article by Ramón Gómez de la Serna in which he proclaims Goya to be the first Spanish humorist. Ramón starts by evoking his childhood, when he would go to the Prado to study Goya's etchings, when he was 'a student at Goya's school, my first real school, the school where I began to suspect what life was'. This was how he became convinced that 'Goya was the precursor of pointed and suicidal humour, what we consider to be the literary ideal for the present moment'. He adds, 'Before Goya, picaresque, epigrammatic, comic, satirical, even caustic elements were mingled with drama, but they had still not learnt the first lesson of contrast, which would become the basis of Spanish humour ... Humour is that which mixes the credible with the incredible, tragedy with comedy, life with death, in other words, everything in opposition. The only inspired conclusion worthy of life seems to come from this spark, always catastrophic, in despair, always baroque and sparing in its dying words'. This 'return from nothing and return to nothing', without moralising or generalising but rather 'taking great chunks out of the truth of life', like 'that etching in which the dead man lifts up his gravestone, on which is written the word *Nothing*', is a concept that is not very far from black humour (surreal or not).

The following year, this article became the chapter 'Los Caprichos' in Ramón's book *Goya*, followed by a chapter on Goya's 'Proverbios y disparates' in which he adopted a position close to surrealism, or at least to the local antecedents of this movement: 'thus superrealism comes to the surface every now and then, that superrealism which has forever lurked in the Spanish psyche because, since our spirit is eminently realist, flights of fancy have always had this realism as their starting point, making great Spanish creations superrealist rather than superfantastic'.

Ramón finishes his book on Goya with a sort of coda about Baudelaire, who in turn had finished his study on Goya by emphasising the painter's modernity, due as much to his peculiar sense of humour as to his development of an aesthetic of 'convulsive beauty', which was to be the battle cry of the surrealists. 'Without doubt', wrote Baudelaire, 'he can dive down into bitter comedy and rise up to total humour . . . Goya is always a great artist, often frightening. He fuses the Spanish grace, joviality and satire of the great time of Cervantes with a much more modern spirit, or at least a spirit more desired in the modern age, the love for the impossible, the feeling for violent contrasts. Goya's great achievement is to have made the monstrous credible. In a nutshell, the seam, the point at which the real and the fantastic meet is impossible to trace; it is an undefined boundary which the most subtle analysis can not mark out, so natural and yet so simultaneously transcendental is his art'.[6]

In the same year that Gómez de la Serna published his biography of Goya (1928), Valle-Inclán, a writer whose aesthetic of the *esperpento* owed so much to Goya, in his novel *Long Life to my Master*, produced a wonderful portrait of the two faces of Spain as exemplified in Velázquez and Goya: 'two Spains intensified their lights on a horizon of grain fields and tile factories, two different souls spread their vast secrets to reach opposite shores, in the quiet of the evening. The mountains thought they glimpsed cold greens, misty pine woods, austere rocks, changeable seas, rain and wind, confronting the African echoes of the burning plain, raucous, stamping gypsy dances and insolent postures, yellow with esparto grass and parched with thirst'.[7]

The superb portrait Velázquez painted of Góngora (which incidentally dates from the year celebrated in the tercentenary: 1627) eloquently presents the affinities between the two Andalusians, painter and poet. Also it is relevant that Valle-Inclán later goes on to say: 'the last civil war fought in Spain was against the Napoleonic invasion, and that this has been forgotten is the fault of the loud-mouthed liberalism that dominated the Parliament of Cadiz and which sought to place a crown of spurious military laurels on the phantom of national unity'. This statement is particularly interesting if we compare it with the opening scene of Buñuel's *The Phantom of Liberty*, which is an explicit visual reference to Goya's painting *Third of May*, repeated throughout the film, while the soundtrack exclaims 'long live our chains!'. This was the cry used on the return to Spain in 1814 of the absolute monarch Fernando VII, by the patriots, bent on destroying the commemorative plaques of the liberal constitution promulgated by the Parliament of Cadiz in 1812.[8]

The homages quoted above were not the only ones to appear in the year of Goya's centennial celebrations. Enrique Lafuente Ferarri, in an article published in *La Gaceta Literaria* on 15 May 1928, ran through the bibliography on Goya already in the bookshops or shortly to appear, like the new edition of Aureliano de Beruete's book, revised by Sánchez Cantón; the etchings and lithographs printed in an affordable collection by Espasa-Calpe; the monograph by Bernardino de Pantorba; and Goya's letters annotated by Guillermo Díaz-Plaja. He also announced the forthcoming works by Ramón Gómez de la Serna, Ricardo Gutiérrez Abascal ('Juan de la Encina') and Eugenio D'Ors, who had published his *Goya's Lifetime* in French in 1926. There are also numerous foreign references which give some idea of Goya's international fame: *La Revue Hebdomadaire*, *Le Figaro*, or the *Illustrierte Zeitung*, for example, all dedicated illustrated supplements to his work.[8]

Lafuente Ferrari at the end of his article refers to the failure of events in the painter's home region, where the only worthwhile thing was an issue of the magazine *Aragón* dedicated to him: 'now we reach the Saragossa chapter. The Aragonese, with a big display of somewhat over-indulged regionalistic pomp, had great plans for Goya. But it all just came down to bullfights. A commentator from Saragossa said bitterly that the only serious events in the Centenary have been the inevitably Goyesque bullfights. The great gatherings and other awesome events came to nothing'.

In fact, it was pointless to try to define Goya from a provincial viewpoint, since his international reputation was not merely greater than Góngora's, but greater than that of any other Spaniard, including Cervantes (and still is today). What is more,

Goya could be more of an inspiration than Góngora in many more artistic spheres, since he had a relevance not just to painting, but also to literature, music (Granados' *Goyescas*), architecture (Fernando García Mercadal's 'Rincón de Goya'), and also the cinema. On 13 February 1926, an influential writer, Ricardo del Arco, came out in support of a proposal for a film about Goya in the most prominent place in the Saragossan newspaper *The Aragon Herald*. He claimed that it was precisely on this new art form that Aragon should place all its hopes, there being no lack of suitable candidates as one of the proposals had come from the famous actor and producer Florián Rey, together with the renowned cameraman José María Beltrán and the budding director Luis Buñuel.[10]

This was by no means the only proposal for a Goya film. The whole of Spain was full of similar projects, for in 1928 Goya was as omnipresent as Columbus was in 1992. Carlos Fernández Cuenca was preparing a short film called *As in Goya's Day*; Federico Deán planned to make *Goya's Maja*; José Buchs had set *El conde de Maravillas* and *The Second of May* in Goya's time, and wanted to do the same for *Pepe-Hillo*, including a Goyesque bullfight (which he had filmed in Saragossa at the same time as *The Second of May*). In the end, the only one who seemed to get what he wanted was Modesto Alonso, judging by the announcement in June 1928 of the start of shooting for *Return of Goya*.[11]

To be able to carry out his project, Buñuel had to overtake his competitors, starting with Valle-Inclán who also wanted to make a film about Goya. Lorca knew about Valle's intentions and told Buñuel who went off to see Valle-Inclán and found him in the company of the theatrical director Rivas Cherif, who got on well with the group of people to which Buñuel belonged. According to the version Buñuel told me, Valle-Inclán gave up his project, with these or similar words: 'Well, I know that you can do the film better than I can because you are a professional, but don't forget to insist on the fact that Goya became deaf when he was fixing the wheels on the Duchess of Alba's carriage'. Buñuel certainly did not forget this. It is practically the only detail common to both the 1926 and the Paramount 1937 versions of his Goya project.[12]

However, the surviving documents do not tell such a favourable or polite story; Valle-Inclán does not seem to have had a

117

particularly positive impression of Buñuel. In a letter dated 21 February 1927, José García Mercadal wrote to Emilio Ostalé Tudela (the secretary of the Goya Centenary Committee in Saragossa) that 'Valle-Inclán told me about the Goya film. Apparently, he spoke to Buñuel, and he believes that if Buñuel manages to do anything, it will be a ridiculous parody, as he thinks Buñuel has not got the knowledge of Goya to do it properly. To make something on Goya with a Russian is bound to be a failure'.[13] However, in December 1926, the press in Saragossa announced Buñuel's project: 'Don Luis Buñuel has been commissioned to do the *découpage* and to start directing with immediate effect. The film will be made next year, 1927. The various characters will be played by very famous actors, both Spanish and foreign. More details will be released as negotiations progress. The Committee has created a group to study the proposal and don Luis Buñuel has left for Madrid and Paris to finalise the plans'.[14]

But the project did not go ahead. This was probably because of clashes of interest and the large number of clichés in the script, when one of the aims of the intellectuals on the Centenary Committee was to rid Goya's image of such things. Guillermo Díaz Plaja's article of 1928 called 'Some brief Goyesque comments. (On the occasion of the Centenary)', contains some significant comment on this aim. After comparing the commemorations of Goya and Góngora, he then emphasises the dichotomy between the two painters which Valle-Inclán had noted, 'Velázquez is a Spaniard for Spaniards. Goya is a Spaniard for tourists. In Goya we can find all the elements of what is thought to be typically Spanish, all the topics needed to paint a crude, picturesque portrait of Spain. Bullfighters, *majas*, witches, horsemen, knives, fans, nothing is missing'. For Díaz-Plaja, Mérimée's Carmen is the spiritual daughter of the nude *maja* and he warns the reader that, 'as Francisco de Goya's life is becoming popular, long-suffering knights appear on the horizon to provide a guard of honour and protection for our illustrious dead. They say 'we must start a crusade' and then 'we must destroy the false myths surrounding Goya's youth!' It is intolerable that Goya be taken for a bullfighter! No more novelettish love affairs! No more persecution by the Inquisition! These are all ludicrous myths which damage our standing in the world! Goya was never a Don Juan out of an operetta!'.[15]

Buñuel's script was more or less a catalogue of all these anathemas, maybe because he thought that would make the film more commercially viable. He did not manage to secure the job, to his great annoyance. First of all, he changed course and joined forces with Ramón Gómez de la Serna to create a script which combined seven or eight of his stories. Apparently, the film's title in Spanish was aptly *Caprichos* and it was due to be premiered in October 1928, to coincide with the First Spanish Conference on Cinematography. However, Ramón's script did not arrive on time despite all Buñuel's efforts, both direct and indirect, and this led him to restart the Goya project in June 1928 with the Julio César company.[16]

In March 1929, this company was going ahead with the Goya film in Paris, although by now Buñuel was working on the filming of *Un Chien andalou*, and the director was apparently to be the Dane, Carl Theodor Dreyer, judging by this note in the press: 'Increasing its joint ventures, the Julio César company has reached agreement with the Société Générale de Films. The first of their films will be centred around the life and times of Goya. The film will be directed by Carl Dreyer, director of *The Passion of Joan of Arc*'.[17]

But the Goya project was not forgotten as far as Buñuel was concerned. In 1937 he came back to it with the project for *The Duchess of Alba and Goya*, and worked on various sequels to it at several points during his career. Reading the 1926 script allows us to put other areas of interest into better focus, like the surprising jump from something so conventional (or so obviously avant-garde in the case of his work with Gómez de la Serna) to the innovation of *Un Chien andalou*. Salvador Dalí always insisted that the impulse for this innovation came from him not Buñuel. According to Dalí, he had written the first draft in private, as he explained in a letter demanding more recognition because he thought the credits inadequate: 'remember yours and Gómez de la Serna's avant-garde projects, contemporary with my writing of the first version of the *Chien*, in which *film surréaliste* was invented'.[18]

It is true that at that moment, both surrealist film and Luis Buñuel as a director were born, both unheard of beforehand. But maybe the long shadow of Goya was not entirely absent from the title and the content of the film, which belong to a context that might well start with the dog wearing a Catalan cap in Miró's painting of 1926, *Dog Howling at the Moon*, and which Dalí took up around 1938 in his *Afghan Hound* and *Endless enigma*. Miró's animal is a result of the fusion of elements from Lautréamont's dogs in *Les chants de Maldoror* and the disturbing *Dog* which Goya painted in the Quinta del Sordo, and which Gómez de la Serna admired in 1928. If this was the case (above all if it was a subliminal memory), we would be faced with another sign of the innovatory current which underlined the Goya Centenary, paving the way for the introduction of surrealism into Spain.[19]

Notes

1 The 1926 script, inaccurately dated to 1928, was published first in a French translation, Paris, 1987. The Spanish original (*Goya*, Instituto de Estudios Turolenses, 1992) has an introductory essay by Gonzalo Borrás Gualís and includes *The Duchess of Alba and Goya*. For this latter text, and my comments, see also L. Buñuel, *Obra Literaria*, Saragossa, 1982, pp. 282–5.

2 M. de Unamuno, *Cómo se hace una novela*, Barcelona, 1977, p. 88.

3 This quotation is from the Saragossan magazine, *Noroeste*, Autumn, 1932. Buñuel, fanatically committed to surrealism after having written the script for *Un Chien andalou* with Dalí, wrote to Pepín Bello (17 February 1929): 'we must fight with all our disdain and rage against traditional poetry from Homer and Goete (sic) to Góngora – the most despicable son of a bitch – and to the pathetic attempts of today's little poets'. See A. Sánchez Vidal, *Buñuel, Lorca, Dalí: el enigma sin fin*, Barcelona, 1988, p. 198.

4 Letter to Rafael Alberti, *La arboleda perdida*, Barcelona, 1975, p. 247. For the context see E. López Campillo, *La Revista de Occidente y la formación de minorías*, Madrid, 1972, pp. 162–73 and E. Dehennin, *La résurgence de Góngora et la génération poétique de 1927*, Brussels, 1962. J. L. Calvo Carillo contrasts the aesthetics of Góngora with those of Goya and Quevedo in his book *Quevedo y la generación del 27 (1927–1936)*, Valencia, 1992.

5 'El gran español Goya', *Revista de Occidente*, XLVII, 1927, p. 192, quoted in Calvo Carilla, *Quevedo*, p. 33. Goya's fortunes are detailed in N. Glendinning, *Goya y sus críticos*, Madrid, 1982, including his representation in the cinema (pp. 251 *et seq.*) and Buñuel's projects (inaccurately dated to 1928 and 1944–1946).

6 All quotations from Gómez de la Serna are from his article 'El primer humorista', *La Gaceta Literaria*, XIII (1927), p. 1; P. Ilie, *The Surrealist Mode in Spanish Literature*, Ann Arbor, 1968, pp. 19–39, links the development of the modern grotesque with the disintegration of romanticism, especially with reference to Baudelaire and Goya for his Quevedian

roots and his subsequent importance for Gutiérrez Solana, Gómez de la Serna and some of the more expressionist elements of Spanish surrealism. Guillermo de Torre extended this heritage to Salvador Dalí, relating him to Solana ('Realismo y superrealismo', *El Sol*, 8 March 1936). Goya's influence is present in artists as important as the Uruguayan Rafael Barradas, whose influence on Dalí and Lorca is well known (see the articles by R. Santos Torroella and A. Kalenberg in the catalogue, *Barradas*, Saragossa, 1992, especially pp. 50–1, also the chapter by E. Carmona in this present book).

7 R. del Valle-Inclán, *Viva mi dueño*, Buenos Aires, 1940, p. 134.

8 In this respect, it is worth recalling that one of the titles which Buñuel considered for his second film (finally called *L'Age d'or*) was *Down with the Constitution!*. Valle-Inclán's play *Farsa y licencia de la reina castiza* and the novels of *El ruedo ibérico* (the series to which the above-quoted *Viva mi dueño* belongs) had an influence on Buñuel's script for *The Duchess of Alba and Goya*.

9 Since Eugenio D'Ors' book is contemporary with Buñuel's script, it is worth pointing out that Buñuel had moved from Madrid to Paris in 1925 in the ultimately vain hope of being appointed D'Ors' secretary in a cultural department of the League of Nations.

10 See A. Sánchez Vidal *El cine de Florián Rey*, Saragossa, 1991, pp. 99–102. José María Beltrán Ausejo (Saragossa, 1898–1962) was one of the most important Spanish cameramen. He worked with Florián Rey (in the silent version of *La hermana San Suplicio*), Nemesio M. Sobrevilla (in what some people consider to be the most important film of the Spanish avant-garde, *El sexto sentido*, 1929), Jean Grémillon (*La Dolorosa*, 1934) and Buñuel in Filmófono. After the Civil War he moved to Argentina, where he is hailed as the person who revolutionised Argentine cinematic photography. He also worked in Venezuela and Brazil.

11 Jose Buchs was planning a 'film based on Goya, although no title nor list of characters has appeared', *La Pantalla*, xvii, 22 April 1928, p. 271. Modesto Alonso's film was sponsored by Gómez de la Serna for its showing in Pombo and was announced as a 'humorous film' in *La Gaceta Literaria*, lxi, 1 July 1929. The abundance of film projects about Goya is referred to in an eloquent poem published by Bernabé Morera in April 1928 in the magazine *Aragón*, the official organ of the 'Circulo de Aragón' in Buenos Aires, which presents several 'filmable scenes' which are not unlike those in Buñuel's script.

12 As Gómez de la Serna recalled (*Goya*, Madrid, 1928, pp. 122–3), the episode started with Charles Iriarte and was expanded on by Ramón himself. The interview with Valle-Inclán is told in a toned-down version in Buñuel's memoirs (*Mi último suspiro*, Barcelona, 1982, p. 102).

13 Documents relating to the Goya Centenary kept in the University Library of Saragossa (Archivo 18.D.6); I am indebted to Ricardo Centellas for permission to consult these. This letter is reproduced in the edition of the script published by the Instituto de Estudios Turolenses (p. 146).

14 *Heraldo de Aragón*, 27 November 1926, p. 3. The edition of the script

published by the Instituto de Estudios Turolenses, incorrectly states (p. 168), 'The exact date of publication in the quoted magazine was 27 September 1926'.

[15] Quoted in his book *Vanguardismo y protesta*, Barcelona, 1975, p. 119. In his introduction to Buñuel's script, Gonzalo Borrás states that his film project was underestimated because it offered an out of date and romantic view of the painter, rejecting the opinion that was due to the 'encounter' (this expression is my own: p. 99 of *El cine de Florián Rey*) with the latter, 'because Buñuel had acquired the exclusive rights of the film for himself' (p. 13). However, this exclusivity was very uncertain, and I believe that the collision with other projects – including Florián Rey's, the nature of which is still unclear – should not be ignored.

[16] Buñuel's participation in this conference is detailed in *La Pantalla*, xxiv, 10 June 1928, p. 384, which sponsored it. It is worth mentioning that there is considerable confusion about all these projects of Buñuel and Ramón. Probably, they are the same with different names, as happened with *Un Chien andalou* and *L'Age d'or*, which each passed through three different titles. In this case we can also list three: *El mundo por diez céntimos*, *Chiffres* and *Caprichos*. The *Revue du cinéma* published 'Chiffres, Scénarios par Ramón Gómez de la Serna' in its issue of 1 April 1930. *La Gaceta Literaria*, XXI and XXIV, 1 November and 15 December 1927, published some of his notes under the title *Caprichos*. Closer to his script for *Chiffres* are the four *Caprichos* in the issues dedicated to surrealism of the *Bulletí de l'Agrupament Escolar*, VII-IX, July-September 1930, pp. 221 and 224.

[17] Loose sheet in the Madrid journal *La Pantalla*, lviii, 10 March 1929, p. 964.

[18] This letter can be found in A. Sánchez Vidal *Buñuel, Lorca, Dalí*, p. 250. In his *Confesiones inconfesionables* with André Parinard (Barcelona, 1975, p. 110), Dalí insisted, recalling the script based on Gómez de la Serna's stories (*El mundo por diez céntimos*), that it was to be read as if it were a newspaper: 'Buñuel had managed to convince his mother to finance a film based on a mediocre idea contained in a childish synopsis: the animation of sections from newspapers, general events, theatres, cartoons. I wrote to him that he had a script capable of revolutionising modern cinema and that it was essential that he came immediately. Buñuel came. The result of our work was *Un Chien andalou*'.

[19] It would be very laborious to list all the times dogs appear from Goya to *Un Chien andalou*. I tried to do it in October 1992 in the opening lecture at the *Jornadas Surrealistas* in Teruel under the title 'Ladran, luego cabalgamos', in an attempt to expand Antonio Saura's comments in his catalogue *El perro de Goya*, Seville-Saragossa, 1992. The comment by Gómez de la Serna quoted is from his article 'Concepto de Goya', *Revista de Occidente*, lviii, 1928, pp. 20–44. Many quotations could be produced to demonstrate Goya's ability to serve as a trampoline for surrealism, but suffice it to remember André Breton's words: 'Goya was already a surrealist' (*El surrealismo. Puntos de vista y manifestaciones*, Barcelona, 1972, p. 291).

16. Oscar Domínguez: *The hunter*, 1933. Oil on cloth

10 / Metropolis and Utopia: Francisco Ayala's *Hunter in the Dawn*

JOSÉ B. MONLEÓN

Hunter in the Dawn, is one of only two avant-garde novels by Francisco Ayala, forming part of a parenthesis in his work that reflects the intellectual atmosphere of the 1920s and Ortega y Gasset's concept of a 'dehumanized art'.[1] Critics have tended to approach this novel on its own terms, as a clear example of artistic experimentation within a tautological argument that validates both theory and practice: if the 'new art' is supposed to be intrascendental and playful, preoccupied with form and disdainful of a referential reality, as Ortega says, then *Hunter in the Dawn* must be, and indeed becomes, the confirmation of such a conception of art.

There is no point in quoting the numerous commentaries which judge Ayala's avant-garde works as being playful experiments in search of metaphorical surprises and games, as stories without any significant plot, and as narrations lacking the possibility of interpretation and, eventually, of meaning. We would need to cover practically the entire critical corpus,[2] with perhaps the sole exception of Ignacio Soldevila Durante. To his credit, Soldevila refuses to surrender his own perspectives on literature and calls for a hermeneutics of Spanish avant-garde prose.[3] Such a task implies moving beyond the theoretical constraints that feed the text, or better yet bringing these same postulates into the realm of interpretation.

The underlying assumption in the present analysis is that there exists an ideology of the Spanish avant-garde, an ideology of the aesthetic, that simultaneously underwrites the individual work and is shaped by it. The question to be addressed, therefore, is not if *Hunter in the Dawn* offers the possibility of unveiling a 'referent' through the reconstruction of the paths that lead from the glass in the window to the garden, in Ortega's famous definition of the new art.[4] I will explore rather the specific articulation in *Hunter in the Dawn* of some of the avant-garde artistic postulates themselves as producers of signification. Torn between modernisation and a vision of the future, between Metropolis and Utopia, Ayala's text will try to transcend the tensions arising from this confrontation between History and the dawn of a 'new civilization'.

The idea that the plot of *Hunter in the Dawn* is simply an excuse for formal experimentation must be contested. It seems to me that its presence is as fundamental as in any other story. The peasant Antonio Arenas goes to the city to do his military service. There he will live through a series of experiences that introduce him to love, urban life and the possibility of social mobility. The chronology of events is basically linear, except for the initial chapter that contains some explanatory flashbacks: the soldier Antonio Arenas is in a military hospital due to an accident – he fell off a horse – and reminisces about his journey from the countryside to the city.[5]

The narration is then, primarily, the portrayal of a process of initiation.[6] In this respect, the sporadic allusions to the Bible, to classical mythology, and to the epic or the chivalresque novel reinforce the connotations of the rite of passage that construct the story. A series of 'falls' will mark the different illuminating moments in the narration. The opening section alludes to St Paul's encounter with God on his way to Damascus: thrown off his horse, St Paul will convert to Christianity and, upon his arrival in the city, join the new civilization that will eventually define the Western world. Section II describes Antonio's discovery of the metropolis and of sex – both presented in relation to the process of commodity exchange: as the market and the product respectively – and is once again portrayed as 'fallen horseman'.[7] Section III frames the peasant-soldier's who last falls before the completion of his transformation. First, he will lose his centre of gravity at the sight of divine love, incarnated in Aurora (p.73); secondly, a providential intervention fallen from the sky (pp. 77 and 79) will announce his future of fame, his destiny as a boxing champion. These three divine signs determine Antonio's new personality in section IV, ('Private Antonio Arenas, how you have changed from Sunday to Monday!' p. 79), which is definitely summarised in chivalresque terms, as a 'hero' with 'a stimulus of clear chivalrous origins' (p. 80).

Sections VI and VII narrate the consummation of the process of change: he makes love with Aurora and, released from his military service, becomes a free man, with 'a new rather than recuperated freedom'(p. 88). He 'completes his transformation'(p. 90) by purchasing new clothes and joining the world of boxing. Paradoxically, or maybe consequently, Antonio's new identity results ultimately in the commodifying of his person: 'his name had begun to circulate like new shares introduced in the stock market, like

currency with which to speculate' (p. 92). The final section ends
with Antonio's last and mysterious fall: after getting drunk, his
head rolls over and lands on Aurora's lap. Suddenly, he awakens
with the shivers. The story thus culminates not with the consecration of the rite of initiation but rather by casting a sombre
doubt over the future.[8]

This brief recounting of the story illustrates that *Hunter in the
Dawn* is not a mere aesthetic game built around the random use of
tropes without plot but rather a text solidly grounded on
narratological techniques that do allow interpretation.[9] Among
the many themes that could be explored, I have highlighted the
inscription of a process of initiation in which Ayala draws from
the literary tradition in order to 'tell' and reproduce the mythical
connotations of his vision: the dawn of a new civilisation. The
rebirth of Antonio Arenas will take place in the urban centre (p.
69), shaped by the signs of a new society and a new culture. Like
St Paul, Antonio will receive enlightening values, although this
time they will descend not from God but rather from the emblematic neon *signs* that *literally* reveal the power of the new order.
Hunter in the Dawn is then a text that covers the distance to the
metropolis – a new road to Damascus – and portrays the transformation of a peasant into a city dweller.

The metamorphosis of Antonio Arenas into the new man of
(post)modernity by the Grace of the metropolis is a tempting
presupposition. It allows us to read *Hunter in the Dawn* as
another expression of the rift between the city and the country.
There are examples that might confirm such an interpretation:
'There , in the country', seasons return every year to corroborate
the slow cyclical nature of Nature, while the world of modernity
(or postmodernity) is impregnated by the inexorable and speedy
succession of time(p. 66). But where exactly is that 'there'? Can
we discern in the text a 'referential' space that would stand in
opposition to the metropolitan topos?

One of Lorca's poems in *Poeta en Nueva York* is entitled 'A Cry
to Rome'. As spokesman for 'the multitudes' that will scream
'until the cities tremble like little girls',[10] Lorca denounces the
Pope. What gives the poet the public authority to interpellate Pius
XI is not only his moral conviction, but also his physical location:
from the new pulpit of modernity, from the tower of the Chrysler

Building, Lorca can assert his voice and proclaim *urbi et orbi* his own Encyclical. In this dialogue, New York and Rome confront each other as universal symbols, as the representative spaces of a new civilisation that is not fulfilling 'the will of the Earth'.[11] The underlying conflict, nevertheless, does not arise from a rift between the earth and the city, but rather from a historical projection, from the fact that the Metropolis stands *as* the Earth, as the engulfing product and universal motor of modernisation.

In *Hunter in the Dawn*, the beginning of the story appears to establish the opposition country – city:

> We all know that during snowy days it is dangerous to approach the hungry bear standing at the fur store. We all have followed, on some occasion, a snake's trail, only to find a dead bicycle tyre, strangled, by the side of the road. . . .
>
> But not everyone has seen the heartbeats of the furious sky, spurred by shining hedgehogs that drive long thorns in its flanks. . . . (pp. 61–2)

The two initial paragraphs portray the experiences of two different worlds: knowledge, praxis and sensibility are framed, in the first one, within the limits of an urban context; Nature (the senses – seeing, hearing, tasting – and galloping) is included in the second one. Yet the difference is subverted by Ayala's narrative strategies. First, the recourse to metaphor blurs the distinction, since the levels of similitude constantly bring together the two realms: bear / store, snake / tyre; cockrel / army, dawn / Chicago. Secondly, the switch in the narrative voice – from 'we all know' to 'not everyone has seen' – presents a more complex situation: the metropolitan experience is universalised, while the rural one, framed within horizons of sulphur, *can* in fact be alien to a sector of humanity.

Ayala elaborates here on the common topic of the tentacular city: 'The smallest and thinnest roots of the industrial world insert themselves deep in the healthy flesh of the country and sensitise its neutral volume' (p. 67). The urban space and life encompass the countryside and are shared by all; the sensual experience of nature is still possible, but belongs to a (privileged or marginal) sector inscribed within the boundaries of modernity.

The 'there' then does not correspond to another space outside of modernity. It refers rather to a temporal designation, to a histori-

127

cal practice that materialises before Antonio reaches the city: 'The military train had incorporated him, without transitions, into a fast rythm unknown to him' (p. 66); 'A jolt, a whistle, the harsh start of the train had thrown him into another pace' (p. 66). Antonio's *process* of initiation into modernity will be completed through his immersion into the urban centre, but modernity was already 'there', ready to assert itself without transitions. The enlightening road to Damascus did not require, ultimately, a displacement since the new means of communication had brought Damascus to Antonio.

The text, therefore, aims at resolving a tension offered not so much by the opposition between rural and urban experiences as by the disappearance of such an opposition through its obliteration within the metropolis. If there is a rift articulated by the story, it does not belong to the 'modern tradition' of city versus country, of History versus Nature, but rather – as we shall see – to the postmodern preoccupation with the relationship between History and the text, between metropolis and utopia.

Michel de Certeau, half a century after Lorca, initiates his *touristic* experience of New York with a gaze that requires a very particular position: 'To *see* Manhattan from the 107th floor of the World Trade Center'.[12] To see – or better, to see a city – implies the recognition of a distance. Immersed in the streets, the modern subject can only live an immediate practice of 'reality' unless he or she is endowed with or has acquired the possibility of mediation, of *changing* the focus of perception. To see, here , is not a passive contemplation but rather a leisurable activity, a dynamic transformation, an aesthetic construction. In order to see, the gaze must first consolidate its peripheral bearings: the 107th floor of the World Trade Center. From 'there', the city and the world can be mapped out.

De Certeau's position is nevertheless a very privileged one. After all, who can be on the top of the trading centre of the capitalist world, and know that this signifies exactly 107 floors? A sense of power and pleasure irradiates from this initial inscription of the point of reference, from this shameless affirmation of a 'transcendental sign'. Paradoxically, there emanates also a confusing projection of arbitrariness, for the 'centre' is no longer 'inside' the city but resides rather on its periphery: it exists in fact within the acknowledgement of distance, in the notation of such a distance. By using concepts such as change of focus, periphery, and distance,[13] I have intentionally subjected de Certeau's text to a reading linked to Ortega's characterisation of the new dehumanised art, a characterisation deeply rooted in spatial and visual coordinates, framed by perceptions that denote the possibility of new shapes and forms, of different angles and focuses in the apprehension and representation of reality.

In the case of Lorca – and of de Certeau – it would seem that the change in perspective and in language arose from *experiencing* New York in all its magnitude.[14] For other writers, Ayala included, such an explanation is less plausible. In order to *see* Madrid and the world, the Spanish avant-garde artists could not rely on the tower of the Chrysler Building. What gave them the new perspective, the new dimensions of reality, and the language with which to textualise it, was a different vantage point: the cinema.[15]

In his *Investigation into the Cinema* Ayala summarises some of the fundamental characteristics of this new aesthetic form: its consonance with the new times, its capacity to create new mythologies, some of its defining formal aspects. 'The minute frames of celluloid coined by its machines are currency of excellent circulation among the children of every corner of the Earth; the only currency universally accepted'.[16] Cinema is not only a window to the world of modernity but also a medium to coin such a world into the World, to universalise modernity. The process of commodification – History – thus penetrates the Earth, overtaking its most unsuspected corners, its most guarded 'innocence': even children become integrated into a circuit of monetary exchange. To *see* the world, to shout *urbi et orbi*, then, does not require reaching to the luminous top of a skyscraper; it can be accomplished by plunging into a darkened cinema. From here, a universe of 'unforeseen perspectives' (p. 41) inscribes itself into humanity's imagination, 'distancing matter' (p. 33) from the familiar representations of realism. From here, everyone has seen the metamorphosis of a snake into a bicycle tyre.

These effects and functions of cinematography are implemented through some specific formal strategies inherent in its condition as a visual art. The framing of the object, close-ups, the combination of light and shadows, the suggestive consequences of editing, etc.,

129

are all artistic recourses whose power is suddenly unbound by one encompassing feature: motion. Cinema becomes the art of moving pictures, of images in their process of formation and transformation. A photograph, on the other hand, represents the horror – or the comicness – of eternity (p. 81), a 'vague danger'(p. 82).

Cinema will provide Ayala and other avant-garde writers with the possibility of exploring the metonymic potential of their prose. As Roman Jakobson has noted,

> [to] the manifestly metonymical orientation of cubism . . . the surrealist painters responded with a patently metaphorical attitude. Ever since the productions of D. W. Griffith, the art of the cinema, with its highly developed capacity for changing the angle, perspective and focus of shots has . . . ranged an unprecedented variety of synecdochic close-ups and metonymic set-ups in general. In such motion pictures as those of Charlie Chaplin and Eisenstein, these devices in turn were overlayed by a novel, metaphoric montage with its lap dissolves – the filmic similes.[17]

Regardless of which exact trope dominates the cinematic production, it appears clear that films offered the vision of *processes* of transformation – and in this respect at least they tended to highlight the influence of metonymy. When Ayala declares that cinema 'transforms – without any effort – a glass into a crystal rose; the rose, into a hand; the hand, into a bird. Or – like in a recent German film – a fruit bowl with two apples, into a woman's breast',[18] the emphasis resides not so much in the completed substitution as in the conversion itself, in the textual unfolding of change – thus the importance that Ayala sees in slow-motion techniques.

Translated into verbal narrative procedures, the metonymic process occupies two main axes in *Hunter in the Dawn*. On the one hand, it permeates the semantic level, constantly referring to a system of images drawn from filmic experience. The windows of a train in motion, for instance, will become the appropriate equivalent of a reel: the framed landscape will be subjected to different speeds, and appear as a deformed representation; the rapid succession of images creates an unpredictable, edited narration; Nature becomes historicised, commodified:

The locomotive pierced the suburban belt . . .

The conscripts, with astonished faces, had never imagined the possibility of nature in a splint, on a corset, full of labels like another commodity in a shop at a railway station.

. . . Suddenly everything became frozen, motionless. (A film which snaps.) (p. 68)

On the other hand, metonymy is introduced at the syntactic level, where the contiguity of words unfolds into movements of displaced meaning: the danger of winter / bear / fur shop. In this sense, the entire narration of *Hunter in the Dawn* can be seen as a metonymic exercise. The initial description of Antonio centres around his 'hanging head', his feverish state in which vague perceptions of escaping from undetermined hunters dominate his sensations (p. 62). When at the end of the story, his head finally rolls over Aurora's lap, the 'deserting winds' have become 'thin air that moves the tender branches of the forest'; his fever, drunkenness; and from being a prey, he wakes up as a hunter at dawn of gazelles – embodied, incidentally, by Aurora. The entire narration, therefore, could be understood as the unfolding of the metamorphosis of a prey into a predator, as the exposition or verbalisation of the transformations underlining every trope. As the *textualisation of processes*.

Cinematography, then, provides avant-garde writers with an aesthetics that deploys a double set of connotations. it embodies, as artistic medium, the universalised process of commodification at the same time as it offers the spectacle of process itself.

Once Antonio Arenas has completed his rite of modernisation, his memories of a pre-urban past begin to fade. His 'prehistory' (p. 93) is depicted in terms that, once again, reproduce Ortega's image of the window and the garden:

The volume of his rural memories had withdrawn to the background; his village was an incomplete drawing over a leaden canvas, behind underlines of rain . . . His entire past was reduced to signs . . . Presence, immediacy, occupied all his attention (p. 93).

The non-metropolitan experience of the new Arenas has been cast out to the background, and all he has left is the possibility of

131

apprehending its signs. Between him and his past arises the artistic text affirming the inescapable presence of mediation. The spell of *seeing* transforms all appearances into commodities, memory into art.

When in the 1980s Michel de Certeau descends from the World Trade Center and re-enters the city, Manhattan has changed: 'New York, this anti-Rome' is 'transformed into a texturology'.[19] As he wanders through the streets, de Certeau will unveil the metropolitan syntax and trace its semiotics. In 1929 Madrid, the soldier Antonio Arenas anticipates such a 'postmodern' attitude. Rambling through the city monuments that serve as notations of its history, the new hero of modernity must acknowledge his illusory condition: 'the cohabitation with such superb characters offered him the illusion of living within the pages of an invented natural History' (p. 69). Even the present, immediacy, that which 'occupies all his attention', is bound to undergo a *process of textualisation*. To live, to experience, becomes paradoxically to inscribe oneself in the pages of discourse. History may not yet be Art, but it already belongs to the realm of invention, and as such will be bound to collapse into the web of textual creativity.

What are the underlying forces behind this process? What are the hidden elements of History that provoke the collapse of experience into discourse? Why the need to sublate modernisation into texturology? *Hunter in the Dawn* covers the rift that it exposes by openly addressing its own internal tensions. History's inexorable colonisation of humanity offers the magic of material progress, but it also reveals, at the same time, its menacing secrets: 'Private Antonio Arenas ignored what the pond's womb conceals – class struggle and Darwin's natural selection – until the fever began to show him its wounded pieces of film, unfolded in front of him its catalogues, and tempted him with its merchandise' (p. 62).

The duality with which Ayala, and the Spanish avant-garde in general, approaches modernity finds a resolution – albeit a fragile one, in need of constant renovation and reaffirmation – in artistic freedom, in textual creativity. Fascinated with technological development yet overwhelmed by its alienating effects,[20] the new writers will unleash the power of language, at once disentailing it from the tyranny of the referent and subjugating it to the demands and arbitrariness of the market.[21] The text, with its capacity for reordering reality,[22] will emerge as the ultimate topos for exorcising social revolution – through artistic revolution.

As Anthony Geist has noted in his analysis of Rafael Alberti's *Sobre los ángeles*, 'language paradoxically separates us from Heaven and gives us a consciousness of that separation. We try to recuperate Paradise through language, yet it constantly eludes us. . . . Heaven is a literal utopia, a no-place and a no-time'.[23] It is indeed a *literal* utopia. Ayala's vision of a totally universalised modernity (both geographically and historically) leaves no room for a sense of utopia outside the text. It is 'here' where liberation from class struggle can be attained, and not in an unreachable, non-existing 'there'. As Ramón Gómez de la Serna said:

> I live fully in novels, in their loose life, through their free paths.
> There is no more beautiful mission than to create the free novel, than to fabricate a world that we will never reach, regardless of how long we live![24]

When the portrayal of the processes of textualisation (the commodification of culture) transforms itself into a depiction of the textualisation of processes (the playful aesthetic game, the pleasure of the text; that is, the culture of commodities, or Culture Inc.[25]) the result leads towards a collapse of the referential function of language. It implies the (illusory) transformation of history from class struggle into indulgence: utopia not as a place outside modernity, nor as a promissory projection in time (bucolic past or revolutionary future), but as a no-place, as a stroll through the intricacies of creativity. Utopia as – to use de Certeau's words – texturology.

The ending of the story, none the less, casts a shadow over the entire aesthetic project: Aurora's womb contains the seeds of a menacing 'reality'. In October 1929, in 1931 and, above all, in 1936, Spain's history refused to be aestheticised. The surface of the pond split in two, spilling its contents once again through the streets.

Notes

[1] Initially published in the *Revista de Occidente*, LXXV and LXXVI, 1929, then as a book, *Cazador en el alba y Erika ante el invierno*, Madrid, 1930. The other

avant-garde work by Ayala is *El boxeador y un ángel*, Madrid, 1929. All page references to *Cazador en el alba* are to the Madrid edition of 1988, with page references bracketed in the text. All translations are mine, except when otherwise indicated.

2 Cf. 'The anecdote is an excuse . . . What is essential is the surprising construction, obtained at each step through the unsuspected associations of words'. R. Navarro Durán, 'Introducción', *Cazador*, 1988, p. 22.

3 I. Soldevila-Durante, 'Para una hermenéutica de la prosa vanguardista española. (A propósito de Francisco Ayala)', *Cuadernos Hispanoamericanos*, CCCXXIX-CCCXXX, 1977, pp. 356–65. For other interpretations see R. Bosch, 'La problemática de *Cazador en el alba* de Francisco Ayala', *Letras Peninsulares*, III, 1990, pp. 101–17, and T. Mermall, *Las alegorías del poder en Francisco Ayala*, Madrid, 1983.

4 J. Ortega y Gasset, *The Dehumanisation of Art and Other Writings on Art and Culture*, New York, 1956, pp. 9–10.

5 The text does not clarify at what moment during his military service Arenas suffered the accident. Nevertheless, we will follow his steps from the time of his incorporation into the army through his discharge. Since the opening scene situates Arenas in the hospital with a high fever, there exists the possibility of interpreting the entire narration as a hallucination or a dream. To take the events face value or as fantasy becomes ultimately irrelevant to the extent that the ambiguity is not problematised. Ayala's experimentation with chronology is not limited to his avant-garde works but appears rather as a constant feature in his production. See A. Alvarez Sanagustín, *El discurso literario de Francisco Ayala*, Oviedo, 1981, p. 117, and E. Irizarry, *Francisco Ayala*, Boston, 1977, p. 34.

6 Prologue to *Cazador en alba y otras imaginaciones*, Barcelona, 1971, p. 34.

7 *Cazador*, Madrid, 1988, p. 72.

8 Is Aurora pregnant? Women are constantly objectified in the text and a case could be built around the fact that this last fall might represent the impossibility of reaching the utopic implications of the initiation process. Is the family institution a threat to the 'heroic' future of Antonio? Is Aurora, like a new Eve, responsible for throwing Antonio out of the reign of fame and back into history?

9 As Ramón Gómez de la Serna indicated: 'What I could not believe is that the purpose was to publicise without offering the public any cipher – that is, without offering the key and the possibility of deciphering'. *Ismos*, Buenos Aires, 1943, p. 371.

10 Federico García Lorca, *Poet in New York*, New York, 1988, p. 153.

11 *Ibid.*, p. 153.

12 M. de Certeau, 'Practices of space', *On Signs*, Baltimore, 1985, p. 122 (italics in original).

13 'Art which – like science and politics – used to be very near the axis of enthusiasm, that backbone of our person, has moved toward the outer rings', Ortega y Gasset, *Dehumanisation*, p. 48.

14 Lorca's 'Paseo de Buster Keaton', none the less, was written before his trip to

the United States and it already contains all the aesthetic elements that will define his *Poet in New York*.

[15] As Victor Fuentes indicates, 'In the narrations of Jarnés and Ayala, the Spanish city – whether Madrid or Barcelona, Saragossa or Granada – refers us to the big urban centres seen in the screen: New York, Paris, Berlin'. 'El cine en la narrativa vanguardista española de los años 20', *Letras Peninsulares*, III, 1990, p. 206. The most complete account of the relationship between cinema and the Spanish avant-garde writers is C. Brian Morris, *This Loving Darkness. The Cinema and Spanish Writers*, Oxford, 1980.

[16] *Indagación del cinema*, Madrid, 1929, pp. 51–2.

[17] *Language in Literature*, London, 1987, p. 111.

[18] *Indagación del cinema*, pp. 35–6.

[19] De Certeau, *On Signs*, p. 122.

[20] Juan Cano Ballesta points out the euphoric attitude of a generation that praises industrialisation and the machine. J. C. Ballesta, *Literatura y tecnología. (Las letras españolas ante la revolución industrial)*, Madrid, 1981, p. 77. Mermall, *Las alegorías*, p. 54, on the other hand, highlights the monstrous character of the city in Ayala's works.

[21] Saussure's (and Roland Barthes') conception of language and, particularly, of the sign reproduces some structures that could be linked to the conception of commodities as analysed by Marx. See J. Baudrillard, *Pour une critique de l'économie politique du signe*, Paris, 1972, and J. Davies, 'The futures market: Marinetti and the fascists of Milan', in E. Timms and P. Collier, *Visions and Blueprints. Avant-garde culture and radical politics in early twentieth-century Europe*, Manchester, 1988, pp. 82–97.

[22] 'The creator moves, guided only by his aesthetic intuition, in a universe of things, of sensations, of ideas which appear jumbled and disorganised to his imagination. In his mind he will have to choose the pieces necessary to construct his machines – perfectly useless and without equivalents in the natural order of the world'. Ayala, *Indagación*, p. 25. The translation belongs to Morris, p. 144.

[23] A. L. Geist, 'Hell's Angels: A Reading of Alberti's *Sobre los ángeles*', *Hispanic Review*, LIV, 1986, p. 178.

[24] *Ismos*, p. 368.

[25] See H. Schiller, *Culture, Inc. The Corporate Takeover of Public Expression*, Oxford, 1989.

17. Joaquín Torres-García: *Street scene in Barcelona*, 1917, Oil on board

11 / Bridges to romance: Nostalgia in Eliot, Salinas, and Lorca

HOWARD T. YOUNG

Cosmopolitanism, diversity, fragmentation – traits that modernism exploited and developed as virtues –[1] serve equally well as badges of the avant-garde artist. In this military metaphor, the emphasis placed on pulling ahead from the main body (other artists) in order to lead an attack on the enemy (also other artists)

136

implies upheaval within the house of art in terms of diversity (different approaches), fragmentation (the crumbling of old forms), and cosmopolitanism (the escape from the parochial).

Nostalgia, from the Greek *nostos* (return home), on the other hand, hardly seems a characteristic associated at first glance with the avant-garde. Soldiers preparing to shatter the old in order to create the new ('Make it new', went Pound's famous dictum) do not grant much privilege to T. S. Eliot's line: 'Home is where we start from'. The cosmopolitan is at home anywhere in the world, whereas nostalgia often accords with homesickness, a term hardly free of opprobrium when applied to military personnel.

Throughout the nineteenth century, until Nietzsche began his assault, history meant continuity. The modernist or avant-garde artists wished to disrupt the temporal linearity of nineteenth century consciousness as manifest in family, progress, and history itself.[2] Nostalgia in relation to history implies a desire to go back to another time conceived of as harmonious and unified in contrast with the futility and fragmentation of the present moment. Writers in the grip of nostalgia tend to deny history and seek to return to something that they probably never had, for memory is treacherous about the paradises of the past. Proust's great novel, a monument of modernism, exposes nostalgia in many guises, all variants of the poignant realisation that the only true paradise is the paradise we have lost.

Proust opens the door, and other writers crowd in. I propose to use T. S. Eliot as a sounding board to explore forms of nostalgia in Lorca and Salinas (the former decidedly avant-garde, the latter more mutedly so): nostalgia for order and innocence (Lorca), nostalgia for romance and high culture (Salinas). The soldiers definitely looked back.

Cosmopolitanism, diversity, and fragmentation are traits that fit like a glove the great modernist set piece in twentieth-century poetry, *The Waste Land*. Yet underneath the polyglot murmur, oscillating voices and dramatic disjunctions, one can trace a blueprint for salvation, a preparation for the absolute.[3] The ostensible biblical voice, structured by polysyndeton in 'The Burial of the Dead', is not parodic, just as the question from Hezekiah, 'Shall I at least set my lands in order?', is not rhetorical. Nor are the quotations from St Augustine and *The Upanishads* merely voices to listen in on (as the famous pub conversation).[4] They deliver messages of hope and preface the famous conversion that will shortly befall the poem's author.

Although nostalgia for a 'still centre' plainly underlies much of *The Waste Land*, another kind of need to return is also present. The urban landscape with its brown fog, grimy scraps, and building sites causes the mind to seek nourishment elsewhere, some other place which offers palpable and at the same time nostalgic evidence of better times. The poem's speaker shores up 'fragments' of European culture's most vaunted moments against his 'ruins'. This obeisance to a cultural whole that is now rent, to epiphanies of literature ('Et o ces voix d'enfants') juxtapose sharply with the degradation and *ennui* of urban life. Palpable examples of a beautiful past – the splendour of Ionian white and gold that is the interior of Wren's St Martyr Magnus compared to the 'pleasant whining' of a mandolin by the fishermen's pub on Lower Thames Street – are made all the more poignant by the joyless present. Unlike Pío Baroja, who was convinced that the plebeian accordion at twilight was the only acceptable aesthetic pleasure, Eliot ever turns to high culture. His heavy recourse to allusion, raising it, as it were, to the level of a trope, implies a perceived structure of history, and an assumed grammar, however fragmentary.[5]

'Mummy. / Embroider me on your pillow', pleads the speaker in Lorca's 'Silly song'.[6] With the same unabashed persistence as Proust, Lorca yearns to return to the paradise of his childhood. It took no madeleine cake dipped in tea to awaken the dormant memories of infancy and of the singular place his talent and congeniality had afforded him in the bosom of his family. The longing to return is expressed with drama, pathos and intensity throughout his work.

The juvenilia eloquently attest Lorca's nostalgia for an age of innocence. After making clear that the nostalgia stems in part from a desire to be rid of the puissance of an awakening sex drive ('May the cup of semen / Be completely spilled, / May neither blood nor warmth / remain in my flesh'), the poet pleads:

> I want to be like a little child,
> Who, pink and silent

In the ermine thighs
Of his loving mother
Hears a dialogue
Between a star and God.[7]

Neither heat nor blood could be denied, however, and when Lorca's sexuality deviated from what was the apparent norm in macho Spain, his longing to return (memory mixed with desire) became laden with pathos and submerged anger. Christopher Maurer (Collected Poems, p. xxiii) perceptively calls Lorca the greatest of Spain's elegiac poets, not for such accomplishments as 'Lament on the death of Ignacio Sánchez Mejías', but for the extended play between presence and absence, the nostalgic yearning to have what is gone, that colours all of his work.

Amidst the welter of avant-garde imagery in *Poet in New York*, the nostalgia of lost innocence refuses to be smothered in a piece like 'Double Poem of Lake Eden'. Its epigraph from the sixteenth-century poet Garcilaso points to a pastoral past and indirectly authenticates the pastoral presence of Vermont, where the poem was written. 'My former voice / Did not know about dense, bitter juices' (Obras Completas, p. 489): the voice that opens the poem belongs to the past of childhood and lies underneath the wet fragile ferns as 'my real voice' (OC, p. 489). The 'former voice' can cauterize the bauble ('talcum') and flashiness ('tinplate') of the present voice. The imagery could not be more modern (like Prufrock's evening sky etherized upon a table), and the message of the 'former voice' could not be more direct and rid of irony: 'I want to weep because I feel like it / Like the children in the back row weep' (OC, p. 490).

The angry denunciation of homosexual prostitution in the 'Ode to Walt Whitman' draws some of its fire from the absent aura of innocence that may have been possible at some point in Spain but seemed impossible in New York. In the words of Derek Harris, Lorca is making a 'clear ethical distinction between Whitman's spiritual, pantheistic homosexual love and the debased sexuality of the 'maricas'.[8] That Lorca turns back to a figure in the past in order to idealize his own sexuality is significant in our anatomy of nostalgia. The ode's conclusion stresses the longing for paradise:

I want the strong breeze of the deepest night
To take the flowers and inscription from the arch where you
   sleep
And a black child to proclaim to the whites and their gold
The coming of the kingdom of corn. (OC, p. 532).

The moral outrage of *Poet in New York* implies an underlying belief in justice, structure, and history. This passionate conviction in 'New York. Office and Accusation' engenders the recurring 'I accuse', that rings with the energy of Zola's 'J'accuse'. The total absence of irony and ambiguity (there must be only minimal separation between the narrating 'I' and the Lorca of flesh and blood) allows us to conflate the individual loss of innocence so keenly felt in Vermont with the fury and indignation that possessed the author in the inhuman New York metropolis.

Towards the conclusion of 'New York. Office and Accusation' comes the question: 'What shall I do, set the landscapes in order?' (OC, p. 518), a query often seen as an echo of Eliot's 'Shall I at least set my lands in order?', referred to earlier.[9] Eliot heeded the injunction from Hezekiah, and it would be answered shortly by the poet's conversion. But if Lorca's use of the concept of ordering simply means the compulsive arrangement of material objects, then the answer for him is a resounding, 'No'. To order lands and old photographs is to lose sight of the injustice that prowls the earth.

At this point, it is useful to consider Lorca's feelings as they can be gleaned from his poetry about the notion of order in general, a concept that because of its implied approval of hierarchy, control and continuity came under attack by modernists. The destruction of the principle of continuity was one of T. E. Hulme's avowed goals.[10] How are we to take the statement of Lorca's speaker in one of *Poet in New York*'s first poems ('1910 [Interlude]'): 'Ask me no questions. I have seen that things / Find their void when they seek their path?' (OC, p. 448). Lament over the absence of sequence and harmony, or recognition that the desire for order usually ended up in a reordering of chaos, that disorder remained the fundamental truth about human affairs?

The 'Ode to Salvador Dalí', published in 1926 a few years before the New York trip, provides clarification. It is written in praise of Dalí's breathtaking representational ability, his uncanny skill at reproducing reality, epitomized in *Basket of Bread* (1926). 'A desire for forms and limits' overwhelms the speaker as he views this painting. It is, however, a still life that in all its perfection lacks vitality. 'You flee', Lorca's speaker lectures Dalí, 'the dark forest of unbelievable forms' (OC, p. 954). A certain kind of world of 'deaf shadows and disorder, / In the foregrounds that humanity inhabits' (OC, p. 954) finds no place in Dalí's canvasses. The ode in its entirety embodies an urgent suggestion to the enormously gifted Catalan painter that, in the pursuit of art, he should not forget love, friendship and the sensuality of the human form: 'You always clothe and bare your brush in the air, / Facing the sea peopled with boats and sailors' (OC, p. 957).

The familiar world of Salvador Dalí with its melting watches and gnomic shapes, was soon to be born, and some critics (Eutimio Martín and Santos Torroella[11]) believe that this shift in content was partly in response to Lorca's ode, for in 1927, just one year later, in *Honey is Sweeter than Blood*, the world of order in the still life of bread and basket is transformed into a 'forest of unbelievable forms'. What seems clear is that Lorca's own artistic vision needed to include disorder, that art for him could not be rigidly measured ('the yellow measure' (OC, p. 953)). In his opinion, a poet's duty lay in making the trip to the 'dark forest', (the heart of darkness, the province of the *duende*, the demonic spirit of inspiration), that was fundamental to the human condition, and forging a trail back blazed by the images discovered in obscurity. In that sense, order would prevail.

Roaming New York's streets and visiting its protestant churches made Lorca homesick for the culture of Europe and the catholicism of his native country. Eliot chose to live abroad and to shore against his ruins fragments of the best that had been thought and written in the European tradition. These shards amidst the lines of Sanskrit are *The Waste Land*'s last message.

Some of Lorca's nostalgia in *Poet in New York* arises from the fact that he was in a New World. And while his letters to his family reveal the exciting tourist aspect of his visit, the poetry struggles with the darker side, the contrast between his roots and the present disorientation.

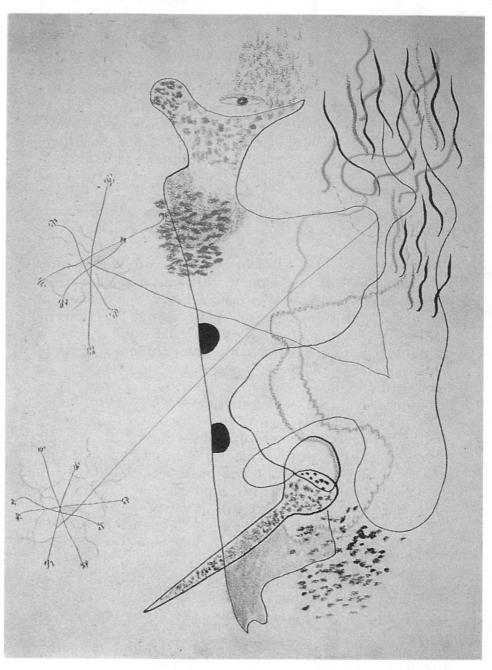

18. Federico García Lorca: *Drawing [Priapic Pierrot]*, c. 1933–36. Ink and coloured pencil on card

A case in point is 'Birth of Christ', where the celebration of the Nativity as glimpsed in New York contrasts with the memory of Spanish scenes. The poem, after foreseeing the crucifixion (the number three, sign of the Trinity, on the Child's forehead is replicated by three bronze thorns in the hay), in the last stanza questions the authenticity of this scene in an American city:

> Manhattan's snow blows against advertising hoardings
> Bringing pure grace to the false ogives.
> Idiot priests and feathered cherubim
> Follow Luther round the high corners. (OC, p. 484)

Swirling among the 'false ogives', a simulacrum of the original Gothic (high culture), only the snow is pure. The priesthood that should function as a guardian of the tradition is cruelly dismissed as an idiotic follower of Martin Luther.

Lorca's reading while in New York of the Spanish translation of *The Waste Land* showed him the significance of Tiresias, the 'vate' of this poem.[12] Lorca would especially have appreciated the situation of Eliot's seer, blind, caught between two worlds, forced to witness sordid and repetitive acts of sexual couplings. Both Lorca and Eliot longed for other times: the lost centre, innocence, Ionian white and gold, pure Gothic. Eliot chose to disguise himself carefully in the figure of Tiresias; Lorca set himself forth unabashedly, with as little disguise as is possible in a literary text: 'Because I am neither man, nor poet, nor leaf, / But a wounded pulse that plumbs for things on the other side' (OC, p. 490).

Among the features of modernity to be found in the poetry of Pedro Salinas, the most obvious is his awareness of the gap between signifier and signified. In a famous statement of his poetics, the poem 'My Faith' from the book *Certain Chance*,[13] the poet announces a lack of confidence in the 'paper rose' (the literary artefact), and displays equal scepticism about the 'real rose' (born from the sun and seasons). Instead, he proclaims his faith in an article that is not a word from his pen, nor a product of the natural cycle: 'In you that I never made, / In you that they never made, / In you I trust, fully / Certain chance'. Salinas does not insist on the arbitrary relation between the word and the object it names; rather, he recognizes the distance between the two (the natural rose and the literary rose) and realizes that poetry (perhaps all

143

communication) depends on a matter of chance, runs an ineluc-
table risk. His 'poetics' in the famous Diego Anthology of 1932
affirms: 'we must let chance run its course, with all that beauty of
risk, of probability, of wager'.[14] In the phrase 'beauty of risk' with
its ready acceptance of probability lie the verve of Salinas and his
appeal to modern readers.

Despite the willingness to live with the hazards of speech (perhaps partly because of it), Salinas's poetry is most famous for its
constant posture of looking back. The search for what is beyond
or behind matter in all its variations – dates, names, faces – is a
salient theme. If Platonism can be read as a philosophy of nostalgia, of seeking the reflection of an ever intangible ideal form, then
Pedro Salinas qualifies as a nostalgic poet. No matter how playfully, whimsically, or humorously, he is forever looking inward or
back (zones that amount to the same bearing on the mental
compass).

It is among the most common and earliest of his themes. His
first book *Presages* (1924) contains a poem addressed to a barren
orange tree, whose fruit has been packed in boxes and shipped to
faraway places. The poem's speaker insists that the barrenness is
only apparent. 'You are left / The dark, round fruit / Of your
shadow on the ground'. (PC, p. 75). The narrator, among the
shadows like Plato's cave dwellers, stealthily enjoys the 'impalpable slices' with the certainty that this thirst for the impalpable
will never be extinguished. The surrender of life to an 'inner
honeycomb' (PC, p. 79), a Proustian belief that 'that within' was
a 'sweet eternal secret' (PC, p. 99) already apparent in *Presages*
becomes explicit in 'Vocations', one of the first poems of *Certain
Chance* that contrasts an Aristotelian cosmos of clarity and
measure, clear lines and shapes (the world that will be Jorge
Guillén's) with an incomplete, unfinished world of shadow, the
view from 'within'.

The unsettling cityscapes of Baudelaire, Eliot, or Lorca are
largely absent in the poetry Salinas wrote before the Spanish Civil
War. After his exile in the United States, he reacts profoundly to
the sterility and madness of the metropolis, and registers his horror at the atomic age. But until that event, he seems content to
handle the artefacts and inventions of modernity with a certain
kind of playfulness that consisted in building 'specific bridges

144

between modern life and romance'.[15] Once we enter into the territory of myth again (in this case, a myth rooted in the *modernista* image of Versailles that is an elaboration with accompanying nymphs, swans, and castles, of an underlying romantic image), we encounter a process of attempting to establish order. In a playful way, Salinas does with his bits of romance what Joyce did with *Ulysses* and Eliot defended him for: introduce a means of ordering the chaos of the present.

Two poems in *Certain Chance* ('35 Candlepower' and 'Underwood Girls') are remarkable for the way they recognize that the modern inventions of the light bulb and the typewriter can be taken possession of by the writer. The muse becomes mechanical, and the mechanical blessed with extravagant meaning. Futurism supplied many an ode to machines, and the results were often robotic, as in this Spanish example contemporary to Salinas: 'Miss, You give the Underwood / A rhythm with a new emotion; / The pure rhythm of the logarithm / Of the "Stock Price" sonata'.[16] It is one thing to speak of stock prices in terms of a sonnet, and quite another to do like Salinas and establish the typewriter's keyboard as a magic casement that opens on to a world of creation: '. . . eternal nymphs / Set against the great empty world' (PC, p. 203). In the first instance, we have an uninteresting metaphor; in the second, an effective appropriation of myth ('fable'). Ironic, tongue-in-cheek, and nevertheless touching is Salinas's embrace of his new muse:

> Just her and me in the room, eternal
> Lovers, she my illuminating
> Docile muse, on guard against
> Hoards of secrets in the night. (PC, p. 136)

Together poet and light bulb set out to decipher the massive secrets of the night. This is a clear and comfortable form of control and order arrived at through the use of fable. No whirling dervish, no visitations by spirits, no opium, perhaps even no wine: just a typewriter and a light bulb, and the entire world to visit the imagination upon.

It is one thing, however, to appropriate these instruments in Madrid, Seville or Paris, and another to see what technology has wrought in New York. The shock of modernity that awaited

Salinas in his exile in the United States was one that Lorca had already undergone. In the case of Salinas, it would have an impact on this themes while not substantially affecting his technique of viewing the present in terms of a romantic past. If anything, his nostalgia becomes more pronounced.

'Advertisement Nocturne' (*Everything Clearer*, PC, pp. 657–60) sets the tone for Salinas's handling of the metropolis. From the ironic use of 'nocturne' in the title to the facile jibe at Coca Cola, the poem employs the time-honoured method of juxtaposing the crass present with a pastoral, romantic past. Overwhelmed by the clamour of the marketplace, the poem's speaker looks skyward towards 'God's publicity' (PC, p. 660), arranged in the form of constellations: Orion, Arcturus, Cassiopeia. The recourse to a divinely arranged cosmos (as in Garcilaso and his sixteenth-century fellow poet Fray Luis de León) is not typical of the early Salinas and undoubtedly bespeaks his consternation at what Times Square provides.

'The nymphs are departed', wrote Eliot in *The Waste Land*, thinking on Spenser. Salinas, harassed by New York's hustle, deplored the same departure: 'a car horn savagely charges through the middle of that group of nymphs that had just emerged a few moments before from the water in lines by Spenser or Garcilaso'.[17] Nor did Salinas find anything romantic in the famous Anglo-American cocktail hour: the intimacy, 'stripped of romanzas, / of swans and illusions', was played out against a landscape formed by the 'rainbow of liquer bottles' (PC, p. 680).

The poet's great romantic adventure described in *The Voice Owed to You* and mourned in *Love's Reason* and *Long Lament* left a deep furrow in his emotional life. His grief is worked out in various ways, many of them revealing his concern to remember that love equalled 'fable'. At the same time, myth could swallow a real person and her love, and this realisation shows the tragic side of myth, fable and nostalgia:

> Myths, in the countryside, always lie in wait.
> I am never sure
> Of what your appearance suggests to me:
> That you are mere mortal, just flesh.
> When you free your body from the silk

A remembrance of nymph or haughty goddess
Turns our embrace to fable.
And so one day in the country
If I let go your hand, you may return
To your myth and leave me weeping
At the foot of a tree. (PC, pp. 540–1)

The beloved herself disappears into myth, lost in signifiers, and removed by the very trope that celebrated her presence: myth. And a modern-day Garcilaso leaves unsaid the famous phrase: 'Let the tears unchecked flow forth'.

Faced with the phenomenon of Joyce's *Ulysses*, Eliot exclaimed that it contained all the surprise, delight and terror that he required.[18] Salinas's quotation from Shelley that serves as the epigraph of *The Voice Owed to You*, reflects the same realisation about love and by extension art: 'Thou Wonder, and thou Beauty, and thou Terror'. In nostalgia, paradise is, as it were, regained, but only at the price of distance and the Proustian realisation, infinitely sad, that the only true paradise is the paradise we have lost. Lorca knew this at once, Salinas came upon it towards the close of his life, Eliot sought salvation through one of culture's overarching myths.

Notes

1 J. Quinones, *Mapping Literary Modernism. Time and Development*, Princeton, 1985, p. 27.
2 Quinones, *Mapping*, p. 88.
3 L. Gordon, *Eliot's Early Years*, New York, 1977, p. 119.
4 C. Bedient, *He do the Police in Different Voices: The Waste Land and its Protagonist*, Chicago, 1986, p. 203.
5 R. Alter, *The Pleasures of Reading in an Ideological Age*, New York, 1984, p. 135.
6 *Obras Completas*, vol. I, Madrid, 1986, 22nd ed., p. 304. Abbreviated in the text as OC.
7 F. García Lorca, *Collected Poems*, New York, 1991, p. xxvii. Abbreviated in the text as CP.
8 D. Harris, *Lorca: Poeta en Nueva York*, London, 1978, p. 61.
9 For Lorca's knowledge of Eliot see H. Young, 'Sombras fluviales: *Poeta en Nueva York* y *The Waste Land*', *Boletín de la Fundación Federico García Lorca*, IV, 1992, pp. 165–77.

10 Quinones, *Mapping*, p. 31.

11 E. Martin, *Federico García Lorca, heterodoxo y mártir*, Madrid, 1986. R. Santos Toroella, *La miel es más dulce que la sangre*, Barcelona, 1984.

12 Young, 'Sombras fluviales: *Poeta en Nueva York* and *The Waste Land*', p. 170.

13 *Seguro azar* in P. Salinas, *Poesías completas*, Barcelona, 1971, p. 158. Abbreviated in the text as PC.

14 G. Diego, *Poesía española contemporánea*, ed., A. Soria Olmedo, Madrid, 1991, p. 379.

15 A. Debicki, 'The Play of Difference in the Early Poetry of Pedro Salinas', *Modern Language Notes*, C, 1985, p. 273.

16 R. Laffon, *Signo + (Poemas)*, Seville, 1927, pp. 51–2. See also C. B. Morris, 'Pedro Salinas and Marcel Proust', *Revue de Littérature Comparée*, XLIV, 1970, p. 198.

17 P. Salinas, *El defensor*, Madrid, 1984, p. 191.

18 T. S. Eliot, 'Ulysses, order and myth', *Selected Prose*, New York, 1975, p. 175.

19. Daniel Vázquez Díaz: *The sleeping factory*, 1925. Oil on canvas

12 / Sociocultural context and the avant-garde in Spain: theory and practice

GERMÁN GULLÓN

Just ten years ago few people in Spain spoke of the avant-garde, the word in fashion when referring to such a multifaceted literary movement was surrealism,[1] whose prestige obscured all the other 'isms' (ultraism, creationism, cubism, dada, etc.). This explains why Spanish critics have never adequately addressed the nature of the sociocultural context surrounding the avant-garde revolution. It is now time to establish the necessary connections between the artist, as such, and man understood as a social being. Without this connection we cannot understand fully the period preceding the

149

Spanish Civil War. An author at the turn of the century lived through an extraordinary cultural period because literary activity had acquired a presence on the national scene. In a country with serious problems, a privileged group of men (the gender here is significant) launched themselves with gusto into artistic life. These *modernista* authors were succeeded by their younger brothers, who formed the avant-garde, although they had been raised in a similar atmosphere of aestheticism, albeit one where they found it harder for them to live such self-absorbed lives since they were often in contact with the world of journalism, with day to day events, which forced the world of everyday into their range of cultural activities.

I will now put forward three theoretical concepts to explain, at least in part, the nature of the context which paved the way for the arrival of avant-garde innovation in literature, and will then apply them to two key poems, one by Antonio Espina, the other by Federico García Lorca.

The first theoretical consideration relates to the idea of eccentricity and marginal discourses. Avant-garde art provokes an unambiguous response, the reader or viewer feels himself faced with compositions which challenge usual artistic norms.[2] These works confront us with the type of art where novelty is reinforced by a spirit of provocation, both at an intellectual and a social level. However, most of the criticism of the avant-garde (including that by avant-garde writers themselves) concentrates on two types of study that do not take this threat into consideration. On the one hand there is a concern with problems raised by the avant-garde's formal innovations, like discontinuous narrative, fragmentation of space – time or new types of image. On the other hand, we find historical – critical analyses of issues relating to the external history of the avant-garde. In both cases, the sociocultural context tends to be disregarded.

That the beginning of the avant-garde in Spain has often been set in 1909, when the Spanish translation of Marinetti's *Futurist Manifesto* appeared, is because we think of the avant-garde in terms of an explosion, as though it were a sudden event in Spanish cultural life, which then rapidly spread through different artistic fields. In metaphorical terms, the manifesto is the starting pistol for the runners in the race. The year 1909 is an important date, a landmark, but the roots of the avant-garde can be found in developments which took place quite a while before, as part of cultural changes associated with the rise of expressionism, the core of all the avant-garde movements of the twentieth century, and with the important sociocultural developments resulting from the constraints put on the imagination by living conditions, the rise of counterdiscourses, and the autonomy of literary discourse compared to that of history or science.

The influence of expressionism in Spain has only been considered, unjustly, in relation to the work of Valle-Inclán, but there were already expressionist elements in the novels of the nineteenth century, in the work of Galdós, Pardo Bazán and Alas. By expressionism, I mean the basic characteristics noted by Kasimir Edschmid in 1917, when writing about poetry:

> The world no longer exists; there is no point in making a copy of it. The basic function of the artist is to study its deepest movements and its fundamental meaning, and to recreate it. Man is no longer an individual tied down by duty, morals, society or the family. In this art, man is just one thing, the grandest and most miserable, he is a man. This is what is new compared to other periods, this is the way to leave behind the bourgeois conception of the world.[3]

This conception of man is exactly the one which appears in the counterdiscourse or in the subtexts of the Spanish novel of the nineteenth century. In *Doña Perfecta* (1876) Galdós presents a narrator whose views challenge those of the fictional official historian of the fictional town where the novel is set. Galdós's version highlights the character of Pepe Rey, a principal protagonist of the novel, who loses control when he has to stay calm, and who is unable to deal patiently with his enemies. In the chapter called 'Light in Darkness', when Pepe secretly meets his fiancée in a dark chapel and tries to embrace her, he accidentally pokes the feet of a statue of Christ into his ribs. The religious image which symbolically interrupts the embrace allows Galdós to illustrate that the obstacle is the religious institution, and not sentiment: the love the two young people feel. The chapter's title suggests the truth that lies beyond the obstacles that religious and political fanaticism place between the young couple. The incident with the statue

151

and the title indicate the author's wish to reach the basic human truth of the two young lovers,[4] which the literary conventions of the period would not have allowed to surface. For the moment, I only want to draw attention to the way the character is revealed in this situation where a conventional action would be insufficient for him to express himself, and to the way the author turns to a figure of speech which breaks the conventional identity of word and referent, when light appears in darkness. There is no shortage of images of an expressionist kind, like the vision the young bride has of the priest through a glass door: 'the canon was on the right-hand side and his silhouette curiously began to change: his nose grew until it was like the beak of a strange bird, and his whole body became a crooked shadow, dark and intense, angular, absurd, thin and scrawny'.[5]

Little by little, the nineteenth-century novel would illustrate the uselessness of absolutist discourses, of stories that explain everything. Incomplete explanations and exceptions to the rule began to appear in the ethical and moral domain. Parallel stories (subtexts and counterdiscourses) began to appear in novels, outside the causal relationships which govern the development of the main story. Leopoldo Alas's great novel, *La Regenta* (1885), concerns the fall of its protagonist, Ana Ozores, into the hands of a provincial Don Juan, a complex story further complicated by the stories of characters who represent very different themes. For example, the cathedral canon, as well as being a formidable opponent of the Don Juan in the battle for Ana Ozores, is also revealed as a man governed by lust and the wish for power, desires satisfied in dealings with maids and through his success in the shady businesses controlled by his mother. As a result the canon presents a more serious situation than that of a simple priest falling in love with a parishioner, and he becomes a man fighting to overcome an uncontrollable passion. This second thematic strand is the one I call eccentric, the door through which literature admits what was unspeakable and was excluded until then.

In Valle-Inclán's *Autumn Sonata* (1902), the primary story line, the last meeting of two lovers, develops into an analysis of the hidden aspects of a man who is able to leave the deathbed of his recently deceased lover to go to the bed of his cousin and make love to her. The two-faced, Janus-like nature of man, with both a tragic and a light-hearted side, suggests a human reality that lies beyond the possible decadent effect of an autumnal romance between cousins. The expressionism of certain passages is self-evident, the following will suffice as an example: 'I was overcome with vertigo and I pulled . . . Concha's body seemed to escape from my arms. I clung to her in anguish and despair. Under her tensed and sombre forehead her waxen eyelids began to open . . . I had to pull brutally until I tore that scented hair I had loved so much.'[6]

Thus, in the nineteenth-century novel a counterdiscourse appears; the novels contain some incomplete stories which are outside the central system of organisation of the work which functions by reason and causality. These incomplete stories abound in eccentricity, marginality, and cannot be explained by the system of values which governs the central story. Nineteenth-century readers became accustomed to texts in which the coherence of the narrative coexisted with textual elements that remained unresolved, open to the hermeneutic chance of whoever might be the reader. Culturally, the novel was beginning to show that it was impossible to explain everything, since some things were beyond bourgeois ideology's capacity to absorb them.

The second theoretical consideration concerns the avant-garde's unconditional rejection of aestheticism, the ideology which had sustained previous literature. When, in 1735, the German, Alexander G. Baumgarten coined the term aesthetics, to designate a science concerned with a special type of perception, different from logic but still concerned with rational thought, the way was opened for literature to take for itself a place of pre-eminence among the sciences, in a realm beyond contact with the real world. In time, philosophical idealism developed an ideology which would justify the leisurely reading of the bourgeoisie in terms of an aesthetic pleasure that would supposedly enrich the spirit of the individual. As a result, any social function in literature was left undeveloped.

When the first history of Spanish literature was written by José Amador de los Ríos in 1861, it carried a dedication to Her Majesty Queen Isabel II which throws some light on the issue:

The book which today I have the honour of presenting to Your Majesty is not the history of bloody acts, nor of the disgraceful aberrations or the terrifying catastrophes which often cloud the brilliant pages of history. I bring to the feet of the constitutional throne of the Queen of Spain the *Critical History of Spanish Literature* in which the great conflicts of this country are presented vividly, while their pain is tempered and sweetened by the peaceful glories of her illustrious sons.[7]

This sharp distinction between the 'facts' of history and the 'peaceful glories' of literature indicates that, from its birth, literary history has been set in an ideal relationship with reality, with the course of history. Literature, as the key phrase of the passage says, tempers and sweetens history, transforming it by aestheticism.

Similar ideas occur in an often quoted passage from Galdós's speech on the occasion of his election to the Spanish Academy, 'Present day society as material for the novel' (1897):

The novel is an image of life, and the art of writing novels consists in reproducing human characteristics, passions, weaknesses, the large and the small, bodies and souls, everything spiritual and physical which we are and which surrounds us, language (the sign of race), homes (the sign of family), and clothes which give the final touches to our external personalities; all of this without forgetting that there should be a fair balance between the accuracy and the beauty of the reproduction. A novel can be approached in two ways: either by studying the image represented by the artist . . . or by studying life itself.[8]

The nineteenth-century novel in Spain as a whole reflects these ideas. Cecilia Böhl de Faber, in the first realist novel in Spain, *The Seagull* (1849), retouched reality in order to make it moral. Juan Valera idealised his imagined worlds to make them aesthetically beautiful. José María de Pereda, Pedro Antonio de Alarcón, and many others also felt repelled by naturalism and the representation of naked reality not mediated through art. Later novelists, less prone to idealism, like Alas, Galdós and Pardo Bazán considered literature almost as an autonomous body, one which exists above reality, despite their preparedness to dally with some of the elements of naturalism. Consider, for example, Alas's comments on Galdós's *The Disinherited*:

> Another technique which Galdós uses, now with even more effect and insistence than ever, is the one used by Flaubert and Zola with great success, i.e. to replace the reflection the author would normally make himself about a character's situation with the reflections of the character itself, in that character's own words, although not as a monologue but rather as if the author were inside the character and the novel were being written inside this character's head.[9]

Realist writers developed a whole series of narrative techniques, from stream of consciousness to free indirect style, which are justified by the lack of intervention on the author's part, implying more autonomy on the part of the character, to make the work seem as though it writes itself, with the author being something like the spark to set the wheels of the novel into motion. Remember the anecdote about the trial of Flaubert when he was accused of immorality over *Madame Bovary*; his lawyer argued that it was not his client who spoke through Emma Bovary, but rather that she spoke for herself. Thus any compromise was pushed aside, and the novel was isolated from reality, floating in the clouds of aestheticism[9]. Remember that Flaubert was acquitted, and today we might say for the wrong reasons.

No further proof is necessary that nineteenth-century literature, realist literature, was paradoxically conceived with relative independence from the reality of the period. The separation between art and the world would increase with *modernismo*, when writers such as Unamuno completely did away with the external world in their theatre, novels and poetry. Literature became speculation, the subject looked at its own reflection in the mirror. From Unamuno's shouts of 'inwards!' and 'I!' to the Juan Ramón Jiménez' line, 'Intelligence, give me the precise name of things!', there are abundant manifestations of the realm of absolute aestheticism, and I am not referring to symbolism or swans, but to literature in general, created with its face turned away from social reality. Rafael Cansinos Asséns, a prominent figure in the early avant-garde, noted that 'the new [*modernista*] writers [in 1898] boasted of total indifference in political matters, as though they

155

were dandies of the pen, and they did not join the Republicans to demand change or to try to bring down the political regime of the time'.[11]

Society, together with the creators of literature, began little by little to institutionalise art. Academies, book publishing, review columns in the press, serialisation of stories in newspapers, to mention just a few things, created in the bourgeoisie the habit of ignoring the everyday world while immersing themselves in the soothing balm of aestheticism, of emotions which permit the mind to become self-absorbed, spoiling it with attention, slowly taking it higher and higher in this bubble created by art until, finally, on the Earth far below people appear smaller than ants who do not work or suffer, and can so be forgotten. Peter Bürger comments:

> The autonomy of art is a category of bourgeois society. It allows the description of art divorced from the context of everyday life as a historical development, which, amongst the members of the social classes who can, even occasionally, live free of the pressing needs of survival, develops a way of feeling which lacks a practical end.[12]

Obviously, there were exceptions. Maybe the clearest in Spain was Vicente Blasco Ibáñez who, like Zola after the Dreyfuss case, wrote some pieces in the service of society, where the reader is always aware that what is written has strong links with life. Blasco even founded a publishing house to make works with social messages available to workers of limited means. But the main tendency during the nineteenth and early twentieth centuries was to steer well away from reality.

The third theoretical consideration refers to the cultural characteristics of the pre-avant-garde. Another central feature of the formation of the avant-garde is the meeting of real events, which come into the cultural arena via the mass media, above all the press in the nineteenth century, with the imagined 'events' presented in literary works. In other words, the factual events coexisted in the social context alongside literary aestheticism; this had never happened before, the newspaper and the book had never coexisted as they did now. In literary reading, all was governed by internal coherence, and a story was told, controlled by universally accepted ideological and moral standards, in which

20. Benjamín Palencia: *Composition*, 1930. Mixed technique on canvas

the characters acted in accord with or against these standards. Also, fictional stories were expected to show a coherent development. In contrast, the daily press was full of unexplainable events, of things which escaped logical analysis and the moral and ethical beliefs of society. Newspapers still maintain the practice of printing extraordinary stories, like the cow born with two heads, in the summer silly season.

In this way a sort of malfunction occurs in the cultural system. There were events filling the daily press at the turn of the century, like the loss of Spain's remaining colonies, Cuba and the Philippines, that astounded the Spanish public, while the *modernista* writers continued to produce novels like Pío Baroja's *Way of Perfection* (1902), although Baroja, despite his propensity to adopt conservative postures, does reveal a muted concern.[13] This divergency meant, to put an extreme case, that while the Spanish navy was being sent to the bottom of the Caribbean Sea by the American fleet in 1898, an important sector of Spanish writers were plunged in literary self-absorption. Readers of the time were living split in two, their cultural lives governed by conventions deeply embedded in literary tradition, while everyday life presented them with an arena of human activity where the unexpected and exceptions to the rule abounded. The reader in the pre-avant-garde period lived with a sense that life was a mixture of ephemerality and permanence. The 'ivory tower' attitudes of the *modernistas* implied an attempt to escape from a social reality filled with news, with immediacy. Even more recently, Spanish intellectuals and novelists have defended the idea that separation from the noise of everyday is an aid to reflection. It is true that it is possible to isolate oneself, what is difficult is to understand the contemporary world without the data provided by the current social situation. It is possible to flee, which implies moving backwards, with prehistory as the goal. The effect of world wars has been to demonstrate the inadequacy of the great nineteenth-century ideologies, and the lack of intellectual coherence in the social life of man. What the witnesses to these wars recall are the memorable episodes, not the bigger picture, because the media were transmitting them almost as they happened. This synchronicity means that events must be explained in a new context, since what is seen is not the great ideological plan, but an isolated event.

158

The avant-garde is best understood in a context where the excentric confronts the aesthetic, where the bourgeois value system sees its space invaded by the unexpected elements of everyday life. This sets us apart from the subject and allows us to understand it as a series of interactions where man refuses to accept a truth, a set of ideas hides life under the mantle of rationality. Reality, the daily encounter with unexpected events, offers us new meanings which refuse to submit to such reasoning. There are events which arrive full of meaning, to which we can add nothing.

As a practical application of these theoretical considerations I shall now look briefly at my two sample avant-garde poems, which show similarities in formal innovation but also, and this is what interests me particularly, dissimilarities in the treatment of the subject, the voice which speaks in the poem and the way this voice is established in the poem.

AN AESTHETE'S WORDS

Society.
Society is not as unjust and as tyrannical as it should be,
Not as militaristic, capitalistic, classbound and hostile
To all those (sad) unlovely slogans of Liberty, Equality and
    Fraternity
That blend the purple and the black into the grey shoepolish
    of mediocrity.
Yes.
There should be Slaves, Bishops, Coats of Arms,
    Straightjackets . . .
Sienna and carmine crowds of the nobility in power.
        Lordly all-powerful government
        Under the absolute rule of
                    A
                    Catholic
                        Demented
                            Despotic
                                Monarch.
        Yes.
Tradition has a place of honour, the stature of Art
        That in this multiform modern life can nowhere be found.
        Who claims we should bow down before the common good?

159

The Spanish avant-garde

Espina's poem[14] begins with a parody of the aesthetic attitude to life, of those who prefer militarism and hierarchy, bishops and coats of arms to democracy because of their beauty, unity, singularity and clarity as opposed to the fragmentation, diversity and enriching multiculturalism of modernity. The poem illustrates the avant-garde's mockery of aestheticism that prefers order, hierarchy and tradition to democratic habits because in a democracy civil liberty is widespread and there is no artistic prestige. In the hierarchy of colour democratic grey shoe polish cannot compete with noble sienna and carmine. Here are the oppositional characteristics referred to earlier that reveal the avant-garde rebellion against all that excludes man. Human Rights (liberty, fraternity, equality) are proclaimed here, as is the right to be different and to follow any lifestyle in modern society.

At the same time, we should note the displacement of the voice that is neither attached to a subject nor demands a specific audience. The irony of the poem leaves both the emission and the reception open to any source of interference, to any that the reader could produce. This refusal to assign things exactly is a characteristic of the avant-garde because it does not assume a closed system of values, but an open one in which two thematic strands are mixed: one social, concerning a collective justice which is difficult to maintain with a 'lordly all-powerful government', and the other aesthetic, concerning those who get drunk on appearances, forgetting the meanings behind the uniforms and the badges. The individual, the voice which speaks in the poem, exists without openly identifying itself with the subject, allowing the contrast of two attitudes which come from different discourses, social and artistic. Let us now look at my other example, the poem by Lorca, quoted here in part.

NEW YORK. OFFICE AND ACCUSATION

There is a drop of duck's blood
Under the multiplication sums;
There is a drop of sailor's blood
Under the division sums;
A river of tender blood under the addition sums.
A river that moves singing
Through bedrooms in suburbs

160

And becomes silver, cement or breeze
In the lie of New York's dawn.
The mountains are there. I know.
And the spectacles to see wisdom.
I know. But I have not come to see the sky.
I have come to see the rushing blood,
The blood sweeping machines over waterfalls
And the spirit into the cobra's mouth.
Every day in New York they kill
Four million ducks,
Five million pigs,
Two thousand doves for the delectation of the dying,
A million cows,
A million lambs,
Two million chickens,
Leaving the heavens smashed to pieces.
. . . .
I accuse everybody
Who is unaware of the other half
The other half beyond redemption
That builds their mountains of cement
To hold the beating hearts
Of forgotten little animals
And where we shall all end up
At the last feast of the pneumatic drills.
I spit in your faces.
. . . .
Saint Ignatius of Loyola
Murdered a little rabbit
And his lips still moan
Around the church towers.
No, no, no, no; I accuse.
. . . .
And I offer myself up to be eaten by the the mangled cows
When their cries fill the valley
Where machine oil makes the Hudson drunk.[15]

This poem exemplifies the avant-garde as we have been defining it here, as a movement in which the author's attention is fixed on the marginal, seeing that the truth lacks the principle of gravity which pulls all towards a fixed centre. The poet knows well that 'the mountains are there' and so are 'spectacles to see wisdom'. He knows it but answers with 'I have not come to see the sky'. He could easily avoid the everyday sights of New York which jar his sensibility by escaping to the mountains or ignoring reality, lose himself in books, but he has come to 'see the turbulent blood'. The change of verb from 'know' to 'see' implies an important change of attitude; knowledge, reason and intellectual justification remain to one side because the testimony of his eyes is impossible to ignore.

Lorca goes much further, he denounces the urban horror of being faced with huge growth, cement blocks, the incredible number of animals sacrificed each day to feed the population and the insensibility this creates. 'I spit in your faces' he says to those who have made the street a hell. He does not want to see a St Ignatius of Loyola who 'murdered a small rabbit / and still his lips moan / around the church towers'. 'No, no, no; I accuse'. We can see in these lines the contrast between two types of attitude to life. St Ignatius's sensitivity to the death of the rabbit causes him to moan. Lorca, in contrast, insists on denunciation, that the poem cry out and cause a sensation. The avant-garde does not allow itself sensitive responses; such a romantic attitude would have been acceptable in *modernismo*, not in the avant-garde; here the poet takes his meanings not only from the individual but from a reality which already contains its own meaning. Lorca sees and understands New York with his sensibility and with what comes from other discourses which allow him to shape his idea of reality. Here we touch on what is, for me, one of the key factors of the movement, the incorporation of other discourses into a personal discourse. Lorca's rebellion against New York and his denunciation are not his alone, others before him have felt the same, and newspapers then, as now, highlighted every day the abuses of businessmen, politicians, environmental pollution, etc. This is what we now call public opinion, in which intellectuals and people from many fields and lifestyles take a formative part. Then, as now, public opinion changed the way the artist and anyone who followed events felt. Lorca's denunciation, then, is based on a personal emotion which is then placed in the field of public sensibility.

When the avant-garde is explained in a broader context than a personal one, it gains its full colouring, like Lorca's poem which seems so arcane if it is only explained in personal terms. His denunciation stands the test of time because it is his and it is also ours. This is because reading his poems creates a fraternity between the writer and his readers, a characteristic of the avant-garde which explains why many of the innovatory writers of the first thirty years of this century sometimes appear at first glance to write like adolescents.

Notes

1 When, in 1981, I published an anthology called *Poesía de la vanguardia española*, all the others on the market had the word surrealism in the title, for example, P. Corbalán, *Poesía surrealista en España*, Madrid, 1974. More recently, there have been anthologies dedicated specifically to one movement: F. Fuentes Florido, *Poesías y poética del ultraísmo*, Barcelona, 1989, and A. Pariente, *Antología de la poesía surrealista en lengua española*, Madrid, 1985.

2 M. De Micheli, *Las vanguardias artísticas del siglo XX*, Madrid, 1979, p. 72.

3 *Ibid.*, p. 89.

4 N. Lynton, *Conceptos de arte moderno*, Madrid, 1986, p. 36.

5 B. Pérez Galdós, *Doña Perfecta. Misericordia*, Mexico, 1977, p. 85.

6 *Obras Completas*, vol. 1, 1944, pp. 383–4.

7 J. Amador de los Ríos, *Historia crítica de la literatura española*, vol. 1, Madrid, Gredos, 1969, p. xv.

8 B. Pérez Galdós, *Ensayos de crítica literaria*, Barcelona, 1972, pp. 175–6. An English version is to be found in J. Labanyi (ed.), *Galdós*, London, 1993.

9 L. Alas, *Teoría y crítica de la novela española*, Barcelona, 1972, p. 231. An English version is to be found in J. Labanyi, *Galdós*, London, 1993.

10 P. Bourdieu, 'Flaubert's point of view', *Critical Inquiry*, XIV, 1988, pp. 539–62.

11 R. Cansinos Assens, *La novela de un literato*, vol. 1, Madrid, 1982, p. 21.

12 P. Burger, *Theory of the Avant-Garde*, Minneapolis, 1984, p. 46.

13 I quote J. Cano Ballesta, who refers here not only to *Camino de perfección* but also to *La lucha por la vida*, which changes our opinion (and his) when we speak only of the 1902 novel: 'We cannot say that Baroja cultivates a rootless 'pure and useless' art to satisfy some personal impulse, to entertain the reader, or simply to denounce the blots in a society. No. Baroja's novels

are not as politically naive as they may seem despite their aesthetic, decadent and individualist appearance. Neither are they pure negation and nihilism as is often said'. *Literatura y tecnología. Las letras españolas ante la revolución industrial (1900–1933)*, Madrid, 1981, p. 53.

14 A. Espina, *Signario*, Madrid, 1923.

15 *Revista de Occidente*, xxxi, 1931, pp. 25–8. This early version of the poem differs from the later definitive form. The lines about St Ignatius, the rabbit and the church towers were subsequently eliminated, possibly because of an ambiguity that makes it unclear whether the lips belong to the rabbit or the saint (editor's note).

21. Rafael Barradas: *Everything at 65*, 1919. Oil on canvas

13 / Exercises in the dark:
Rafael Alberti's cinema poems

EDGAR O'HARA

Buñuel remarked that when the talking pictures arrived the cinema ceased, inevitably, to be an international form. The silent cinema had created an entirely new visual narrative language of cross cut, close up, fade, montage, and many other techniques that are difficult or impossible to reproduce linguistically. The poets of the time were deeply aware of this other language whose expression took place in the space between silence and movement, somewhere between a voice and a blank page. Some poets sought to write this new language perhaps because of the sympathy they felt for the subversive nature of the silent comedians, which they associated with their own lack of respect for poetic tradition.[1]

The paradox of tradition and innovation characteristic of the Spanish avant-garde is, however, clearly present in the poems that Rafael Alberti wrote in 1929 as a homage to the stars of the silent screen. They have a collective title, *I was a fool and what I have seen has made me two fools*, that seems to have a typical avant-garde quality, although it is, in fact, lifted from two lines in a well-known play, *The Daughters of the Air*, by Calderón, the seventeenth-century master of the Spanish classical theatre. The Spanish avant-garde's willingness to accept the tradition of classical literature encompasses much more than the celebration of the Góngora tercentenary in 1927 which gave Alberti's generation its name. This collection of cinema poems is a fine example of the way one section of the avant-garde in Spain was prepared to operate simultaneously on different stylistic levels. For all the Calderonian title, Alberti's poems were intended for public performance by their author, sometimes even wearing a disguise, at the film club in Madrid that was founded by Enrique Giménez Caballero, who was also the editor of the central avant-garde magazine, *La Gaceta Literaria*.

The beginning of the mutual interaction between literature and cinema can be traced to a number of French writers, most particularly André Maurois and his 'Poetry of the cinema' of 1927, who tried to use a literary set of references to *see* the cinema as a kind of visual poetry composed of images and rhythms. During the 1920s and 1930s words like 'image', 'music', 'poetry', and 'rhythm' could be found in frequent use in essays on the cinema published in Spain. There was only one exception to this, as C. B. Morris has noted, in a brief critical commentary on the avant-garde poetry of Gerardo Diego, who is described as actually producing cinematic effects rather than bringing a literary focus to bear on the cinema:

And an anonymous critic (Anon., 'Noticiario', *La Gaceta Literaria*, xxiv, 15 December, 1927) did at least look at the disposition of words on a page when he observed in 1927 that the *creacionista* poet was the one who wrote 'the most disconnected cinematographic poetry'; alluding to the disconnected images and disjointed rhythms pursued as ends in themselves by Gerardo Diego in *Imagen* (1921) and *Manual de espumas* (1923), that the critic suggested perceptively that 'his lines of poetry operate on great planes in the same way that films do. To prove it take a poem, number its lines consecutively, and you will have transformed it into a screenplay'.[2]

For such a poet the cinema provided a spectacle of the unexpected, the possibility of seeing as normal, things that were not part of normality or were even impossible, the possibility of transferring visual stimuli into words. The cinema provided, above all, a context for self-recognition: '. . . when through it a poet learned more about himself and projected himself through situations and characters he saw in films'.[3]

I was a fool contains not just allusions but specific references to the world of the screen: Chaplin, Harold Lloyd, Buster Keaton, Harry Langdon, Laurel and Hardy, Wallace Beery, Bebe Daniels, Ben Turpin, Adolphe Menjou, and others now less well-known. What is more, the different characters in the poems aim to communicate explicitly, via telegrams or newspapers, an explanation of the unfortunate episodes that befall them. Moreover, the titles of some of the poems strongly recall the explanatory captions of the silent screen, rewritten sometimes in an avant-garde mode: 'Buster Keaton searches through the forest for his fiançée, who is a genuine cow'; 'Larry Semon explains to Stan Laurel and Oliver Hardy the telegram that Harry Langdon sent to Ben Turpin'; 'Stan Laurel and Oliver Hardy accidentally smash up 75 or 76 cars and then claim it was all the fault of a banana skin'; 'The fireman, Wallace Beery, is dismissed from his post because he did not answer the alarm call quickly enough'.[4] One particular aspect of this communication between the poem and its recipient is the importance held by the number of direct questions asked in the poems but not answered. These are not necessarily rhetorical questions, instead they tend to be concerned with the development of a plot that the poem is unable to resolve because it shares the curiosity or complicity the author has with regard to the films.

167

The Spanish avant-garde

Consider these examples: 'Have you got the umbrella?' (p. 165); 'If my shoes do not fit these four footsteps / Then whose are these four footsteps?' (p. 170); 'Who has died? ... What does good morning mean?' (p. 174). This makes it possible to read Alberti's texts as poems derived from sources in the cinema, as well as from other sources. It is evident that the acting of the poem, and not just its recital, was of interest to the poet because one of the poems has the author himself as protagonist, 'Alberti is very worried by that dog casually peeing against the moon' (p. 181). The interest in the cinema is also on occasions linked to painting – Alberti's early training was as a painter – and to avant-garde writing in general. This is Alberti's own description of the moment to which his cinema poems belong:

> It was the age of the avant-garde's innovations, which had reached Madrid with some slight delay, and of the last great moments of the silent cinema just before the advent of talking pictures. ... The new names of René Clair, Germain Dullac, Cavalcanti and Epstein were spread before our eyes in a cavalcade of astonishing images, a montage of absurd, unexpected metaphors very much in accord with the poetry and art of the Europe of the time (Tzara, Aragon, Eluard, Desnos, Péret, Max Ernst, Tanguy, Masson, etc.).[5]

From the literary point of view there is also a connection with the deep personal crisis expressed in *Concerning the angels*, written a year or two earlier. Morris indicates that the verbal clowning of *I was a fool* 'overlays a gravity of purpose and feeling' closely linked with the earlier book.[6] Certainly Alberti's poems are not just commentaries on the films, although the abundant information C. B. Morris has provided in his edition of *I was a fool* enables the reader to capture many of the hidden comic references. Sometimes the auditorium retains its shadows, the eye projecting and the eye receiving the reflection of light on the screen are not exactly the same.

Images develop without a definite chronological order on the screen of the mind. The similarity between what occupies our brain while we dream (be it awake or not) and cinematic sequence was an idea which circulated freely in everyday life during the 1920s. For example, we only have to recall Antonin Artaud's

168

remarkably poetic–biological concerns, or how productive dreaming was for Buñuel. It is not that surrealism identified itself with the cinema, but it is, none the less, the aesthetic (or moral or ethical) movement which makes its own all the implications of writing that recognises the impasse confronting literature in the years after the First World War.

For Alberti, the difficult moment came after he had left the cinema because he had to find, as Morris says, 'a verbal equivalent for the slapstick comedians',[7] although he could also make these same clowns do something 'they could not do on the screen: speak'.[8] Moreover, the poetic text and the performance on screen had similar aims: to take possession of 'a different personality, a different manner of being'.[9] This goes far beyond those who saw or pretended to see poetry in films or those who sought the imprint of films on poetry, some of whom saw a connection between them no deeper than that between images on the screen and images on a page, to paraphrase Morris again.[10]

What links all of these different points of view is, one might say, precisely the act of seeing. What was 'new' in the 1920s and 30s was that the poet could contemplate moving pictures, in the cinema, as well as seeing static pictures, as Alberti did in his repeated visits to the Prado Museum in Madrid. In both situations, 'the poet has to translate a visual stimulus into words.'[11] *I was a fool* reflects this in its obsession with communicating via telephone, telegramme, newspapers, letters, and even an alarm call. There are also other functions, such as assuring (metalinguistically) the use of a code, even though this might be merely a sensorial one: 'Truely, / there is nothing as pretty as a bunch of flowers / when the goat has left one or two of its little round black things on them. / Can I have realised that there is nothing as pretty as a bunch of flowers, / especially if the goat has left one or two of its little round things on them?' ('Harry Langdon makes love to a girl for the first time', p. 175); or the phatic function of guaranteeing the continuity of communication: 'What, what, what, how? / Say that again. / Oh yes!' / Fire!!! ('The fireman, Wallace Beery, is dismissed from his post . . .', p. 189). However, it is clear that the poet speaks from linguistic security, – 'I won't be insubordinate if I confess / That my uniform is not to be found at the scene of the fire. / No, no. / And what I say is (no) no.', says the same Wallace

Beery (p. 188), – however much he may seek to transgress grammatical good manners. Alberti does not put forward any poetical grammar, and perhaps this was not his intention anyway. The verbal game becomes simply a series of transpositions that the reader can easily decode. In this sense, the weight of tradition acts as an emblem which we must de-cypher in different ways. For example, these grammatical garglings: 'What, which, who, whose.' mouthed in the poem 'Harold Lloyd, the student' (p. 165), '. . . because j'aime, / Tu aimes, / Il aime, / If you all forget the sea is like a neutral background for flirting . . .', which occurs in the poem 'Five o'Clock Tea' (p. 191), or the declension attributed to Buster Keaton in the poem 'Press report about a melancholy schoolboy':

NOMINATIVE	The snow
GENITIVE	of the snow
DATIVE	To or for the snow
ACCUSATIVE	The snow
VOCATIVE	O snow!
ABLATIVE	With the snow
	From the snow
	In the snow
	Through the snow
	Without the snow
	Over the snow
	Behind the snow

The moon behind the snow
And those personal pronouns lost by the river
And that sad conjunction lost among the trees. (p. 180)

These are all attempts to find something that only conclude with an even bigger question to answer: where is the corpse? Could such a question refer to the corpses, perhaps even the dismembered corpses of a decaying poetic tradition, incapable of expressing 'the new'? The question 'who has died?', in the middle of the poem 'On the day of a death by gunshot', immediately after another exercise in grammatical nonsense conjugation, receives an *indirect* answer, based on a series of alternatives:

Tell me once and for all if all that was not happy.
5×5 then was not 25

170

Nor had the dawn thought about the existence of evil knives.

I swear to you by the moon not to be a cook,
You swear to me by the moon not to be a cook,
He swears to us by the moon to be not even the smoke from
such a

                                        sad kitchen.

Who has died?

The goose regrets being a duck;
The sparrow regrets being a teacher of Chinese;
The cockrel regrets being a man,
And I regret having talent and admiring how unhappy
A shoe's sole can be in winter.

A queen has lost her crown,
A president his republic, and his hat:
I have lost . . .

I do not think I have lost anything,
That I have ever lost anything,
That I have . . .

What does good morning mean? (pp. 173–4)

'Chinese' is a popular metaphor for the incomprehensible, so to be the teacher of something that other people cannot understand is tedious. But the poem ends with another question, this time unanswered, that represents a common-place of meaning. Could it not then be this that the speaker has lost? A loss of breath, the breath of life, his verbal soul. There are repeated references to death and corpses in these poems, references which can be read as linguistic metaphors: 'A naked corpse is evaporating in the pharmacy' (p. 164); '. . . it is not that I believe in the premature death of lovely neckties / nor in giving a Christian burial to cats that have not even got a name' (p. 182); '. . . if my sweet love of that time was a synonym of a broom / Today it is rather like that dog that explodes on the highway' (p. 183); 'I too have died' (p. 184); '. . . you are suffering from the very serious mistake of confusing / the police station with a greengrocer's when I want to die / tell me truely if I want to die' (p. 187); '. . . the demise of the most poetic forests in front of my jacket' (p. 193); '. . . if you tell me that your fiancée has a hoarse body and a little head of dead sneeze, / In San

171

Francisco in California a father of the church will give birth to a beautiful daughter' (p. 197); 'All the seraphim wear their toupees when they walk along the river. / Except you, / Deceased cherub, / Cherub who died of love for an enchanting housemaid' (p. 198); 'The body of a raped angel has been found in a London hotel' // 'Goodbye, / I now know that you are that dead neck that ascends for ever in an aeroplane pulled by 6 loves of chocolate' (p. 199). This is why, within the absence of words itself there is being conducted a desperate search for bearings or direction, accompanied by an obssessive use of other languages, the languages of science, mathematics, mechanics.

The first thing to observe is that in order to proceed the loss must be made explicit, or rather be assimilated creatively: 'I cannot advise you to ask me how many balconies my house has / Nor if my bicycle is a hired bicycle / Nor if I get on the tram on the other side from everybody else' (p. 176); '. . . they made you redundant as a chauffeur because you used to drive by all the cities on the left-hand side of the road' (p. 186); 'Why does this corpse choose to lean to the left / And the other one prefer to lean to the right?' (p. 193). In addition there is the mention of the demise of 'the most poetic forests' (p. 193), the preoccupation for the 'speed of a stationary horse / And the stillness of express trains that predict the future death of trams' (p. 185), and the predicament of a character reduced to tears because 'this morning a gas lamp murdered my bicycle' (p. 186). This, then, is the context in which a type of stasis produces an interest in other languages.

Something else that must be noted is the frequency with which numerals appear in these poems, as a stylistic device like the use of the conjunction 'and' by romantic poets who employed it to prolong the poetic *narrative*. Alberti's poems suffer an invasion of numerals that is quite gratuitous in most cases. Sometimes numerals replace words: 'I am, gentlemen, 900,000 years old . . . The saddest thing, sir, is a clock: / 11 o'clock, 12 o'clock, 1 o'clock, 2 o'clock.' (pp. 161–2); 'And for this unconscious fly, nightingale of my flowering spectacles. / 29, 28, 27, 26, 25, 24, 23, 22. / 2π / $\pi r2$' (p. 166); '1, 2, 3, 4. / My shoes are too big for these four footprints . . .' (p. 170). At other times numerals disrupt meaning: 'One kilo is 10 metres. / One metre is equal to 20 litres' (p. 194).

There are many other examples; the few quoted serve to show how the poet searches for resonances between words and numerals, that is, of course, numerals said as words. This could be simply a case of an avant-garde pirouette, but it also indicates, for me at least, the profound difficulty the poet experiences in trying to escape from rhyme as principle resource of poetic tradition. However much he may wish to break free, he will always gravitate back to the familiar resource. Even semantic games carry the weight of this anchor in rhyme:

> At three o'clock precisely a pedestrian will die.
> Moon, you do not need to be frightened;
> You, the moon of taxis that are late,
> Moon of firemen's soot.
>
> The city is burning in the sky,
> A suit just like mine is bored in the countryside.
> Suddenly I am twenty-five years old.
>
> It is snowing, snowing
> And my body is turning into a wooden hut.
> Why don't you rest, wind.
> It is much too late to dine on stars.
>
> But we can dance, lost tree.
> A waltz for the wolves,
> For the chicken's dream without the fox's claws . . .
>   ('Chaplin's sad tryst', pp. 162–3)
>
> She came by at one o'clock eating herbs.
> Cuckoo,
> The crow was cheating on her with a mignonette flower.
> Caw, caw,
> The owl was cheating on her with a dead rat.
>
> Gentlemen, forgive me, I am going to weep!
> (Wah, wah, wah.)
> ('Buster Keaton searches the forest for his fiançée . . .', p. 171)

I hope that these observations are seen as merely descriptive. Under no circumstances do I want to detract from Alberti's avant-garde 'credentials' in these poems, although occasionally a critic has sought perhaps to over-emphasise the avant-garde nature of certain passages. For example, Morris refers to the fantasy and impertinence of these lines from 'Harold Lloyd, the student': 'And Nebuchadnezzar was turned into a mule / and your soul and mine into a royal bird of paradise. / The fish no longer sing in the Nile / Nor does the moon pose for the dahlias of the Ganges' (pp. 166–7). I would prefer to see these lines as a jokey display of *modernista* exoticism. They are another example of the way the avant-garde Alberti combines, whether consciously or not, widely different materials from both traditional and experimental sources.

Let us now consider the other languages which show a desire to produce something 'surprising' within Spanish poetry. Sentimental reflections suddenly come under the influence of mathematical expressions: 'Le Printemps pleut sur Les Anges. // Spring rains on Los Angeles / At the time when the police / are still unaware of the suicides of isoceles triangles / as well as the melancholy of a Napierian logarithm' (p. 167); 'At this sad moment when the moon is almost equal / To the integral disgrace / Of this love of mine multiplied by X' (p. 168). Or it is maybe a symptom of a genuine desire to escape, very characteristic of the avant-garde, in order to then take refuge in other mysteries: 'The fact is I am very worried by silence and astronomy' (p. 185); 'and my scientifically preoccupied soul knows that steam treatment of cocoa is not aided much by crying' (p. 186). Despite the fact that each of the quotes I have selected can be 'explained' through the plots or scripts of the films on which the poems are based, a task for which much credit is due to C. B. Morris for uncovering storylines that in many cases had disappeared for ever due to the deterioration of the filmstock, it is still possible for me to read these poems in accord with a number of different possibilities available to the poet as he processed his material. For example, the inventiveness referred to in the poem 'Charles Bower, the inventor' is also the poet's inventiveness, as is the urge in the poem to classify things: 'But you we will classify as a holm oak. / And this one would like to be called Charles, / Although it is a dead cypress' (p. 193). This might suggest to us what Hugh Kenner described in the work of Eliot and Pound as the incorporation into poetics of the functional values (or the desire for exactness) of technology. 'Charles Bower, the inventor' ends like this:

174

And so many other scientific conundrums, my dear Odette,
to die in anger and at the hands of a sardine.

Mechanics.
Love.
Poetry.
Oh! (p. 195)

What sort of effects was Alberti after other than the equivalence
between cinematographic image and poetic composition? The fact
that he never published these poems as a separate book (they were
published together for the first time in the Buenos Aires edition of
his *Complete Works* in 1961), gives us a clue about the stylistic
achievements the poet felt in his collections like *Concerning the
Angels* and *Sermons and Mansions*, with which the cinema poems
are contemporaneous. What is clear to me is his later reluctance to
play with the spatial distribution of his verses. In Alberti's most
sucessful work, from the point of view of the avant-garde, the
verbal weight of his long lines and the density of meaning take
control of the page, maybe filling it (in a baroque manner, for not
in vain did Alberti seek to pay homage to Góngora by writing a
continuation of his unfinished *Soledades*), in an attempt to counter
the vacuum or to underline a more historical presence, that would
take him 'on to the street' in his political poems written immediately after his tribute to the silent screen.

Although novels, or literary texts in general, have inspired
works for the cinema, the obverse has hardly ever happened
because a screen play fulfils the function that the novel, the story
of the play, fulfils in a literary context. Despite the abundance of
images, a film, explicitly or implicitly, has a textual guide. This
simple fact should indicate to us that Alberti's literary sources
have an influence on the extent to which his expression seeks to
establish an analogy with the language of the cinema. It is the case
of having a mediating text that provides support and for his
adaptation of cinematic language, making it more acceptable
although at the same time limiting the 'inspired' quality of the
writing. This can either result unconsciously or be part of the
tradition of literary games to which Alberti had attached himself,
the tradition that embraces seventeenth-century poets like
Góngora and Quevedo as well as Gómez de la Serna's *greguerías*.

Alberti then expands this tradition and 'gives a new dimension to humour in Spanish literature by translating into poetry the spirit as well as the substance and personalities of comic films'.[12]

In *I was a fool* the poems' sources cannot all be cinematic. A principle mediator was *Alice in Wonderland*, translated into Spanish in 1927. Another literary mediator would be the nonsense poems called *jitanjáforas* by the Mexican poet Alfonso Reyes and published in magazines in Buenos Aires, Havana and Rio de Janeiro in 1929 and 1930. The dates coincide directly with Alberti's poems, although it is of no significance if Alberti knew Reyes' nonsense verses, since he was extremely familiar with the antecedents of this type of poetry to be found in Góngora and in the *modernismo* of Rubén Darío. Alfonso Reyes' comment on the first of the *jitanjáforas*, Mariano Brull's 'Verdehalago', is particularly relevant here: '. . . this poem is not addressed to the reason, but rather to feeling and fantasy. The words have no utilitarian purpose here. They are simply at play, almost . . . In short: some words create, others neither create nor destroy, and others destroy because they create so much'.[13]

What is extraordinary is how what we might call this gratuitousness of sound takes its place in Alberti's poems, sometimes in the form of a mingling of languages: 'Alice, I have the hippopotamus. / L'hippopotame for you. / Avez-vous le parapluie? // Oui. / Yes. / Sí.' (p. 165), and sometimes in the form of a semantic tongue twister: '. . . the facial unibusquibusque' (p. 167). Such elements are, of course, part of the always playful intent of the avant-garde to break communicative codes. But in this case, alongside this intention, the poems can also be read as parallel lives of the cinema characters, lives in which everything is possible. But since poetry is a linguistic art we should ask exactly what can poets do or cannot do. In principle everything, but in practice, as we have seen, things do not work like that. The problem is the weight of the poetic tradition that causes Alberti almost to violate his mother tongue. However, blasphemy in Spain is a way of consecrating the religious canon.

Notes

1 'The attitude of impudent disrespect shown by comic films towards authority', noted by C. B. Morris, *This Loving Darkness. The Cinema and Spanish Writers 1920–1936*, Hull, 1980, p. 62, could be applied to the majority of comic films. In a literary context authority might be represented by the poetic tradition.

2 Morris, *This Loving*, p. 44.

3 *Ibid.*, p. 79.

4 All references to Alberti's poems are from *Sobre los ángeles. Yo era un tonto y lo que he visto me ha hecho dos tontos*, edited by C. B. Morris, Madrid, 1981. Page references are bracketed in the text.

5 R. Alberti, *La arboleda perdida*, Barcelona, 1975, pp. 278–9.

6 Morris, *This Loving*, p. 90.

7 Morris, Introduction to R. Alberti, *Sobre los ángeles. Yo era un tonto y lo que he visto me ha hecho dos tontos*, Madrid, 1984, p. 34.

8 *Ibid.*, p. 36.

9 *Ibid.*, p. 40.

10 Morris, *This Loving*, p. 43.

11 *Ibid.*, p. 50.

12 *Ibid.*, p. 92.

13 A. Reyes, 'Las jitanjáforas', *La experiencia literaria*, Buenos Aires, 1969, pp. 183 and 185.

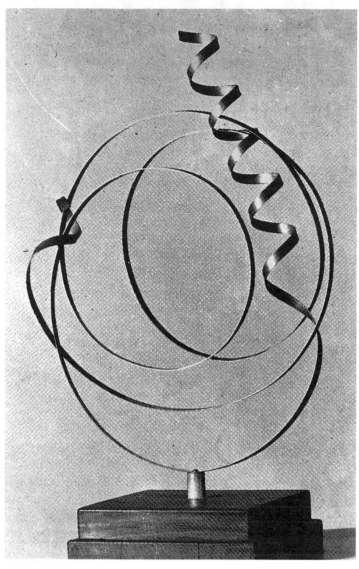

22. Leandre Cristòfol: *From the air to the air*, 1933. Aluminium, metal and wood

14 / Rafael Alberti's *Concerning the Angels*: a representation of alchemical process   ALISON SINCLAIR

Avowedly triggered by a crisis in Alberti's life, *Concerning the Angels* (1928–1929) charts a descent into the chaos of an infernal world in which forces in the form of angels focus and embody different elements of the poet's psyche or of pressures upon it.[1] The poems are painful, disrupting, disorientating. The linguistic forms are simple, but the syntax often interrupted, departing from expected conclusions. Despite the confusion, a sense of form emerges, partly in the verse forms adopted, but more so in recurrent patterns of imagery: images of the elements, fire, earth, air, water, and images of burning coals, and of charred remains.

Alberti emphasised in his autobiography that the collection was rooted in crisis, using images of material destruction (rubble, splinters), and the angelic forms in which mental states were contained.[2] Two other contemporary versions by the poet of what the collection was about are also revealing. The summary in the *Autobiographical Index* of the 1961 edition of his *Complete Poems* runs simply: '1928 Love. Wrath. Anger. Rage. Failure. Disorder. *Concerning the Angels*'.[3] The thematic clusters here relate to differences of feeling, and appear to indicate a type of progression. The statement in *La Gaceta Literaria* in 1929 is generally held to be mischievous or simply puzzling:

> 1927–1928. *Concerning the Angels* (Forthcoming in Editorial Ibero-Americana). I have rent my poetic garments (because I had them). I covered my head in ashes. I am burning myself alive. I take out a red handkerchief – last trump –. And from the charred remains come Bosch, Breughel (the Elder and the Younger), Bouuts [sic], Sedenborg, W. Blake, Baudelaire and the apostle's eagle. Suffocate me with braziers and surround me with blue chafing-dishes, because I am in a bad mood. (On the importance of this book, consult Pedro Salinas, Jorge Guillén, Antonio Marichalar, Dámaso Alonso, Juan Chabás and José Bergamín).[4]

The impression that here Alberti is merely indulging in the personal peacock behaviour typical of many avant-garde artists is not unreasonable. Both imagery and reference suggest, however, a more serious content. Alberti speaks of willed self-destruction, of penitence, of ordeal by fire, or conceivably cauterisation, after which a red rag of triumph or defiance is waved. It is from these

179

burned remains of the poet that the strange and disparate list of artists emerges.

Closer consideration of the names in the list suggests that it is not so disparate. Bosch's allegorical paintings have attracted numerous alchemical interpretations.[5] Likewise, Breughel the Elder (1525–1569) has received commentaries based on alchemical imagery, and his engraving *The Alchemist* (1558) may well have come to mind.[6] 'Bouuts' almost certainly refers to the Dutch painter Dieric Bouts (1415–1475) who is not known for alchemical reference, and it is possible that the name here appears for alliterative purposes. It may be worth noting, however, that the work of his contemporary Van Eyck (1390–1441) is sometimes discussed in an alchemical interpretation.[7] 'Sedenborg' (presumably Emmanuel Swedenborg) and William Blake are both known for their links with mysticism and an interest in hermetic knowledge.[8] Baudelaire seems a more marginal case for this list, although Van Lennep suggests the theory of 'correspondances' was an adaptation of ancient theories of analogy, and that his vision of a counter-religion based on the theological vision of the power of Satan Trismegistus, initiator into forbidden knowledge, link him to alchemy.[9] The eagle of the apostle is much harder to place, though within alchemical thought the eagle represents one of the higher transformations, or the state of the spirit, and, with the serpent, symbolises the cycle of eternal return.[10] The eagle is also said to devour its own wings or feathers, thus being linked to the image of the serpent or 'uroboros', and to the image of the wingless bird which will appear in the vision of the poet with clipped wings at the end of the collection.[11] The references point to a strong connection between *Concerning the Angels* and alchemy, although I do not suggest we should speculate about Alberti's possible interest in alchemy, but rather that we might see him as an example of the link between personal process and alchemical process as understood by Jung.

The ancient origins of, and arcane beliefs in alchemy were revived and re-interpreted by Jung in a series of major works produced in the latter part of his life.[12] The most significant proposal he made concerned the essentially inner nature of the quest of the alchemists. In contrast to the popular view of the alchemist as someone engaged in strange quasi-scientific experiments to convert base matter to gold, or to produce the philosopher's stone, Jung argued that these scientific processes and theories were related to the internal processes externalised in the descriptions of experiments.[13] When faced by the mystery of matter, he believed that the alchemist involuntarily projected into it the contents of his mind, and that when the unknown was contemplated it would always take this inner projected form.[14]

Alchemy centres around a process of transformation, which has four stages linked to colour changes: blackening (*nigredo*), a state of chaos or confusion which is either there at the start, or consequent on a separation and further processing of elements; whitening (*albedo*), achieved when the elements have been separated out, opposites have been united, and the product of the union has died, by mortification, calcination or putrefaction; yellowing (*citrinitas*) which forms the transition from the dawn of the *albedo* to reddening (*rubedo*), reached by the raising of heat to the highest intensity.[15] The goal of alchemy is the union of opposites, but can also be understood as the restoration of the fallen Adam, or, in psychological terms, a search for a form of the self which can survive destruction. The quest for the alchemical product, the philosopher's stone, which would be incorruptible, and thus immortal, can thus be construed as the quest for immortality, a quest which is easily understood in the light of fears for personal survival which attend serious breakdown.[16]

A brief example will show the degree to which an alchemical reading may alter our understanding of *Concerning the Angels*. In C. B. Morris's commentary on the poem 'Death and Judgement', he refers to the second section where the poet's body is seen to descend to the bottom of the sea to join 'quicksilver, lead and iron', noting that the body has been characterised as a 'lifeless charcoal', and that the minerals it goes to join are 'equally dead'.[17] The poet's body has, however, been perceived throughout, in pathetic compassion, as that of a 'child'. While we might read his descent to the ocean floor as his destruction, the capacity for transformation and resurrection is indicated in the image of the wood partly burned, that is, partly transformed by fire, and in the image of the child which can be construed as the divine or saviour child, product of the alchemical process. The minerals the body goes to join are, within the alchemical context, all used as images of the *prima materia*, forms of base life which can be transformed through the alchemical process. This capacity for transformation is alluded to in the immediately surrounding text: 'And since you sank down to the depths of the tides, / To the urns where quicksilver, lead and iron seek to be human, / To have the dignities of life' (p. 56). The descent can thus be construed not as one of defeat, and return to dead matter, but of the necessary descent to join with other types of *prima materia*, all of which represent our capacity to grow and change. The aspiration 'to have the dignities of life' can be read as the hope of resurrection. The most suggestive view underlying form or process to *Concerning the Angels* is that of Jiménez-Fajardo for whom the move is 'from a realisation of inner chaos to a correlative vision of surrounding chaos, to a consequential return within the self, an attempt to reach deeper layers of the spirit, from which to begin a reconstruction'.[18]

Alberti's description of his initial crisis state speaks of being in a 'well of darkness, that obscure pit where I would thrash about violently'.[19] The initial poem of *Concerning the Angels*, 'Lost Paradise', refers to an environment which is terrifying for its lack of containment. It appears to evoke a formlessness not of the poet, but of the surroundings, a perception that can be construed as the projection of the poet's own formlessness or state of *nigredo*. This is a post-lapsarian world, the world from which Adam (the symbolic figure of man prominent in alchemical writings) has fallen, made the more devastating because of the previously known vitality, in which birds sang, there was wind, sun. This place, formless as it is, is the 'melting pot' of the world. Although this initial poem does not suggest the hermetic nature of that alchemical vessel in which the process of alchemical transformation will take place, we will find in the collection a succession of spaces, partially closed – galleries, trenches and wells, or wholly closed – tombs and sepulchres.[20] The reference back to a pre-lapsarian world, before the introduction of knowledge, difference or gender, is also made nostalgically at the start of the third section of *Concerning the Angels* in the 'Prologue' to the 'Three Recollections of Heaven'.

Formlessness, or *nigredo*, is expressed mainly through placelessness and non-recognition. 'Eviction' (p. 20) and 'The

Uninhabited Body' (pp. 21–5), using the traditional motif of the body as the house of the soul, announce eviction as the action by which the placelessness of the poet's psychic self is achieved.[21] The projection of a hostile force which denies the poet his form is alluded to in the title of 'The Angel of Sand' (p. 52), which in the face of the poet's dream of exuberant life in the form of 'a boy who went leaping naked' is annihilated by the gaze of the angel which 'awakening, engulfed me in your eyes'. The significance of the title derives from the association of sand not just with the evocation of sand-dunes of the poet's youth,[22] but with the meaning of 'sands' as 'shapes' or ideas, and referring to the 'bodiness' of the four elements, who thus deny recognition as a shape, or discrete being, to the poet.[23]

Poems evoking particularly the formlessness of unbeing are not restricted to the first section. Among them we might note 'The Angelic Angel' (p. 38), where the formlessness of the implied protagonist comes from deprivation of a source in the earth, the element most closely associated with the cold dampness of the alchemical *prima materia*. Thus while other elements give the poet / angel attributes ('the sea . . . a name . . . the wind gave a surname . . . a body, the clouds . . . and a soul, the flame'), the earth renders nothing. The result is the lack of human shape able to produce a shadow (the touchstone of material being and humanity): 'Her shadow never wrote / The semblance of a man'. Unbeing is also implied in the impotence of the poet so graphically evoked, particularly in the early poems. By being no more than the passive recipient or sufferer of outside forces (albeit projections of his inner turmoil), he is experienced for himself and for the reader as a non-subject, a nonbeing. The collection as a whole is characterised by strong verb forms in the present indicative, which have as their suffering object the poet, rarely allowed to 'possess' or use his own verb form.

The progression from the formlessness yet potentiality of the *nigredo* stage towards the *albedo* stage results from separation of elements and conflict – all necessary steps before the first stage of union can be achieved. That separation is linked to conflict is outlined in 'The Ashen Angel' (p. 31), where a summary of the four elements in conflict is placed around a brief and graphic evocation of rage:

> To break chains
> and set the wind and the earth face to face.
> Unseeing, irate.
>
> To break chains
> and set the wind and the earth face to face.

'The Furious Angel' (p. 32), standing in penultimate position in the first section of the collection, appears to address the organising force which has set in motion the powerful feelings holding the poet under their sway. Alberti's angels, which we can now firmly view both as his projections but also as his potentialities, have been set in motion by an angel characterised as raging, an avenging angel lacking a precise reason for revenge.

Because conflict is characteristically represented as taking place between two elements, it is polarised and absolute. Thus in 'The Warlike Angels' (p. 27) the conflict is between North and South. The stark lines 'wind and wind fight it out' which bring the poem to a close insist on a conflict of cosmic proportions, in which North stands against South, and in the midst of which the poet is a 'tower in no man's land'. The suggestions of alchemical symbolism carry the impact of this particular confrontation much further than mere geographical opposition. The conflict, however, is a necessary and productive one. The South Wind was associated with wisdom,[24] and with the dawn – an event unfailingly associated in alchemy, as elsewhere, with resurrection and rebirth. By contrast, the North was frequently associated with the opposite of Wisdom, with 'unknowing', so that clouds were envisaged as being the form of the devil in the North. The necessary nature of the conflict lies in the need for the attributes of the South to be brought into contact with the attributes of the North, not only so that unknowing might be tamed by wisdom, but also so that wisdom (in the form of 'civilised' knowledge) should be tempered by the experience of 'unknowing' – a state which had to be passed through in order to reach the deity.[25]

Another poem which emphatically opposes North with South is 'The Hound of Flames' (p. 42). Associated by Morris and Gagen with the dog that accompanies Santo Domingo de Guzmán with the flaming brand of truth in its mouth[26] and by Connell with the star Sirius, possibly representing passion or energy,[27] the flaming dog is of cosmic proportions, standing between the North Wind (devil-bearing) and the South Wind (wisdom-bearing), and may be related to the dog Kerberos.[28] Within Roman mythology, the dog Cerberus was guardian to the infernal regions, and the origin of the fable may derive from the Egyptian custom of guarding tombs with Gods. In the light of these associations, we might regard the dog as presiding over mighty conflict within Hell or the enclosed death-cell of the tomb. A more powerful suggestion derives from a reading of the dog as the symbol of Mercurius, as representative of the initial *nigredo* state.[29]

Noticeable in Alberti's use of the elements in this work is the degree to which one of the four may be either denied or omitted. Thus in the 'Song of the Luckless Angel' (p. 28) of the first section, in the form of a puzzle, and alluding to the changing state of the element of water (water, wave, snow), the elements of water, air and earth are there, but no fire. This might be the answer to the puzzle, but will also be the crucial element for the process of calcination. In 'The Angelic Angel' (p. 38), water, wind and fire name the angel, but the earth gives nothing.[30] In 'The Soul in Torment' (46), where air is not only present but powerful and destructive, and where earth (associated with man) and water are suggested in the disquieting unbalanced conflict of 'Birds against ships, / Man against rose,' (p. 47) we are told that fire is dead.

The vacillation between the naming of three or four elements, which might be seen as artistic playfulness, or evasion of a set and enclosing form that would run counter to the suggestion of the poet's confusion, can be read as significant within alchemical belief. The alternation between four, and three elements found in alchemical writings is a pointer to the dynamic urge towards transformation, since four, or the quaternity, is symbolic of wholeness, while three signifies a state of incompletion. At the same time four is held to signify the feminine, motherly, physical, while three signifies the masculine, fatherly, spiritual, so that clusters of three or four elements indicate the movement within the alchemical process itself towards union, or the *coniunctio*, between masculine and feminine, in order for the alchemical product to emerge.[31]

Burning in hell-fire is an image traditionally associated with descent to the infernal regions. The paradox within the alchemical construction of the world is that descent and burning (by corros-

ives or fire) are necessary processes for the attainment of the hard
and durable form of the self. Images of burning are present in the
collection from the start, while Part 7 of 'The Uninhabited Body'
speaks simply, forcibly and with total impact of the burning
process:

> You fell asleep.
> And angry angels, in trouble,
> Charred it into rubble.
> They charred all your dream to rubble.
>
> And wild angels, in their fury,
> made black cinders of your soul,
> your body. (25)

In 'The Two Angels' (p. 33), the *calcinatio* is not merely
suffered, but desired, indicating a more advanced understanding
of the process, while the identified principals in the drama are no
less than Luzbel, the sun and the moon, these last two being
symbols of the masculine and the feminine in the alchemical
union. 'The Sooty Angel' (p. 39), however, is rejected, still of
earthly *prima materia* being 'of mud and soot', and still to be
further burnt: 'Hell burn you!'. These reminders of as yet uncon-
verted matter populate the collection, including the earthy damp
suggestions of 'humidity' and 'wells' in 'The Angel of Mystery' (p.
44), in which a horse, emblem of the passions and the physical life,
runs wild, as yet untamed, and 'Ascension' (p. 44), in which the
atmosphere of damp imprisonment is the setting for the urge to
ascend and where the self is water where hooks may trawl.[32]

The characteristic way that alchemy appears in the collection is
in brief allusion to elements and processes which can be read
alongside, or within, the scenario of infernal suffering. Occasionally a much fuller reading is possible. In 'The Uninhabited Body',
having cast out from his body something that is only indicated as
being lifeless and feminine in part 2, the poet is overtaken by
forces of the earth, of chaos, confusion in part 3. The dislodging of
the feminine (whether the soul, truth, or the feminine principle in
man) is significant, because the alchemical process will require a
subsequent *coniunctio* of masculine and feminine properties. In
part 4, opening 'You. I. (Moonlight).', the idea of contrasts and

separation comes to the fore, leading to the crashing eddies of aimless wandering of the body without its feminine aspect in part 5. Part 6 speaks of the potential within the self – 'He bore a city within him', though this as yet is no more than earthy *prima materia*, even less than this, the space occupied by it: ' he's a tunnel / Pitch-black and dripping' yet opaque, 'down which nothing can be seen'. The process of calcination is recounted in part 7, while the final part provides a recapitulation of the disorientation of the whole process. In this way it is analogous to the form of the whole collection, in that there is no absolute linear progression from beginning to end, but constant re-treading of previous ground.

The poems of the final section are recognisable at a glance from their line-length, and paint a bleak, post-catastrophe landscape, in which debris of past existence is littered over a sterile planet. Insistent use of past tenses, whether preterite or imperfect, emphasises a sense of impotence, of tired acceptance of what has happened. The number of references to petrification here might be thought of as a possible allusion to the attainment of the alchemical goal of the philosopher's stone, but it would be erroneous to suggest that the end of the work outlines the attainment of that goal.

The final image, however, in 'The Surviving Angel' (p. 65), leaves us with a striking alchemical motif, that of the wingless bird. In the final recounting of bare survival of humanity, one survivor remains:

> A man's last outcry stained the wind with blood.
> All the angels lost their lives.
> Save for one, wounded, with clipped wings.

We are familiar with the image of the phoenix as an emblem of resurrection, as we are also familiar with the commonplace of the bird that represents the spirit or the spiritual life. The bird with wings clipped, however, evokes the wingless bird of alchemical illustrations. Senior's *De chemia*, for example, shows a wise old man displaying a tablet on which a winged bird and a wingless bird are joined together, each holding the tail of the other in its beak. As a pair they represent the urge to rise, held back by the earthbound nature of the lower world.[33] Thus the final image is not necessarily of a man reduced by his experience, having survived the onslaught of his projections, but a man reaffirmed in his earthly state of possessing the will to rise, but the inability to do so.

Notes

1 *Concerning the Angels* is the title of the translation of *Sobre los ángeles*, by Geoffrey Connell, London, 1967. All page references will be to this edition, bracketed in the text.
2 *The Lost Grove*, Berkeley, 1959, pp. 259–60.
3 Alberti, *Poesías completas*, Buenos Aires, 1961, p. 12.
4 See, for example Geoffrey W. Connell, 'The Autobiographical Element in *Sobre los ángeles*', *Bulletin of Hispanic Studies*, 40, 1963, pp. 160–73 (p. 161), and C. B. Morris, *Rafael Alberti's 'Sobre los ángeles': Four Major Themes*, University of Hull Occasional Papers in Modern Languages no. 3, Hull, 1966, pp. 11–12.
5 See, for example, J. Chailley, *Jérôme Bosch et ses symboles*, Brussels, 1978, Madeleine Bergman, *Hieronymus Bosch and Alchemy*, Stockholm, 1979, and J. van Lennep, *Alchimie: Contribution à l'histoire de l'art alchimique*, Brussels, 1984, pp. 309–340.
6 See van Lennep, *Alchimie*, pp. 340–66 on Breughel and alchemy.
7 See, for example, van Lennep, *Alchimie*, pp. 290–6.
8 See, for example, M. O. Perceval, *William Blake's Circle of Destiny*, New York, 1938, pp. 197–215, D. Hirst, *Hidden Riches: Traditional Symbolism from the Renaissance to Blake*, New York, 1964, pp. 134–6, and A. A. Ansari, 'Blake and the Kabbalah' and P. Nanavutty, '*Materia prima* in a page of Blake's *Vala*', both in *William Blake: Essays for S. F. Damon*, edited by A. H. Rosenfeld, Providence, 1969, pp. 199–220 and 293–302. On Swedenborg see E. A. Hitchcock, *Swedenborg, a Hermetic philsopher. Being a Sequel to Remarks on Alchemy and the Alchemists*, New York, 1858, reprinted 1973.
9 See van Lennep, *Alchimie*, p. 414; J. Pommier, *La mystique de Baudelaire*, Paris, 1932 and P. Arnold, *Esotérisme de Baudelaire*, Paris, 1972.
10 C. G. Jung, *Mysterium Coniunctionis*, in *Collected Works*, 20 vols., translated by R. F. C. Hull, London, 1953–79, vol. 14, p. 323, n. 254 and p. 342, n. 328. All references to Jung will be to this edition of the works.
11 Jung, *Mysterium coniunctionis*, p. 144, n. 266 and p. 445.
12 See the *Collected Works*, vols. 12, *Psychology and Alchemy*, 13, *Alchemical Studies*, and 14, *Mysterium Coniunctionis*. There are also essays on alchemy in vol. 9, *Aion*.
13 'The Psychic Nature of the Alchemical Work', *Psychology and Alchemy*, p. 242.
14 *Ibid.*, p. 244.
15 Jung, 'Basic Concepts of Alchemy', *Psychology and Alchemy*, pp. 228–32.

16 See M.-L. von Franz, *Alchemy: an Introduction to the Symbolism and the Psychology*, Toronto, 1980, p. 93: 'The search for immortality was . . . the search for an incorruptible essence in man which would survive death, an essential part of the human being which could be preserved'.

17 C. B. Morris, *Rafael Alberti's 'Sobre los ángeles': Four Major Themes*, Hull, 1966, pp. 53–4.

18 S. Jiménez-Fajardo, *Multiple Spaces: the Poetry of Rafael Alberti*, London, 1984, p. 51. The motion suggested by Jiménez-Fajardo is reminiscent of the *circumambulatio* of alchemy. See Jung, 'The Symbolism of the Mandala', *Psychology and Alchemy*, pp. 145–8.

19 *The Lost Grove*, p. 258.

20 See A. Leal, 'Acerca del tema del vacío en *Sobre los ángeles* de Rafael Alberti, *Dr. Rafael Alberti: El poeta en Toulouse*, Toulouse, 1984, pp. 113–21.

21 See D. Gagen, ' "Thy fading mansion": the image of the empty house in Rafael Alberti's *Sobre los ángeles*', *Bulletin of Hispanic Studies*, xliv, 1987, pp. 225–35.

22 As noted by C. B. Morris, in his edition of *Sobre los ángeles*, Madrid, 1989, p. 128.

23 von Franz, *Alchemy*, p. 82.

24 *Ibid.*, p. 200.

25 *Ibid.*, p. 208.

26 C. B. Morris, *ed. cit.* of *Sobre los ángeles*, p. 110, and D. Gagen, ' "Invitación al aire": the imagery of ascent in Alberti's *Sobre los ángeles*', *Modern Language Review*, lxxxiii, 1988, p. 874.

27 G. W. Connell, 'The Autobiographical Element in *Sobre los ángeles*', p. 169.

28 von Franz, *Alchemy*, p. 69.

29 See Jung, 'The Spirit Mercurius', *Alchemical Studies*, p. 232.

30 A. L. Geist, 'Hell's Angels: a reading of Alberti's *Sobre los ángeles*', *Hispanic Review*, liv, 1986, p. 179.

31 Jung, *Psychology and Alchemy*, pp. 26–7.

32 The stage of (bitter) divine water as part of the process is a necessary element in the achievement of the *albedo* stage. See von Franz, *Alchemy*, p. 89. It is the unformed element of life, the corresponding solid state of which is the stone of the philosopher (von Franz, *Alchemy*, p. 174).

33 See von Franz, *Alchemy*, pp. 109–111 and 125–7.

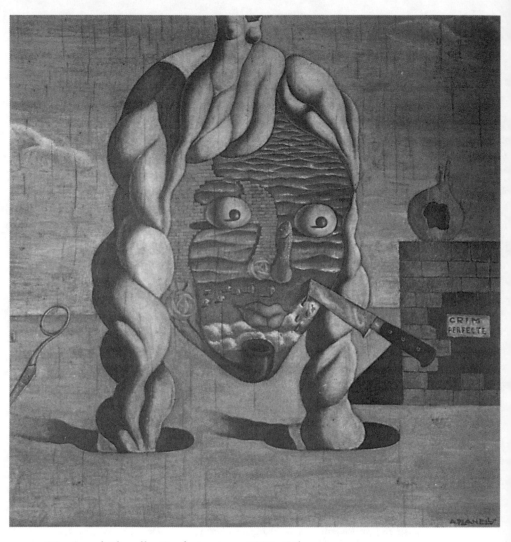

23. Angel Planells: *Perfect crime*, 1929. Oil on canvas

15 / The oblique language of Luis Cernuda: creative ruin or fragments shored? C. BRIAN MORRIS

The fragments to which Eliot refers in the last passage of *The Waste Land* are a cluster of phrases and quotations that, although they may have been thrown up by his memory, according to his earlier 'Rhapsody on a Windy Night', as 'a crowd of twisted things', are assembled as a defence against disintegration, which is more likely to be textual and literary than emotional. If we further interpret Eliot's avowal as a positive measure against a negative threat, then *The Waste Land* can be seen as a sustained and distinguished product of a process that Paul Klee defined in an apparently startling paradox as 'the creative ruin'.[1] A parallel product, on a smaller scale, can be seen in some of Cernuda's surrealist poems, notably 'Where were cast down' from the collection *Forbidden Pleasures*, especially if we detect in the poem's first words a violent, exaggerated version of the venerable topic of *ubi sunt*. When we read later in this same poem 'Hang yourself in my young arms', we may be tempted to interpret this version of the amorous topic 'Die in my arms' as evidence of the central principle of Harold Bloom's contention about Poetic Influence, which is not as 'outrageous' as he claims:

Poetic Influence – when it involves two strong, authentic poets – always proceeds by a misreading of the prior poet, an act of creative correction that is actually and necessarily a misinterpretation. The history of fruitful poetic influence, which is to say the main tradition of Western poetry since the Renaissance, is a history of anxiety and self-saving caricature, of distortion, of perverse, wilful revisionism without which modern poetry as such could not exist.[2]

Such words and phrases as 'misreading', 'misinterpretation', 'self-saving caricature', 'distortion', 'perverse revisionism' appear to be an indictment of a process that Bloom regards as vital to modern poetry. The process is an essential part of the surrealists' profound concern with language, which is evident in poems such as Eluard's 'The Word' (from *Capital of Pain*, 1926), in which the word is the speaker; Aragon's 'Poetry' (from *Poetry's Destinies*, 1925–1926), in which language mocks itself; and Péret's 'The Language of Saints' (from *The Great Game*, 1928). These poems are matched in Spain by Aleixandre's 'My voice' (from *Swords like Lips*) and Cernuda's 'Misfortune' (from *A River, A Love*), in

191

which the protagonist, identified only as 'he', is represented as a parrot uttering words ineffectually:

> But he with his lips,
> With his lips only knows how to say words;
> Words directed at the ceiling,
> Words directed at the ground,
> And his arms are clouds that turn life
> Into navegable air.[3]

The repetition of 'lips' and 'words' devalues the human voice and the sounds it makes with a sadness absent from Aleixandre's vigorous assault in 'Words' (also from *Swords like Lips*), in which he barracks his own efforts in parenthetic asides and in an inventory that undermines and deprecates through semantic content and grammatical disconnection the very activity in which words are engaged:

> Paper. Language of mourning. Menace. Charnel house.
> Words, words, words, words.
> Wrath. Bestial. Lewdness. Yellowness.
> Dirty words directed at belly and thighs.[4]

By indicting words as 'dirty', Aleixandre lets words be their own judge and jury, creating a verbal texture that is, through the overall theme and individual components of the theme, incontrovertible evidence of its own fallibility. In his essay 'The crisis of language', Richard Sheppard connects the ideas of fallibility and redemption as he explains why 'the modernist poet rejects all notions of art as description or mimesis':

> because the 'real' world is felt to be 'fallen' to questionable ends, the task of art cannot be to reproduce this fallen world or manufacture a beautiful 'surface' for it with a language which is equally suspect. Thus the task of the modern poet becomes the creation of a redeemed, visionary world of langue in which, as André Breton put it in *The Disdainful Confession* (1924), 'something fundamental' is given back to form and in which the lost dimension of language and the human psyche is rediscovered or preserved.[5]

192

The oblique language of Luis Cernuda

Sheppard returns to the idea of the surface when he lists the 'shock tactics' with which the dadaists and surrealists set out 'to break down conventionalised responses to words, to defeat the censorship which the surface areas of the personality, the conscious intellect and the will, had imposed upon the profounder levels of the psyche' (p. 333). One of the tactics he names – 'violently incongruous images and surprise effects' – offers the most provocative challenge and constitutes the most enduring appeal of surrealist art, films and literature. In his important essay 'La métaphore filée dans la poésie surréaliste', Michael Riffaterre stresses, like Sheppard, that unconventionality, which he defines as arbitrariness, can be perceived and then gauged only in relation to 'our logical habits, . . . our utilitarian attitude with regard to the reality of language'.[6] Surrealist images and metaphors do not refer to the world that exists: they force us to see the distance between what they conjure up and what we are conditioned to expect, often using a correct and totally familiar syntactic structure to generate a tension between that structure and what is expressed within it. This tension between structure and content is one of the most subversive features of surrealist language, and may be seen at its most disturbing in these examples from Breton, Eluard, Aleixandre, Cernuda and Lorca:

> The hollow flowers' and protruding cheekbones' timetable
>   invites us to leave the volcanic salt-cellars for the bird-
>   baths.[7]
> The sweet red-hot iron of dawn
> Gives sight back to the blind.[8]
> A mouth with wings the size of snow
> Places its burning coal on your neck.[9]
> A mollusk moan
> Seems of no importance;
> But at night the waves are a moan
> Of burning marble,
> Weary corolas
> Or lascivious columns.[10]
> The joyful fevers fled to the ships hawsers
> And the Jew pushed open the gate with the frozen chastity of
>   a lettuce's heart.[11]

193

The two lines by Eluard were chosen by Riffaterre, who perceives 'total incompatibility' between 'sweet' and 'red-hot iron'. At first sight, he seems justified: in normal circumstances 'sweet' or 'gentle' is not appropriate to a red-hot iron – unless one thinks of the joy felt by the blind on recovering their sight. In any case, this image illustrates the fundamental point he establishes at the beginning of his essay, that 'the arbitrariness of these images only exists in relation to our logical habits . . .';[12] and arbitrary images, Breton declared in his first surrealist manifesto, are the ones that take longest to translate 'into practical language'. Conditioned and constrained by our 'logical habits', we can do no more than recognise cases of arbitrariness and incongruity in Breton's volcanic salt-cellars, in Lorca's joyful fevers, in Cernuda's mollusk moan and burning marble and in Aleixandre's mouth with wings the size of snow. To read and follow Breton's sentence is to find within a perfectly correct syntactic structure both a total lack of rational content and an invitation to do something that we do not know how to do.

In these images we see perfectly encapsulated one of the great paradoxes of surrealist literature: the freedom to choose new themes and to renew poetic language does not necessarily lead to thematic or emotional clarity, and what we experience when reading many poems, and viewing many paintings, is ambiguity, ambivalence, unformulated ideas and unfiltered emotions. The surrealist poem creates holes and spaces, which we have to breach, if our will and our experience allow it, without being sure of ever retracing the complex processes in the mind of the writer, who is often conscious of the conflict between his own complexity and the language he has to use. One of the most revolutionary contributions, and lessons, of surrealism is that words, whether in a single image or in an entire poem, do not have to collude or to harmonise in order to create a single meaning: the tensions they cause generate resonances, ideas and emotions free from the tyranny of clarity, coherence and fixed meaning.

This revolution, which to me is a constructive one, obliges us to pose alternative questions. Instead of asking what a poem means, we should ask whether it is possible to extract a meaning, whether we have the right to expect to decipher one, whether the poem has a key and whether the key we think we have found opens all or

194

only part of the poem. We could ask these questions about many poems written in Spain under the influence of surrealism; poems by Aleixandre, Alberti, Cernuda, Lorca, Hinojosa and Prados present difficulties that are not easily resolved. One particularly challenging example of this type of expressive revolution is Cernuda's 'Where were cast down', because it sends us in different directions, emits diverse signals and generates reactions that we may or may not be able, or willing, to order and reconcile:

> Where were cast down those cascades,
> All those lovers' kisses. that pale history,
> With venemous signs, then presents to the pilgrim
> In the desert, like a glove
> That asks, forgotten, for its hand?
>
> You know where, Corsair;
> Corsair enjoying yourself on tepid reefs,
> Bodies screaming beneath the body visiting them,
> And they only think about caresses,
> They only think about desire,
> Like a block of life
> Slowly melted by the cold of death.
>
> Other bodies, Corsair, know nothing;
> Leave them be.
> Pour, pour yourself over my desires,
> Hang yourself in my young arms,
> And I, with drowned eyes,
> With the last word to burgeon from my lips,
> Bitterly shall say how much I love you.[13]

The poem's initial phrase contains one of the two coordinates that help us to situate it in a literary context: the topic of *ubi sunt*. The poem's last words, 'I love you', offers us the other. To recognize these two venerable topics is to perceive at the same time the modifications to which they are now subjected. In formulating his question, Cernuda modulates the sadness traditionally associated with the topic, overlaying an emotion that may be rage, or indignation, or exasperation, by means of a violent verb and a mode and tense of the verb that suggest that someone behaved aggressively, and through a noun, 'cascades', which adds violence and

195

drama to the rivers evoked in the most famous Spanish antecedent of the theme, the fifteenth-century 'Verses on the death of his father' by Jorge Manrique, as simply: 'Yonder are the mighty rivers, / Yonder the other smaller ones, / ... and the littlest'.

The adverb 'bitterly', which dominates the poem's last line, should warn us that 'I love you' does not occupy that plane of spiritual selflessness that might be found in the Renaissance tradition of erotic poetry, which distinguished between the 'ardent virtue' of love and the 'grossness', as defined in the well-known sonnet by the seventeenth-century poet, Francisco de Quevedo. That distinction between 'love' and 'desire' is one that Cernuda's speaker blurs in the explicitly erotic entreaties of the final stanza. The exigent and egocentric temper of the speaker clashes with the abnegation evoked by 'love', which stands as a kind of forlorn postscript to the erotic texture of the poem. The love that the speaker promises is one that is aware of sexuality and names it as a factor in his entreaties, fully conscious of the two poles of pleasure and pain, of life and death, that he links throughout the poem in the 'Corsair enjoying himself on tepid reefs', in the 'bodies screaming beneath the body visiting them', in the equation of 'caresses' and 'desire', and in the pleas to 'pour yourself' and 'hang yourself'.

All this may remind us of the very traditional death from love, but Cernuda converts the topic into a means of underlining the role of martyr that he assigns to his speaker; blind and on the point of exhaling his last sigh, he will not shout as other bodies (not persons) shout, but offers himself as a passive and compliant victim of the sexual activity denoted by verbs of excess, either of indulgence or of violence: 'cast down, enjoy, scream, visit, pour, hang'. Although 'visit' does not appear violent at first sight, its sexual meaning – penetration – emerges as the cause of the bodies yelling when we read in erotic poetry of the Golden Age the salacious confessions that anonymous poets impute to indulgent and popular women, who state unashamedly 'Many friars often / Come to visit me' and, even more mischievously in its capitalisation, 'His Visitation / Stirs me up'.[14] Other erotic poems from the same period contain the verb 'pour', which, together with 'irrigate' and 'spill', and in connection with hot water and 'broth', signifies with little subtlety ejaculation. One of the male players in these sexual games utters an urgent warning about the imminent risk to which his passion exposes him: 'I'm really in a hurry now, / The water's on the fire, / And if I don't get there soon / I swear it will boil over'.[15]

Although 'pour' and 'hang' appear to be synonymous, the dominant association of the former points us towards heterosexual love and the latter hints at homosexual love; in that case, 'hang' is a consequence of 'pour', a sinister, lethal invocation that perpetuates the association with death central to the picturesque indictment of a homosexual pronounced by an anonymous Golden Age poet: 'With hanged man's teeth and hangman's noose / You exercise Merlin's craft'.[16] When Cernuda's speaker imagines himself, through a bold synaesthesia, 'with drowned eyes', he shares the fate of another poet, the mythical Thamyris, of whom it was said that he was 'the first man who ever wooed one of his own sex', Hyacinthus; for boasting that he could sing better than the Muses, the latter punished him by removing his sight, his voice and his memory for playing the harp.[17] Both Thamyris and Cernuda's protagonist are victims of their pride: the first, in the power of his voice, the latter in the power of his love. If Cernuda had Thamyris in mind, then he offers, consciously or unwittingly, a connection with homosexuality that, according to Octavio Paz, is the starting-point of his poetic activity.[18] If homosexuality is the point of departure, how can we tell where it leads him? How do we detect the poetic result of that sexual identity? Critics who have studied homosexuality in literature have posed other questions, such as those listed by George Stambolian and Elaine Marks in their introduction to the volume *Homosexualities and French Literature*. How does homosexuality affect the language, style, and structure of a writer's work? Is there a connection between a writer's sexuality and his or her literary practices? How do the dominant sexual myths and erotic fantasies of a period shape a work or determine a writer's reputation? In what ways does a text produce semiotic connections that can be read as homosexual? How does a work reflect, consciously or unconsciously, the prevailing discourse on homosexuality? In what ways does all writing on homosexuality struggle with the polarities male / female, homosexual/heterosexual?[19] The answers are as complex as the questions, but all of them would have to start from the same point:

that the vigour of the literature of homosexuality lies in what Robert K. Martin, writing of Whitman, has called 'the strategies of concealment', strategies that create what Gregory Woods terms 'its obliquity, arising from the need to resort to metaphor to express sexual meaning'.[20]

In 'Where were cast down' obliquity is indispensable to the double apostrophe to the Corsair, which is set in an appropriately aquatic context evoked directly or suggested by 'cascades', 'tepid reefs', 'block of melted life', 'pour' and 'drowned eyes'. The Corsair is a forceful Romantic prototype, celebrated by Berlioz in a lively overture and singled out by Byron in a long poem as 'That man of loneliness and mystery / Scarce seen to smile, and seldom heard to sigh' (Carto II., pp. 173–4). As a figure of adventure, he appears as the Red Rover in Fenimore Cooper's tale of that title, which was translated into Spanish in 1893 as *El corsario rojo*, and as The Black Pirate in a silent film of that title (1926) featuring Douglas Fairbanks, Sr.; as one more victim of boredom and aimlessness, he meanders through Robert Desnos' novel *Liberty or Love* (1926) with the designation of *Corsaire Sanglot*. The sexual freedom enjoyed by Desnos' protagonist is a version of the licence that governments granted to merchant ships in their campaigns against pirates or enemy vessels. Whilst Corsaire Sanglot has his yacht, Cernuda's Corsaire enjoys the liberty to wallow 'on tepid reefs', to enter and to leave (coves, bays, bodies) whenever he pleases. In his poem 'The rainbow and the cataplasm' (from his unpublished *The Andalusian Dog*), Buñuel asks a number of provocative questions, one of which is: 'Are sailors pederasts?' The literature of homosexuality shows them to be essential actors in homosexual fantasies: they are some of the 'divine beings' reported by John Addington Symonds in a letter from Venice to Edmund Gosse;[21] Christopher Isherwood's George, the protagonist of his novel *A Single Man* (1964), recalls the first time he saw his lover Jim, 'not yet demobilized and looking stunning beyond words in his Navy uniform'; and Cernuda himself announces in the title of another poem from *Forbidden Pleasures* that 'Sailors are the wings of love'. The danger of drowning – represented in this poem as something pleasurable through his longing 'I want to go alone to the sea and drown' – is one factor of the magnetism that, according to John Lehmann, is exercised by sailors:

198

Sailors are adventure seekers. Homosexuals are adventure seekers, rejecting the rules that tie conventional society together. Freedom, yes, that's it, they are symbols of freedom, in spite of the fact that they're under close discipline. Perhaps, paradoxically, because of? Then, their closeness to death. The sea as an image of death. The sea as an image of boundless orgasm. All those stories of them being allowed to choose their boyfriends after a warship's been ninety days at sea.[22]

In his poem 'Through the Looking-Glass', Auden uses the metaphors of rudder, wind, reef and landfall to express the consequences of control and the lack of it, which are represented as a choice between a successfully negotiated berthing and missing the entry to the reef:

> Lost if I steer. Tempest and tide may blow
> Sailor and ship past the illusive reef,
> And yet I land to celebrate with you
> The birth of natural order and true love.[23]

In order to wallow on 'tepid reefs', Cernuda's Corsair has to swim or sail in what Quevedo, once contemptuously referred to as 'the high seas of the flesh'.[24] The activity that sailing entails, together with the activities ('pour', 'hang') that the speaker entreats, makes of him a dynamic figure, more menacing in his mobility than the passive Greek 'beautiful boy', who is categorised by Camille Paglia as 'an androgyne, luminously masculine and feminine . . . beardless, frozen in time . . . physicality without physiology'.[25] Physicality is precisely what is displayed in Thomas Eakins's painting *The Swimming Hole* (1883–1885), whose naked males – standing, lounging, swimming – offer their nakedness as unselfconsciously as the young boys in a rowing boat painted in 1894 by H. S. Tuke under the title 'August Blue'.[26] To find a poem in Alan Stanley's *Love Lyrics* (1894) with the same title and on the same theme is to see the fascination exercised on poets and painters alike by a topic whose frequency made it into an easily decipherable code. Whitman had already plotted the scene in the passage from 'Song of Myself' (1855) beginning 'Twenty-eight young men bathe by the shore, / Twenty-eight young men and all so friendly'; many boys were to follow their example in Uranian poetry, and many soldiers would bathe in whatever pools they could find in poetry written during the First World War. As it blandly changes the boy's sex, Stanley's tribute to him in 'August Blue' – 'A very nymph you seem to be / As you glide and dive and swim' – confirms Paul Fussell's contention that 'pederastic bathing verses . . . could . . . seem innocent, romantic, and sentimental – homoerotic rather than riskily homosexual'.[27] Innocence is what E. M. Forster was at pains to suggest in the episode, in chapter 12, of *A Room with a View* in which Mr. Beebe, Freddy and George 'forgot Italy and Botany and Fate' and 'began to play' in a small woodland pool.[28] If we are familiar with the topic, our reactions to the scene are likely to be ambivalent; and we may evince no surprise at all to find homosexuals in Edgar Michael Bravo's film *I'll Love You Forever . . . Tonight* spending so much time in a Palm Springs swimming pool, or to find Isherwood's George, in *A Single Man*, plunging naked into the Pacific Ocean in the company of a male student 'to receive the stunning baptism of the surf'.

If we return to Cernuda's poem, it is clear that he did not let himself be deluded by the idealisation of homosexuality that the topic of the bathing scene fostered: the glove that 'forgotten, asks for its hand', the 'tepid reefs' and the 'block of life / Melted by the cold of death' have negative elements: the glove is given more importance, and life, than the hand; the water is tepid rather than hot; and life has to be colder than death if it can be melted by death. Such eccentricities endorse the connection Jonathan Dollimore postulates 'between perversity and paradox' as 'a single criterion of that dubious category, the homosexual sensibility'.[29] In the first stanza Cernuda is quick to follow 'All those lovers' kisses' with 'venemous signs'; Oscar Wilde had good reason to insist on the metaphor of poison, describing what he called the *Amour de l'Impossible* as 'the poison of unlimited desire' and sharpening the paradox in his evocation of 'an unknown land full of strange flowers and subtle perfumes, a land of which it is joy of all joys to dream, a land where all things are perfect and poisonous'.[30] A century later, a homosexual poet, Sal Farinella, identifies similar difficulties in similar terms: 'To see you this night / I can not go / but swim in deep waters / poisoned blue'.[31]

In its assault on the conventionally positive response to the blue sea, 'waters poisoned blue' subverts our reactions as forcefully as

The oblique language of Luis Cernuda

Cernuda's conjunction of kisses and 'poisonous signs', of yells and visits, of caress and cold, of desire and death. These are not clearly defined contrasts: they fuse and overlap to create a verbal texture that reminds us of, yet swerves away from, such familiar utterances of erotic poetry as: 'Put our arms around . . . and hold me tight, / The rage for death is in me'.[32] To read 'Hang yourself in my young arms' is to encounter a modification that disconcerts, one that makes us into active readers. Before a poem like this, or before any number of surrealist paintings, passivity is impossible. Breton declared in his first surrealist manifesto that man has received the gift of language to make a surrealist use of it; I would add that without a surrealist mind to respond to it, that language would fall into a void, and we would deny ourselves the chance of piecing together for ourselves those fragments, and our responses to them, that Cernuda shored not so much against his ruins as against his silence: fragments that – perverse, paradoxical, incongruous – we have the opportunity to assemble into an experience very different from reading, say, Jorge Manrique's 'Verses on the Death of his Father', which Cernuda's poem may acknowledge. In that case, 'Where were cast down' is like the rock pool at the end of Isherwood's *A Single Man*, which, 'swarming with . . . deepdown sparkling undiscovered secrets, ominous protean organisms motioning mysteriously, perhaps warningly, toward the surface light', awaits the ocean of consciousness. If we as readers are that ocean, then our role is to both illuminate and to give life to the poem.

Notes

1 R. Crone and J. L. Koerner, *Paul Klee. Legends of the Sign*, New York, 1981, p. 22.
2 H. Bloom, *The Anxiety of Influence. A Theory of Poetry*, New York, 1975, p. 30.
3 *Obra Completa*, vol. 1, Madrid, 1993, pp. 155–6.
4 *Espadas como labios. La destrucción o el amor*, Madrid, 1972, p. 85.
5 R. Sheppard, 'The crisis of language', in M. Bradbury and J. McFarlane, eds., *Modernism 1890–1930*, London, 1987, p. 329. I approach surface and subsurface from another angle in 'The cultural underground of Eliot, Alberti and Lorca', in K. M. Sibbald and H. T. Young (eds.), *T. S. Eliot and Hispanic Modernity (1924–1933)*, Boulder, 1993, pp. 9–29.

6 M. Riffaterre, 'La métaphore filée dans la poésie surréaliste', in Riffaterre, *La production du texte*, Paris, 1979, p. 217.

7 A. Breton, 'Cartes sur les dunes', *Clair de terre*, Paris, 1966, p. 55.

8 P. Eluard, 'Le bâillon sur la table', *La Vie inmédiate*, Paris, 1962, p. 66.

9 'Aurora insumisa', *Destrucción*, pp. 144–4.

10 'Mares escarlata', *Obra Completa*, p. 158.

11 'Cementerio judío', Poet in New York, London, 1990, p. 136. This translation by Harris.

12 'La métaphore filée', p. 217.

13 'Adónde fueron despeñadas', *Obra Completa*, p. 176.

14 P. Alzieu, R. Jammes, Y. Lissorgues, *Floresta de poesías eróticas del Siglo de Oro*, Toulouse, 1975, p. 173; p. 107. Cernuda's poem would have been included, along with four others of his, in the anthology *Poesía erótica en la España del siglo XX*, Madrid, 1978, had authorisation been granted to its editors, J. López Gorgé and F. Salgueiro (p. 12 note).

15 Alzieu, *Floresta*, p. 143. Camilo José Cela does not list *caldo, regar* or *verter* in his *Diccionario del erotismo*, but *derramar* is crisply defined as 'Ejaculate semen' (Barcelona, vol. I, p. 379).

16 Alzieu, *Floresta*, p. 253.

17 R. Graves, *The Greek Myths*, vol. I, Harmondsworth, 1978, p. 78.

18 Paz's words are quoted by S. Jiménez Fajardo in his introduction to *The Word and the Mirror. Critical Essays on the Poetry of Luis Cernuda*, London and Toronto, 1989, p. 17.

19 G. Stambolian and E. Marks (eds.), *Homosexualities and French Literature. Cultural Contexts / Critical Texts*, Ithaca and London, 1979, p. 29.

20 R. K. Martin, *The Homosexual Tradition in American Poetry*, Austin and London 1973, p. 7; G. Woods, *Articulate Flesh. Male Homo-Eroticism and Modern Poetry*, New Haven and London, p. 2.

21 Symonds' letter is quoted in R. Croft-Cooke, *Feasting with Panthers. A New Consideration of some Late Victorian Writers*, New York–Chicago–San Francisco, 1968, pp. 140–1.

22 Lehmann's words were published in *Gay News* in 1976 and 1977, and are quoted in Woods, *Articulate Flesh*, p. 80.

23 Auden's 'Through the Looking-Glass' was written between 1933 and 1938; it appears in *Collected Shorter Poems 1927–1957*, New York, 1966, pp. 74–6; the lines I quote are also adduced by Woods, *Articulate Flesh*, p. 179.

24 Quevedo, 'Pinta el suceso de haber estado una noche con una fregona', *Obras completas*, I, *Poesía original* (ed.), J. M. Blecua, Barcelona, p. 1131.

25 C. Paglia, *Sexual Personae. Art and Decadence from Nefertiti to Emily Dickinson*, London and New Haven, 1990, pp. 110, 114, 117.

26 See G. Hendricks, *The Life and Works of Thomas Eakins*, New York, 1974; *The Swimming Hole* is plate 29.

27 *Male Homosexuality in English Literature from 1850 to 1900*. An Anthology selected with an Introduction by B. Reade, New York, 1970, no. 71, p. 348; a reproduction of Tuke's *August Blue* appears on p. 293. P. Fussell has a section entitled 'Soldiers Bathing' in *The Great War and Modern Memory*,

London–Oxford–New York, 1977, pp. 299–309; the quotation I adduce appears on p. 305. See too T. d'Arch Smith, *Love in Earnest. Some Notes on the Lives and Writings of English 'Uranian' Poets from 1889 to 1930*, London, 1970.

28 Hindsight, particularly the furore generated by the publication of *Maurice* in 1971, encourages us to interpret the pond scene in *A Room with a View* as an example of what Forster called 'the flesh educating the spirit'. See C. J. Summers, *Gay Fictions. Wilde to Stonewall. Studies in Male Homosexual Literary Tradition*, New York, 1990, for illuminating chapters on Forster and Isherwood: 'The Flesh Educating the Spirit; E. M. Forster's Gay Fictions', pp. 78–111; and 'The Waters of the Pool: Christopher Isherwood's *A Single Man*, pp. 195–249.

29 J. Dollimore, *Sexual Dissidence. Augustine to Wilde*, Freud to Foucault, Oxford, 1991, p. 309.

30 Wilde, 'The Critic as Artist', in The Portable Oscar Wilde, Harmondsworth, 1982, p. 86. The second quotation belongs to a letter from Wilde to Harry Marillier of January–February 1886, and is quoted in Croft-Cooke, *Feasting with Panthers*, p. 203. A woman poet, 'Marie Madelaine' (Baroness von Puttkamer) represents a lesbian encounter as a 'Crucifixion' and confesses to her lover: 'I gave you of the poison that was mine . . .': in S. Coote (ed.), The Penguin Book of Homosexual Verse, th, 1983, p. 281.

31 S. Farinella, 'Howl at the Moon', in I. Young (ed.), The Male Muse. A Gay Anthology, New York, 1973, p. 31.

32 Alzieu et al., *Floresta de poesías eróticas*, no. 135, p. 271.

24. Wladislaw Jahl: 'Waterfall'. Woodcut, published in *VLTRA*, Madrid, XVI, February 20, 1921

16 / Subversions of the sacred: the sign of the fish   PATRICIA MCDERMOTT

On the inside cover of the first issue of *La Révolution Surréaliste* (1 December 1924), the magazine published by the French surrealists under the aegis of 'The Central Office for Surrealist Research', was the announcement: 'We are on the eve of a RÉVOLUTION. You can take part'. Its advertisement was dominated by a drawing of a fish inscribed 'SURREALISM', an appropriate emblem for research into the unconscious. According to Cirlot, the fish is 'a psychic being' which 'came to be taken as a symbol of profound life, of the spiritual world that lies under the world of appearances . . . representing the life force surging up', symbolizing as cosmic fish, 'the whole of the formal, physical universe'.[1] The fish is the arcane substance of alchemy and, as a symbol of fecundity and regeneration, is common to all the mystery religions, gods of the underworld and lunar goddesses of the waters, from Orpheus and Venus to the rebus ICHTHUS depicting Jesus Christ Son of God Saviour. Small wonder that the fish should be found, alive or dead, in the symbolic systems of the Spanish vanguard when poet-playwrights such as Alberti and Lorca attempted to revive the public theatrical playing space as a modern holy place in which to play rough games with the old eschatology in the light of the new psychology.

In a society of strong social control and sacralized institutions which strictly delimits the boundaries between purity and impurity, the Durkheimian model of a society in which God is Society and Society is God, all moral and sexual deviance is in contravention of the law of that society and its religion. The anthropologist Mary Douglas, who interprets philosophical controversies about the relationship of spirit to matter or mind to body as condensed statements about the relationship of the individual to society, has pointed to the inevitability in such a society of social change being expressed in a revolt against its ritual, of alienation being expressed in a de-sacralisation of its images.[2] Small wonder that in a society of strong social and bodily control such as Spain in 1929–1931, caught up in the crisis of a discredited military dictatorship and foundering (Catholic) Monarchy, dramatists such as Lorca and Alberti, working out individual sexual / spiritual crises in therapeutic dramatic images, should signal the sexual / social revolution of the avant-garde *âge d'or* in a secular parody of the sacred drama of Spain's Golden Age, the *auto sacramental*. In the genealogy of morals, new wine does indeed come in old bottles.

The dramatic revolt against the ritual of the old cosmology, enacted in the Catholic mystery / morality tradition as restrictive code and system of control, paradoxically exploits that same tradition as system of communication in a reenactment of it as sacrilegious act. The resulting anti-ritual theatre of inverse holiness administers a scandalising shock to orthodoxy as the body of man replaces the Body of Christ and the law of desire replaces the law of His grace.

On the eve of the collapse of the Spanish monarchy and the establishment of the Republic, Rafael Alberti had a *succès de scandale* with *The Uninhabited Man*, premiered on 26 February 1931, which divided its audience in its response into 'putrescents and not putrescents', vanguard epithets for reactionaries and revolutionaries. The young author, en route from lost faith in Catholicism to faith in Communism, responded to a final curtain-call with the now legendary anarchic cry: 'Long live extermination! Down with the putrescence of Spanish theatre today!'[3] Alberti transmutes that putrefaction, the sexual guilt of a body-negative culture, which simultaneously hallows the body in relation to the Incarnation of Christ and represses sexuality in relation to His Virgin Birth, in the crucible of a dramatic piece which he laconically summed up as 'a sort of *auto sacramental*, but with no sacrament, of course.'[4]

Alberti's modern morality inverts the traditional drama of salvation, the Biblical plot of Creation, Fall and Redemption, charting the perdition of Everyman in his discovery of self as sexual subject, prey to salvation anxiety. Here there is no Incarnation, no Eucharist, no Mystical Body to redeem man from his human condition, only the incarnation of concupiscence in allegorical bodies on stage. The omissions and inversions of Christian paradigms ironically alert an audience bound in that culture to the demonic dissent of one schooled by a pre-Liberation-Theology Society of Jesus in the tradition of didactic drama and spiritual exercises.

For those familiar with Ignatian spirituality, *The Unihabited Man* is a dramatic parody of the exercises of the first week in which the retreatant, 'considering my soul imprisoned in its corruptible body, and my entire being in this vale of tears as an exile among brute beasts', reviews his life and his attachment to the 'creatures' in the light of the end for which he was created: 'to praise, reverence, and serve God our Lord, and by this means to save his soul'.[5] The meditations for the first week – on the sin of the angels, of Adam and Eve, of the subject himself and of the damned in Hell – are designed to purify the soul and end in loving colloquies of gratitude for the merciful bounty of the crucified Saviour and the recitation of the Lord's Prayer. The sting in

206

Alberti's tale comes in the Epilogue when the damned Man condemns his Maker as a sadistic criminal. But the clues to inverse interpretation are laid in the Prologue. Alberti adapts Jesuit training in the mental composition of place exercising all the senses to the composition of a scenic triptych which distorts the positive image of a triune God of Love by setting the central panel of Paradise Lost between two designs of Hell Mouth: chaos and darkness flank light. The mystical ascending pattern of celebration of conversion from ignorance to enlightenment through faith is twisted into an infernal circle of defiant despair.

The initial stage direction transforms Dante's Inferno into modern Wasteland, dominated centre-stage by a closed sewer before which flickers a red lamp within a make-shift triangle of twisted iron bars, a visual parody of a Christian altar where the sanctuary lamp indicates the Real Presence of the reserved Sacrament. The action begins when Man emerges from the sewer in a blown-up diving bell to be cut free by the Night-Watchman, using a giant pair of scissors, in a grotesque visualisation of the creation of the soul or of baptism as an act of castration. Man is born again as [Christian] Gentleman, not in a state of *nuditas naturalis*, but wearing a moustached mask and frock-coat which symbolise bourgeois morality. Stage objects out of scale or out of context are part and parcel of the surreal 'world upside-down' spirit of Alberti's amoral satire, in which the oil-skinned figure of the Creator wears a blackened mask. At first sight Man presciently identifies the Watchman with his search light as 'a nocturnal bird with a single shining eye to disturb a man's sleep',[6] and in the event the All-seeing Eye will become the Cyclopian eye of destruction. In Alberti's reworking of the Calderonian model of sacred allegory such as *Life is a Dream*, there will be no intervention of figures of the Divine attributes of Power, Wisdom and Love in the provision of salvation by the grace of the sacrifice on Calvary channelled through the Eucharist.[7]

Equally, the infusion of a rational soul into the hollow man, ostensibly releasing him from the vegetative condition of a humankind symbolised by the plastercast masks and empty costumes on the despirited carnival carousel in the background which the Night-Watchman likens to 'a grieving for death by sleepwalking dummies who have lost their souls' (p. 11), is not incarnated on stage by figures of the powers of the soul such as Understanding and Will who regularly do battle against figures of the Devil, the World and the Flesh in the allegorical drama of Calderón and in primitive *autos* such as the *Farce of the Sacrament of the Five Senses*. Instead the stage is dominated by monstrous emblematic figures of the windows of perception of his 'soul shut inside a body' (p. 13), which is how the Night-Watchman defines the Gentleman in a pointed direct aside to the audience.

Man remains in Thomist terms a sensitive soul and the remainder of the Prologue is taken up with the education of the Five Senses as agents of desire according to the pleasure principle, but with disturbing hints of the reality principle which will prevail in the final judgement. Sight, the first of the senses, is opened with a vision of the stars, accompanied by a reminder that man's sphere is earth. Hearing is aroused by celestial music which is the sound of a heavenly battle in which the defeated are cast into nothingness. Smell is stimulated into desire of an as yet unknown object by the perfume of a white rose, the flower of Venus, goddess of love, and Christian symbol of purity. The Night-Watchman, as educator–tempter, reserves Taste and Touch for Man's promised domination of the world, using weasel metaphysical words ('the passion for the infinite . . . for infinite caresses' p. 16) as he titillates Man's physical appetites. He presents Man first with an orange, replacing the apple in representations of the Fall and Redemption, and then, in a parody of the resurrection of Lazarus, raises up a mummy: 'a mystery wrapped round in white ribbon' (p. 116). Unbandaging reveals a sleeping-beauty dressed in a white body-stocking, representing *nuditas virtualis*, the symbol of purity and innocence. The Senses surround her in a roundel of desire lit by their red lanterns, the colour of blood, of passion, of love and hate, the colour of fire and Pentecost, of martyrdom and revolution. Under instruction from the Night-Watchman, Man awakens the Girl with a triple kiss, the heavenly number representing soul, and is entrusted with turning her into Woman in the chaste relationship of monogamous couple. The Night-Watchman sends him out into the world, reiterating his promise of happiness but with an ominous warning regarding Man's control of the senses: 'Your salvation and perdition are to be found in them' (p. 18).

The set of the main act is dominated stage right by a garden with a tree (the Tree of Life / of Knowledge of Good and Evil) in the centre beside a round pool, the fount of origins, symbol of the unconscious, Christian symbol of salvation and eternal life. In a fools' paradise, secure in a belief in the protection afforded by purity of soul in their quest of unknown experience, Man and Woman review a world journey in the mirror of the pool as memory, discreetly silencing a moment of sexual union precipitated by the sensual communion of an ice-cream served in a glass goblet. Woman desires to be kissed in the water of the pool, dismissing Man's fear that their kiss might be interrupted by a goldfish (Christian morality?). The kiss leads to a game of catch in which the quarry is Woman's body, pursued into the feminine symbol of the house. In the garden the Senses celebrate Man's physical joy, equating it with happiness of soul, in a round passing game with a red fish which Touch extracts alive from the water and to which he returns it dead from the hands of Taste. Blood mixes with water in an inverse consecration which coincides with the cries for help of Temptation: the dead fish, symbol of Christ, is transubstantiated into the living body of a woman, like Aphrodite, rising from the waves of the sea beyond and pointing to her bleeding feet, phallicly symbolic of man's relationship with the earth (*Ecce mulier*).

Traditionally identified in Christian culture as sexual experience, Temptation is personified as a beautiful half-naked female, *nuditas criminalis*, the symbol of lust. The female body, demonised as occasion of sin for the heterosexual male, is *Eva*, the polar opposite of *Ave*, Woman now depicted feeding her doves in her high tower (emblems of purity of the Queen of Heaven): warring sisters of Man's anima in the battle for possession of his soul / body, in which Woman as white dove of innocence will be killed. Temptation engages the Senses in a conspiracy to win control of Man's desire in a waiting game of promise and postponement of enjoyment of her body (*Noli me tangere*) which provokes Man's agony of body / soul in the garden. In an unequal contest, Man abandons himself to Temptation, accepting her dagger as the instrument of his liberation. The ritual wife-murder is enacted in slow-motion, a window-framed picture on high which is blacked out as the stage is plunged into total darkness, a sensory-deprivation immersion effect essayed for the first time in this play.

Man emerges completely alienated, obsessed with washing the blood from his hands, which Temptation proceeds to do for him in the waters of the pool into which she has thrown the dagger. In an ironic reprise of the opening episode in the garden, Temptation, offering the joy of her body, invites him to contemplate their reflection, but all Man now sees in the pool as mirror of conscience is a dagger and a dead fish – Eros, Thanatos and lost innocence – and their kiss is interrupted by his guilt. He allows himself to be led slowly into the granary stage left, with great spider-webs painted on the wall, symbolic of destiny and Christian symbol of the devil ensnaring sinners. Union in the darkness with Temptation is sundered by Woman's ghost, the dead fish transubstantiated into punishing conscience, who shoots him dead with a revolver supplied by the Night-Watchman, ironically echoing, as she does so, the last words of Touch: 'Love! Love!' (p. 41). The dyad is transformed into Man's dying three-fold call, 'Lord! Lord! Lord!', as he falls back on abandoned sheaves of wheat, untransformed into saving Host, and a giant black spider covers his face.

Synchronous with his execution is Man's personal judgement in the Epilogue, in which dawning light at the end of the Act turns to dusk. The Night-Watchman subjects Man to a cat-and-mouse inquisitorial game in order to extract a confession of his double crime of desire, to which Man pleads not guilty, claiming divine *force majeure*. Grace is mentioned for the first and only time in order to draw the Night-Watchman close to receive a reversed charge of criminal responsibility for Man's perdition. Divested of his Senses in an inverse act of damnation in which the light of the stars is extinguished, Man is condemned to an un-beatific vision of a dagger covered in blood, revivified by hell-fire. The knife-fish is a symbol of severance, of the mutually exclusive hatred of creature and Creator in an underworld of darkness in which the Divinity plays the role of Devil controlling the World and the Flesh, a Goyesque Saturn devouring his sons.

The Creator's judgement may be a profound mystery, according to His closing words, but the judgement of His creator-destroyer Alberti is less opaque. In a post-Nietzschean world-view, the Epilogue is an incitement to a retroactive transvaluation of values in the darkness of the all-too-human cave converted into revolutionary light: the impure will become pure, the criminal natural, in a baptism of blood and fire, a pre-Foucauldian *coup de grace*, aimed at freeing (uninhabiting) the body from the prison of the soul, resurrecting the fish as phallus drowned in the waters of Christian conscience.

Earlier in 1929 Lorca had been thwarted by the censorship in his attempt to illuminate forbidden erotic pleasure within the darkness of the theatre-frame in the unveiling of the body of Belisa and its hidden object of desire towards which the phallic fish swims in her opening song off: 'Love. Love. / The sun swims like a fish / Shut inside my thighs'.[8] The glorious vision of her body produces a complete revaluation of values beyond the old social morality of honour in the male gaze of the lost innocent Don Perlimplín, his coming of age in dishonour symbolised by his crowning with golden horns. The defeat of the Calderonian world-view by that of Nietzsche is expressed in his letter to her in which

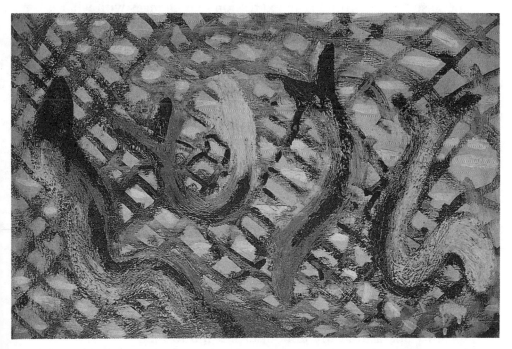

25. Pancho Cossío: *Still life with conger eels* or *The nets*, 1927. Oil on canvas

211

he cuckolds himself in the persona of new man of desire: 'For what purpose do I want your soul? – he says to me. The soul is the heritage of the weak, of crippled heroes and of sickly people. [. . .] Belisa, it is not your soul that I desire, but your white, trembling, delicate body!' (p. 278)

His impotence to possess her in the flesh in his agony in the garden is resolved by self-immolation, designed to transmit his 'soul' to the body of Belisa, that is, the imaginative capacity not only to anticipate the joy of erotic pleasure but also to suffer the pain of frustration of impossible union. As a victim of love, the enigma of Perlimplín's desire is cloaked in the red of passion and martyrdom, a profanation of the Host as a sacrifice for human love. If Alberti materialises the spirit as a first step to engagement in historical materialism, Lorca spiritualises the material in his mystification of subjectivity, loathe to abandon hope in the myth of transcendence, if not of absolutes: 'The poet's mission is this: to give a soul . . . But do not ask me about what is true or false, because "poetic truth" is an expression that changes with what is being said, what is light in Dante can be ugliness in Mallarmé'.[9]

In the hypothetical game of consequences which opens Scene 2 of *The Public*, the quest for Pan in the ever-changing Proteus, the cloud and the eye of Divine Omniscience are scatologically transmogrified into the shit and fly of the organic cycle, while the apple and kiss of Edenic appetite are explicit translated into a homosexual embrace between sheets whose whiteness is symbolic of sterility and death. The real 'shock of the new' in Lorca's work is the presentation of the second Adam as a homosexual, opting out of heterosexual reproduction in the light of death as the end, and his mythification as a secular Christ beyond Redemption. Almost half a century before the successful blasphemy prosecution against *Gay News*, Lorca dared to tread where even Breton in the surrealists' *Researches on Sexuality* had turned aside in disgust.[10] The *mauvaise foi* of surrealist debate may be parodied in the sexual–spiritual wrestling for authenticity among the figures and masks of *The Public* (1930), which to the date of its first performance in Spain in 1986 remains the most revolutionary piece in twentieth-century Spanish theatre in both theme and form.

Focusing on the author's role as producer and the role of audience response in the production, the play contains within itself the dramatic verdict on its own impossibility in terms of 'coming out' in public performance in the contemporary theatre. In spite of the Nietzschean joy of revolutionary students prepared to follow the Gay Science, reactionary spectators kill the male actors playing Romeo and Juliet as homosexual lovers and the Director himself. The dramatic revelation of the conflictive homosexual artistic consciousness judging itself from the point of view of the dream of life that is death would have to remain underground, buried in its format as *theatre beneath the sand*. The formula of sand representing the sterility of the grave may have been inspired by the desert of burning sand in Canto XIV of the *Inferno* in which Dante meets the Violent against God, Nature (Sodomites) and Art, in turn inspired by the account of the destruction of Sodom and Gomorrah in *Genesis*, xix, 24.[11] Paul Smith in a brilliant exegesis of *The Public* quotes Foucault on the language of homosexuality as a 'reverse discourse',[12] and this is amply borne out by the dramatic 'turning upside-down' of Biblical discourse from *Genesis* to *Revelation* in the text of Lorca's play. In a ritual reversal in Scene 1 the Horses of instinct, an ironic parody of the Four Horsemen of the Apocalypse, lift the anathema placed on the homosexual in the Judaeo-Christian tradition: 'FIRST HORSE. Abominable! / HORSES 2, 3 and 4. Blenamiboa'.[13]

Dalí called Freud 'a great upside-down mystic',[14] a term equally applicable to Lorca in his dramatic subversion of the *auto sacramental* tradition in *The Public*, typified in the condensed statement of the 'Foolish Shepherd's Solo'. Agreeing with Rubia Barcía that the unnumbered solo would stand most appropriately in its traditional place as prologue,[15] the shepherd's song and dance routine, accompanied by a suitably carnivalesque hurdy-gurdy, is a parody, in profane terms, of St John of the Cross's parody, in divine terms, of the pastoral mode. A parody of John the Baptist in his animal skins, the Fool is a voice crying in a post-Christian wilderness as he pushes his portable *armario / almario* of masks to the music of 'the wounded spikes and the flask' (p. 149): a broken crown of thorns and an empty grail. The masks which bleat in mocking chorus are those of beggars and poets who have killed the Creator as *carnivorous buzzard*, of masturbating children rotting under the mushroom-womb of life and of eagles with crutches, mutilated symbol of St John the Divine and the Resurrection of Christ. All of this in the riddle of the great theatre of the world, a vast cemetery presided over by the death-mask of God. Against a

backdrop of blue, symbolic colour of truth, not of Divine transcendence here, but of the Void and the self-reflexivity of
the human condition, the Fool is no more the foolish shepherd of
the Divine Comedy who becomes wise following in the footsteps
of the Good Shepherd. Rather he is the Nietzschean genealogist
whose role is 'to push the masquerade to its limit and prepare the great carnival of time when masks are constantly
reappearing'.[16]

His performance is a fitting curtain-raiser to the first scene, the
Director's room, symbol of individuality, which will be filled with
the unstable figures and masks of his schizoid personality. Its blue
set is dominated by a great hand impressed on a wall with X-ray
windows, the map of man's life and psyche, reflecting the corre-
spondence between man and the cosmos. It is not the hand of God
the Creator emerging from a cloud, but the hand of the artist as
creator, that of the masturbator whose onanism, sterile in terms of
sexual reproduction, is transformed into the creative play of art.
One thinks of Lorca's portrait of Dalí as a clown with a red fish
over his heart and red fish-fingers covering the genital area, the
phallicly erect thumb penetrating the hole in the artist's palette
and indicating a column, part gold speckled with blood-red, dis-
secting a moon, 'murdering the moonlight'.[17] The shadow-boxing
of the two in the period of their friendship in the paintings and
drawings of the self and the other as shadow-self with their mutual
obsession with the fish as sign of erotic communion / crucifixion /
artistic creation is translated into the homoerotic encounter of two
mythical figures in Scene 2 of *The Public*.[18]

Set in a Roman ruin, symbolising the fall of antique cosmology
/ sexuality to the Christian, a figure covered in red vine leaves,
sacred to Dionysos and emblematic of the Eucharist, the colour of
Priapus the Red God, plays the flute, seated on a column, both
lingam and pillar of flagellation, whilst a figure decked in golden
bells, attached to figures of Priapus in Bacchic rites and emblematic of the Consecration in the Mass, dances. The dance, watched
by the Director and his personae, is the dialogue of the desire for
homosexual integration destined to difference and disintegration.
The dance of Eros is the dance of Thanatos and the repeated figure
of the calculus ends in ambivalent images of the phallus and its
castration or death: a mythical moonfish and knife:[19]

214

FIGURA WITH BELLS. Supposing I was to change into a moonfish
FIGURE WITH VINELEAVES. I would change into a knife (pp. 57 and
59).

In the final scene 6, set as in Scene 1 with the addition of a
severed horse-head stage left and an enormous eye with trees and
clouds, propped against the wall stage right like the discarded set
of a divine *auto*, a woman in black weeds comes looking for her
missing son Gonzalo (identified with the First Man and the Figure
of Vineleaves, who had ordained that his love-head should be left
in the ruin). The mother has been presented with a rotting
moonfish as the body of her son, linking this discovery with the
dead fish-body of the poem 'Abandoned Church' in *Poet in New
York* which symbolises the dead Christ, the poet's lost faith in the
Redemption of Calvary, his own unbegotten son. The audience
has already witnessed the death agony of the First Man in Scene 5,
ignored by the public on stage in simultaneous actions which
report the revolution and counter-revolution that is taking place as
Romeo and Juliet are forced to replay the grave scene before being
killed. In a parody of the Crucifixion and the Consecration of the
Mass which crosses visual echoes of Cimabue Cross and Expressionist operating theatre in a perpendicular bed, a Red Nude
is mockingly done to death, pronouncing the Seven Last Words
between the proclamation of the Sanctus by two thieves. At the
consummation, this set swings round to reveal the First Man, the
alter ego who had not disguised his homosexuality, whose repeated last words 'I die!' punctuates the rest of the scene. The Red
Nude is not the Red King of alchemy, the Androgyne, the Fish, the
risen Christ of immortality, he is mortal flesh, a persecuted phallus, alone at the moment of truth in death.

The Director-Enrique-Figure with Bells, his warring twin, faces
death in the last-beginning scene in the figure of a Magician, for
the first of the Tarot trumps whose gesture signifies 'as above,
so below'. But the Divine Gaze of the Calderonian *auto* has been
displaced by the self-referential human gaze of the theatre beneath
the sand which leads to a dead, not a happy, end.[20] As the curtain
falls on the narcissistic spectacle with its mocking echo, white
gloves conjured up by the Magician rain slowly down on the fallen
figure of the Director, the slow handclap accorded to the failure of

transcendence in the material cycle of destruction. The gloves turn
to the snowflakes of oblivion, creating a final tableau of frozen
vitality, paradoxically a stimulus to that libertarian lust for life, in
whatever natural shape or form, denied by the Christian order.

The homosexual *The Public*, trapped in the closet, stands with
the heterosexual *The Uninhabited Man*, out in the open, as the
dramatic *non serviam* to orthodox morality by the Spanish avant-
garde in a war of national values in which the victory of the old
cosmology would condemn their authors, dead or alive, temporar-
ily to the silence of the damned.

Notes

[1] J. E. Cirlot, *A Dictionary of Symbols*, London, 1962, pp. 106–107. See also J.
C. Cooper, *An Illustrated Encyclopedia of Traditional Symbols*, London,
1978 and G. Ferguson, *Signs and Symbols in Christian Art*, Oxford, 1974.

[2] M. Douglas, *Natural Symbols. Explorations in Cosmology*, Harmondsworth,
1973, pp. 179 and 195.

[3] R. Alberti, *La arboleda perdida. Libros I and II de memorias*, Barcelona, 1976,
p. 305.

[4] *Ibid.*, p. 304.

[5] *The Spiritual Exercises of St. Ignatius*, New York, 1964, pp. 54 and 47
respectively.

[6] *El hombre deshabitado*, Buenos Aires, 1959, p. 10 (subsequent references
bracketed in text).

[7] See T. S. Beardsley, 'El Sacramento desautorizado', *Studia Iberica Festchrift für
Hans Flascher*, edited by K. H. Körner and K. Rühl, Bern-Munich, 1973, pp.
93–103.

[8] *Amor de don Perlimplín con Belisa en su jardín*, Madrid, 1990, p. 255.
Subsequent references are bracketed in the text. This play is attributed to
1925–1926.

[9] 'Imaginación, inspiración, evasión', *Obras Completas*, Madrid, 1967 (13th
ed.), p. 85.

[10] *La Révolution Surréaliste*, XI, 15 March 1928, pp. 32–40.

[11] See *The Divine Comedy: Hell*, Harmondsworth, 1964, pp. 156–60.

[12] *The Body Hispanic. Gender and Sexuality in Spanish and Spanish-American
Literature*, Oxford, 1989, p. 129.

[13] *El Público y Comedia sin título*, Barcelona, 1978, p. 37. (Subsequent references bracketed in text).

[14] R. Santos Torroella, *La miel es más dulce que la sangre*, Barcelona, 1984, p.
32.

[15] 'Ropaje and desnudez de *El público*', *Cuadernos Hispanoamericanos*,
CCCCXXXIII–CCCCXXXIV (1986), pp. 385–97. For the traditional figure see J.

Brotherton, *The Pastor-bobo in the Spanish Theatre before the Time of Lope de Vega*, London, 1975.

16 Quoted by Smith, *The Body Hispanic*, pp. 112 and 130.

17 1927. Reproduced by M. Hernández, *Line of Light and Shadow. The Drawings of Federico García Lorca*, London, 1991, p. 10.

18 See Dalí's *Fish and Balcony (Still Life by Moonlight)* and *Still Life by Mauve Moonlight* (1926) reproduced by Santos Torroella, *La miel*, pp. 111–12.

19 See J. A. Valente 'Pez luna', *Trece de Nieve*, I–II (1976), pp. 191–201.

20 'DIRECTOR: The only way the play can justify itself is by breaking down all the doors, seeing with its own eyes that the law is a wall that dissolves in the tiniest drop of blood. The dying man who draws a door on the wall with his finger and then sleeps soundly disgusts me. The real drama is a colonnaded arena where the breeze, the moon and creatures enter and exit with nowhere to rest' (p. 159).

Index

Index

Index